Contemporary history on trial

Manchester University Press

Contemporary history on trial

Europe since 1989 and the role of the expert historian

edited by
**Harriet Jones,
Kjell Östberg and Nico Randeraad**

Manchester University Press
Manchester and New York
distributed exclusively in the USA by Palgrave

Copyright © Manchester University Press 2007

While copyright in the volume as a whole is vested in Manchester University Press, copyright in individual chapters belongs to their respective authors, and no chapter may be reproduced wholly or in part without the express permission in writing of both author and publisher.

Published by Manchester University Press
Oxford Road, Manchester M13 9NR, UK
and Room 400, 175 Fifth Avenue, New York, NY 10010, USA
www.manchesteruniversitypress.co.uk

Distributed in the United States exclusively by
Palgrave Macmillan, 175 Fifth Avenue,
New York, NY 10010, USA

Distributed in Canada exclusively by
UBC Press, University of British Columbia, 2029 West Mall,
Vancouver, BC, Canada V6T 1Z2

British Library Cataloguing-in-Publication Data is available

Library of Congress Cataloging-in-Publication Data is available

ISBN 978 0 7190 9130 8 paperback

First published by Manchester University Press in hardback 2007

This paperback edition first published 2013

The publisher has no responsibility for the persistence or accuracy of URLs for any external or third-party internet websites referred to in this book, and does not guarantee that any content on such websites is, or will remain, accurate or appropriate.

Printed by Lightning Source

Contents

List of contributors		page ix
Introduction *Harriet Jones, Kjell Östberg and Nico Randeraad*		1
1	The responsibility of the historian *Peter Mandler*	12
2	Public uses of history in contemporary Europe *Klas-Göran Karlsson*	27
3	Coming to terms with the (post-)colonial past in Belgium: the inquiry into the assassination of Patrice Lumumba *Georgi Verbeeck*	46
4	The Bloody Sunday tribunal and the role of the historian *Paul Bew*	62
5	Between scholarship and politics: experiences from the Commission on the Swedish Security Services *Karl Molin*	81
6	Historical research where scholarship and politics meet: the case of Srebrenica *Hans Blom*	104
7	Negotiated history? Bilateral historical commissions in twentieth-century Europe *Marina Cattaruzza and Sacha Zala*	123
8	The Italo-Slovenian historico-cultural commission *Raoul Pupo*	144
9	The state, the historians and the Algerian War in French memory, 1991–2004 *Raphaëlle Branche*	159
10	The German historians' debate about the upheavals of 1989 *Martin Sabrow*	174
	Conclusion *Harriet Jones, Kjell Östberg and Nico Randeraad*	193
	Index	201

The editors should like to express their gratitude to:
The British Academy
The Summer University of Southern Stockholm
The Netherlands Organisation for Scientific Research (NWO)

Contributors

Paul Bew is Professor of Irish Politics at Queen's University Belfast. He was a special adviser to the Bloody Sunday Tribunal. Author or co-author of eleven books on modern Ireland, he is currently attempting to complete *Policy And Enmity: Ireland And Britain Since 1789*, a volume in the Oxford History of Modern Europe.

J.C.H. (Hans) Blom is director of the Netherlands Institute for War Documentation (NIOD) and professor of Dutch History at the University of Amsterdam. His main recent publications in English are: J.C.H. Blom and E. Lamberts (ed.), *History of The Low Countries* (New York and Oxford: Berghahn Books, 2005²) and J.C.H. Blom, R.G. Fuks-Mansfeld and I. Schöffer (ed.), *The History of the Jews in The Netherlands* (Oxford and Portland, Oregon: The Littman Library of Jewish Civilization, 2002). As director of the NIOD he was responsible for the report (2002) of the investigation about the fall of the enclave Srebrenica in Bosnia in 1995, commissioned by the Dutch government.

Raphaëlle Branche is Lecturer in Contemporary History at the University of Paris-I-La Sorbonne. Her main recent publication is La guerre d'Algérie: une histoire apaisée? (Paris: Le Seuil, 2005). Her previous book, *La torture et l'armée pendant la guerre d'Algérie, 1954–1962* (Paris: Gallimard, 2001) is about to be published in English (Nebraska Press University).

Marina Cattaruzza is Professor of Contemporary History at the University Berne. Her recent books include: *Socialismo adriatico. La socialdemocrazia di lingua italiana nei territori costieri dell'Impero asburgico* (Manduria: Lacaita, 1998, 2001); editor, with Marco Dogo and Raoul Pupo, of *Esodi. Trasferimenti forzati di popolazione nel Novecento europeo* (Napoli: Edizioni Scientifiche Italiane, 2000), editor of *Nazionalismi di frontiera* (Soveria Mannelli: Rubbettino, 2003); editor of *La Nazione in*

Rosso. Socialismo, Comunismo e "Questione nazionale": 1889–1953 (Soveria Mannelli: Rubbettino, 2005); Political Religions as a Characteristic of the 20th Century (Special issue of *Totalitarian Movements and Political Religions*, 2005/1).

Harriet Jones is a Senior Research Fellow at the Institute of Historical Research, University of London. Formerly Director of the Institute of Contemporary British History, her most recent book is *A Companion to Contemporary Britain 1939–2000* (Malden, MA: Blackwells, 2005) which she co-edited with Paul Addison.

Klas-Göran Karlsson is Professor of History at Lund University. Among his recent publications are: with K. Gerner, *Nordens Medelhav. Östersjöområdet som historia, myt och projekt* (Stockholm: Natur och Kultur, 2002); *Terror och tystnad, Sovjetregimens krig mot den egna befolkningen* (Stockholm: Bokförlaget Atlantis AB, 2003); with U. Zander (eds), *Echoes of the Holocaust. Historical Cultures in Contemporary Europe* Lund: Nordic Academic Press, 2003); with U. Zander (eds), *Holocaust Heritage. Inquiries into European Historical Cultures* (Malmö: Sekel Förlag, 2004); with U. Zander (eds), *Historien är nu. En introduktion till historiedidaktiken* (Lund: Studentlitteratur AB, 2004); with K. Gerner, *Folkmordens historia. Perspektiv på det moderna samhällets skuggsida* (Stockholm: Bokförlaget Atlantis AB 2005).

Peter Mandler is Reader in Modern British History and Fellow of Gonville and Caius College, Cambridge. He is the author of, among other books, *History and National Life* (London: Profile Books, 2002) and a forthcoming history of the idea of the English national character. From 1998 to 2002 he was Honorary Secretary of the Royal Historical Society and is currently co-editor of *The Historical Journal*.

Karl Molin is Professor of History at the Stockholm University. His main fields of research are Swedish domestic and foreign policy, and industrial relations during the twentieth century. He has been in a charge of a PhD project on Swedish foreign policy and public debate during the Cold War. He was a member of the Swedish Commission on the Security Services 1999–2003.

Kjell Östberg is Professor of History and research director at the Swedish Institute of Contemporary History at Södertörn University College. Research interests have primarily focused on issues of democratisation and bureaucratisation in twentieth-century Sweden, with special attention to folk movements and social movements. His main recent publications are *När allting var in rörelse, 60-talsradikaliseringen och de sociala rörelserna,*

(Stockholm: Prisma förlag, 2001); and with Yvonne Svanström, *Än män då?* (Stockholm: Atlas förlag, 2004).

Raoul Pupo is Associated Professor in Contemporary History in the Faculty of Political Sciences, University of Trieste. His main recent publications are: *Il lungo esodo* (Milano: Rizzoli, 2005); with Roberto Spazzali, *Foibe* (Milano: Bruno Mondadori, 2003); 'Med zgodovino in geografico. Razmisljanja o italijanski vzhodni meji', in *Prispevki za noveiso zgodovino*, XL, 2000, 1, pp. 285-99; *Guerra e dopoguerra al confine orientale d'Italia 1938-1956* (Udine: Del Bianco, 1999).

Nico Randeraad is Lecturer in History and European Studies in the Faculty of Arts and Culture, Universiteit Maastricht. His main recent publications are: editor of *Formation und Transfer städtischen Verwaltungswissens. Jahrbuch für Europäische Verwaltungsgeschichte* 15 (2003); with D. J. Wolffram, 'Dutch Administrative Culture in a Historic Perspective', in: F. Hendriks and T. A. J. Toonen (eds), *Polder Politics. The Re-invention of Consensus Democracy in the Netherlands* (Aldershot: Ashgate, 2001) 41-59; with D. J. Wolffram, 'Constraints on Clientelism: The Dutch Path to Modern Politics, 1848-1917', in: S. Piattoni (ed.), *Clientelism, Interests, and Democratic Representation. The European Experience in Historical and Comparative Perspective*, (Cambridge: Cambridge University Press, 2001) 101-21.

Martin Sabrow is Professor for Contemporary History at the University of Potsdam and Director of the Centre for Research on Contemporary History Potsdam (CRCH). His recent publications are: *Das Diktat des Konsenses. Geschichtswissenschaft in der DDR 1949-1969*, Ordnungssysteme. Studien zur Ideengeschichte der Neuzeit, vol. 8 (München: Oldenbourg, 2001); with Klaus Große Kracht and Ralph Jessen (eds), *Zeitgeschichte als Streitgeschichte. Historikerkontroversen nach 1945* (München: Beck, 2003); (ed.), *Skandal und Diktatur. Formen öffentlicher Empörung im NS-Staat und in der DDR* (Göttingen: Wallstein-Verlag, 2004). His main research topics are the German history of the twentieth century and of historical culture.

Georgi Verbeeck lectures both general European and German history at the universities of Maastricht (The Netherlands) and Leuven (Belgium). Among his publications are: *Geschiedschrijving en politieke cultuur. De weg naar het fascisme in de DDR-historiografie* (Amersfoort: Acco, 1992); with J. Tollebeek and T. Verschaffel (eds), *De lectuur van het verleden. Opstellen over de geschiedenis van de geschiedschrijving* (Leuven: Universitaire Pers Leuven, 1998); editor of *De verdwenen gaskamers. Over de ontkenning van de Holocaust* (Leuven/Amersfoort: Acco, 1997).

Sacha Zala is Lecturer in Modern and Contemporary History in the Department of History at the University of Berne, Switzerland. His main publications are: *Gebändigte Geschichte. Amtliche Historiographie und ihr Malaise mit der Geschichte der Neutralität* (Bern: Schweizerisches Bundesarchiv, 1998); *Geschichte unter der Schere politischer Zensur. Amtliche Aktensammlungen im internationalen Vergleich* (München: Oldenbourg Verlag, 2001); with M. Herren, *Netzwerk Aussenpolitik. Internationale Organisationen und Kongresse als Instrumente der schweizerischen Aussenpolitik* (Zürich: Chronos Verlag, 2002).

Introduction

Harriet Jones, Kjell Östberg and Nico Randeraad

Historical practice today is characterised by such growing diversity that there are now many ways of being a professional historian. This volume focuses specifically on the rise of those who Carole Fink has recently referred to as the 'new historians', who choose to play the role of 'expert' in public debates about the past. As she puts it,

> Although they mete out no sentences and impose no reparations, these expert historians now inhabit a complex world of memory and forgetfulness, politics and bureaucracies, verdicts and judgments far remote from their university training. Also, these scholars have renounced the privacy and protection of their classrooms and research institutes to become public figures serving a specific paymaster, subject to strict external deadlines, exposed to blistering press and official criticism and also subject to the laws of supply and demand.[1]

Scholarly history and public history are coming closer together, not only widening the scope of what the professional historian is called upon to do, but also fostering debate about the increasingly precarious balance between professional standards and degrees of moral, political or social engagement. Generally speaking, the historical community has been kindly disposed to a greater openness to the world. The public use of history, writes Nicola Gallerano, 'is not a practice to be rejected or demonized on principle'.[2] It is no longer tenable, according to Ludmilla Jordanova, to 'dismiss public history as "mere" popularisation, entertainment or propaganda'. She envisages a world where scholarly and public history enter into meaningful co-operation, primarily based on the recognition and development of the skills that historians traditionally possess.[3]

But is it possible to mobilise that expertise to the benefit of the common good without eroding the same expertise? What consequences do these developments have for the professional practices and attitudes of historians? We set out here to explore the various ways in which 'expert historians' have been confronted with questions of justice, guilt, responsibility, torn memories and reconciliation, and the extent to which these challenges have affected their views on scholarly objectivity and social responsibility.

Since the beginning of the 1990s, Europe has witnessed a series of heated and politicised debates that question the 'truth' about painful episodes in the recent past. There are a number of possible explanations for this. Of course, the political consequences of the quite sudden collapse of Communism in 1989 have been far-reaching, quite simply because the Cold War had been the framework through which Europeans had made sense of politics in the years since 1945. Thus the breakdown of the old political order east of the Iron Curtain suddenly released long-suppressed controversies about ethnic conflict, political and intellectual culture, and past atrocities. The collapse of the Soviet threat west of the Iron Curtain was followed by an end to old certainties about the welfare state, the mixed economy and the desirability of a 'third way' between Communism and capitalism. Issues surrounding restitution for those who had been dispossessed by Soviet occupation encouraged and became connected to renewed pressure to see the crimes of the Holocaust finally resolved while there were still living witnesses to testify and to see justice done. The end of the European empires, which in many cases had taken place against a bloody backdrop of Cold War politics and intrigue, could finally be addressed. There were now new pressures, moreover, to expand the European project, integrating central and Eastern European neighbours into liberal democratic approaches to public life. The end of the familiar Cold War narratives sparked an intense and public interest in finding new narratives to replace them, and in arriving at a new understanding of the context of the extreme violence of the twentieth century. The end of the Cold War has thus led to the revival of public interest in history, and in particular to an intensity of pressure to set the record straight, so that 'justice can be done'.[4]

Specifically, once the Cold War had ended, it was inevitable that painful and contested memories of past events would have to be confronted and resolved, before new narratives could begin to emerge. Inquiries and fact-finding commissions have become a common device employed by governments to deal with the consequent pressure of public opinion. While the structure of these procedures has varied from country to country, many have placed contemporary historians in the ethically ambiguous role of professional interpreter of the past. As difficult as this may be, contemporary historians have been given the opportunity to climb down from the ivory tower and engage fully in public debate.

The changing role of the historian has been discussed recently by Olivier Dumoulin in a broad perspective.[5] Starting in the second half of the nineteenth century, he follows various phases of the social role and self-understanding of the profession, paying particular attention to the 'invention of the historian as expert' in the past two or three decades. Examining case studies mainly from France and the United States, where historians have frequently been called up as expert witnesses in courts of law, he wonders whether this new social role compromises the legitimacy of the discipline. Although Dumoulin points to a striking difference between France, where the expert historian is more likely to be involved in cases related to public interests, and the American and Canadian practice, where private interests are often being served, he concludes that the implications for the social responsibility of historians are equally large. Deciding *wie es eigentlich gewesen* acquires a new meaning and can have an incomparably more profound impact, when communicated in court rather than in a lecture hall or in print. According to Richard Evans, who has served as a defence witness for the US historian Deborah Lipstadt in the David Irving Holocaust denial libel trial in 2000, historians may encounter more difficulties than they had envisaged, when acting as expert witnesses.[6] Evans focuses on the position that Henri Rousso, the French contemporary historian, had defended when he refused to stand as expert witness in the trial against the French war criminal Maurice Papon. Basically, Rousso argued, 'the argumentation developed in a trial is not of the same nature as that produced by scholars'.[7] Although sympathising to some extent with Rousso's decision, Evans concludes that not all trials are the same, and that sometimes historians can gain from their work for the courts. While Rousso believes that our historical understanding of the Vichy regime has been obfuscated by events in the courtroom, Evans argues that the decision in *D. C. J. Irving* v. *Penguin Books Ltd. and Deborah Lipstadt* was an important victory for the profession. The court decided that Lipstadt was justified in describing Irving as a 'Hitler partisan' in her book.[8] The verdict was a victory for the importance of academic historical scholarship in the establishment of historical truth.[9]

Similar observations have been made for the roles of historians in American courtrooms. David Rothman, a medical historian who specialises in bioethics, for example, has written of his experiences as an expert witness. He distinguishes between 'serving the client' in court and 'serving Clio', but in his view the former can be done without undermining the latter.[10] John Neuenschwander, combining the functions of professor of history and municipal judge, sensibly argues that first of all we should not forget that even in a judicialised country such as the United States, historians constitute only a small minority of experts in court. He points out that they are especially useful in some circumstances, such as cases concerning native American rights, voting rights, deportation and denaturalisation, and the potential dangers of products such as tobacco, asbestos or pharmaceuticals – that is, in contrast to Dumoulin's opinion, cases that involve both public and private interests. In his 'view from the bench', Neuenschwander claims that judges are aware of the subjectivity inherent in historical practice, but that they look for the same qualities in historians as in other experts: 'appropriate specialisation, thorough research, and conclusions that are well supported by the record'.[11] But real life can be more complicated than these reassurances would suggest, especially in a litigious culture such as the United States. In 2003, the possibility of legal action seeking restitution for African-American descendents of slaves, for example, prompted the first African-American President of Brown University, Ruth Simmons, to appoint a 'Steering Committee on Slavery and Justice' composed entirely of academic members of staff. Simmons was worried that Brown, which was founded partly on profits from the slave trade, was vulnerable to embarrassing legal action. And while in theory the purpose of the Committee is laudable – 'to organize academic events and activities that might help the nation and the Brown community think deeply, seriously, and rigorously about the questions raised by the national debate over slavery and reparations' – its underlying purpose of thwarting formal action has placed its members in an ethical position which is unenviable to say the least.[12]

To act as witness is thus just one of the roles of the expert historian. They have also served as salaried consultants, historical advisers, business historians or members of fact-finding and reconciliation commissions. This volume investigates such roles in a broad European context. In comparison with Dumoulin's study, we have considerably extended the number of countries under scrutiny, which also increases the variety of themes that are discussed. As well as the common experience of the Second World War and the Cold War, there are many problematic legacies in different parts of Europe which contemporary historians have been asked to pass judgment upon. Depending on the issue, of course, but also on the political or juridical culture of the country involved, the public memory of catastrophe can be manifested in markedly different ways, through public commemoration, lawsuits, reparations or official inquiries, for example. The historians in this volume cover the public response to events as diverse as the mass killing at Srebrenica, Bloody Sunday, the assassination of Lumumba, the surveillance activities of the Swedish Security Services, collaboration with totalitarian regimes and the Algerian War. It would be too ambitious to cover the experiences of all European states in one volume. We think, however, that our selection can contribute to more informed and more varied discussions in countries or about issues that are not discussed here. We decided not to dwell on controversies related to the Second World War or to the fall of Communism, which are amply discussed elsewhere.[13]

Common to all of these examples is the central and generally problematic role of the state, both in terms of its role during the events being examined and in terms of its attempts in the present to resolve popular controversy.

Introduction 5

For example, in many of the cases considered here, the state has deliberately suppressed at least some factual details and documents for decades, a decision generally defended on the grounds that core state interests (national security or political stability, for example) are at stake. But there seems to be a 'tipping point' when popular pressure to examine and resolve such controversies reaches a scale which makes it in the best interests of the state to hold some sort of public process of examination. Needless to say, it remains in the interest of the state to satisfy public opinion that an impartial and fair examination has been held, while simultaneously avoiding unnecessary embarrassment or by putting at risk any genuine national security concerns, however they may be defined by the government in power at the time.

For several years the Bergier Commission, installed in 1996 and dissolved in 2001, dominated discussion about the historian's role in a society's recovery from a difficult past. A combination of lawsuits and public pressure [14] led to its formation, charged with investigating the origins and trajectories of assets, mostly Jewish, moved to Switzerland before, during and immediately after the war.[15] Bergier (formally 'the Independent Commission of Experts') set the example for a series of similar commissions which followed, in Austria,[16] Sweden,[17] France [18] and the United States.[19] In general, their recommendations have been accepted and it is true that they were able to shed light on facts that had remained hidden for too long. These commissions attracted considerable public interest and played an important role in the increasing attention given to the Holocaust and its continuing implications (an issue discussed later in this volume by Klas-Göran Karlsson). To this extent the expert historians associated with them usually came out looking well.[20] But they also gave rise to debates about the ways in which such painful episodes should be investigated; there is evidence, for example, that anti-Semitic and extreme nationalistic elements in Swiss society were stirred up as a result of the Bergier Commission.[21]

As a form of inquiry into public affairs, the commission has a long history. The British royal commissions go back to 1815, for example.[22] Many other states also have a tradition of using parliamentary or ministerial commissions to investigate national crises, scandals or controversies. But the expert historian has only gradually emerged in the sense that we are familiar with today. It is true that governments in the twentieth century sometimes commissioned specialists (diplomats, historians, archivists) to collect and publish documents relating to war and international relations; for example, we have the German and allied series on the origins of the First World War, projects which formed part of the national process of coming to terms with the huge losses of that generation.[23] A relatively new phenomenon are the so-called truth commissions, 'bodies established to research and report on human rights abuses over a certain period of time in a particular country or in relation to a particular conflict', which often appoint historical advisers.[24] The idea of a commission of inquiry, therefore, has come to be generally accepted as a suitable administrative format for investigating complex and controversial issues. Of course, historical input in commissioned investigations is not self-evident; but the participation of historians has increased considerably in recent years. Out of these different experiences it is possible to distil a preliminary typology. For any commission, it is useful to consider:

1. its *legal basis* (for example, is it a tribunal or an inquiry; what are its terms of reference; to whom does it report) and *composition* (is it unilateral, bilateral or multilateral; is it composed of historians only, is it a mixture of experts; or are there one or two historical advisers). The commissions discussed in this volume show remarkable differences in these aspects, with interesting consequences discussed by the authors;

2. its *subject*, which can, for example, be recent (Srebrenica), distant (Italo-Slovene or German-Polish), or somewhere in-between (Algeria, Bloody Sunday, Lumumba); relatively provable and objective (events, decisions, acts of war) or speculative and subjective (divided memories, nationalist legacies, construction of new narrative);

3. its *purpose* and *public use* (fact-finding, reconciliation, restitution, juridical, moral, or satisfying public indignation).

This volume starts with two contributions exploring the general context of the changing role of the historian. Peter Mandler addresses the fundamental problem of the historian's professional, political and moral responsibilities. He emphasises the multiple responsibilities or roles that historians may or may not claim, drawing many examples from the contributions in this volume. Mandler argues that there can be no higher responsibility for the historian than to remember the long historical context of contemporary debate and controversy. His argument is carried further by Klas-Göran Karlsson, who questions the ethical role of contemporary historians in constructing the parameters of acceptable political behaviour through the example of Sweden's 'Living History' initiative, through which the state attempts to educate young people about the lessons of the Holocaust. The chapter reflects upon the different uses of history on a more general level, varying from the need to reconstruct, to forget, to rediscover or to illustrate.

The contributions by Blom, Bew, Verbeeck and Molin consider at length recent public inquiries in which professional historians have been employed in a variety of capacities. With the exception of Verbeeck, the authors themselves participated in the highly sensitive investigations they analyse. As editors, we encouraged them to reflect critically upon their experiences.

Introduction 7

They candidly discuss the organisation of the inquiries, the political and public pressure put upon them, and the limitations of researching contemporary history. Hans Blom, who led the Dutch official inquiry into the Srebrenica killings (1996–2002), looks back at this tragedy and overtly discusses the problems that the inquiry team faced: the assignment and conditions under which the inquiry would be conducted, the period of fact-finding and editing, and the presentation of the report, which had far-reaching political consequences for the then sitting government. Paul Bew served as historical adviser to the Saville Tribunal on the Bloody Sunday events in Northern Ireland. He reflects upon his role in the process and the new evidence that it has revealed. He analyses different views of the tragedy, and compares the Tribunal's tasks and responsibilities with those of the historian more generally. His sharply critical opinion of the Tribunal throws interesting light on its proceedings from the point of view of an insider. As a contemporary historian, Karl Molin sat on the official commission which investigated the activities of the Swedish Security Services from 1945 to the present day. He analyses the work of the commission in the light of its terms of reference and the more general historical context that led to its establishment. He concludes that the commission focused on questions related to the violation of personal integrity in a narrow sense, and was restrained in its consideration of the wider political and social implications of surveillance during the Cold War, an aspect of the report that drew criticism upon its publication.

The chapters which follow, by Cattaruzza and Sala, Pupo, Branche and Sabrow, examine the contribution of historians to the process of coming to terms with a recent totalitarian, colonial or otherwise problematic past. Although their primary concern is not fact-finding, the problems that historians dealing directly or indirectly with *Vergangenheitsbewältigung* (coming to terms with the past) face are similar to the first four cases: a large amount of contradictory evidence, divided and torn memories, closed archives and reluctant or conditional help from governments. In each example, these problems have left many unresolved questions from the point of view of the professional historian. Commissions of inquiry have not always been confined to a single country. In their chapter, Marina Cattaruzza and Sacha Zala analyse the workings of bilateral historical commissions since the First World War, for example, those funded by UNESCO after 1945 to re-write history textbooks as part of the wider process of denazification. Many Communist countries also established bilateral commissions in an attempt to suppress long-term, 'pre-revolutionary' antagonism. Raoul Pupo discusses the problems encountered by the bilateral commission that investigated Italo-Slovene relations from the end of the nineteenth until well into the twentieth century, including the First and Second World Wars and their aftermath. His chapter reflects upon the troubled history of this relationship and discusses the impact of the commission's report, which was published in 2000.

The former imperial powers have been confronted in the past decade with uncomfortable questions resulting from the process of decolonisation after 1945. Cold War imperatives meant that metropolitan elites were particularly determined to hand power to compliant native political elites, not only to safeguard existing investments, but also to ensure that newly independent countries were free from Communist (or imagined Communist) influence.[25] For example, in 1999 the new evidence brought to light by a Belgian researcher led to a parliamentary inquiry into the government's involvement in the assassination of the Congo's first prime minister, Patrice Lumumba, in 1961. Georgi Verbeeck analyses the context of this recent official Belgian investigation into the assassination. He follows the activities of the commission, and the role of historical experts in the inquiry. He evaluates the findings of the inquiry against the background of changing attitudes at the national and international level, and reflects critically upon the role of the historians in this process. Raphaëlle Branche describes the re-emergence of the Algerian War in French public debate in the early 1990s, and its continuing reverberation. She pays particular attention to the different views on torture practices carried out by French soldiers, and the difficulty of maintaining an impartial position in such circumstances. Notwithstanding the differences between the Belgian fact-finding on government acts and the French reconstruction of cruelties committed by the armed forces, Verbeeck and Branche show the similarities in the difficulties in reconstructing the colonial past, given an historical context at once less than fifty years old, but yet far away both in time, place and culture.

Martin Sabrow's contribution discusses the consequences of regime change on the way that the historical profession is organised and how historical inquiry is conducted. Historians in the East were profoundly affected by the 1989 *Wende* in Germany. Sabrow discusses the consequences of the fall of the German Democratic Republic in 1989–90 for the discipline of history in the German academic world. He analyses different 'strategies' of dealing with a difficult past, and reflects upon the role that Western historians were forced to play in making judgements about the methodologies and credibility of their Eastern colleagues.

It should not be forgotten that official inquiries are initiated as the result of public controversy. This places enormous public and political pressure on historians to draw conclusions where there might not be sufficient evidence to do so, or to temper their conclusions to suit the climate of opinion. Although the inquiries themselves are not necessarily expected to pass judgement in any political, moral or juridical sense, historians should be aware that there can be political, moral and juridical consequences, for example, when ministerial responsibility is at stake or when criminal acts are discovered.

Moreover, since Ranke, the historical profession has sought to distance itself from the role of serving the state or nation by constructing or reinforcing nationalist narratives. This might be a function that is easier to identify in totalitarian regimes, but with hindsight, it has often been the case that historians have played – consciously or subconsciously – an active part in constructing national myths. The risk for the expert historian is that this function is elevated at the expense of historiographical independence and integrity, even in the service of an objective which can be identified as contributing to the public good (for example, Holocaust education).

The case studies included in this book strikingly illustrate the different ways in which societies come to terms with memories which are painful or divisive. Not only is this bound up with different political and juridical cultures, but it can also be influenced by recent events, such as regime change. Thus judicial processes, in France or the United Kingdom for example, would be unfamiliar in Sweden or Holland, where consensus has been reached on the basis of investigations led by historical experts. The fall of the German Democratic Republic was bound to have profound consequences on the way postwar German history would be written. Interestingly, when the authors of these chapters met in Sweden in 2002 to share their experiences, each to some extent was envious of the position of the other. In other words, there is no trouble-free model for the resolution of such problems, which will always involve controversy and compromise. 'We know', François Bédarida wrote, 'that contemporary history ["l'histoire du temps présent"], more than any other, is unfinished by nature: a history in continuous movement reflecting the sweeping changes that unfold in front of our very eyes, and hence an object of unending renewal'.[26]

Notes

1 C. Fink, 'A new historian?', *Contemporary European History*, 14 (2005), 147.
2 N. Gallerano, 'History and the public use of history', in F. Bédarida (ed.), *The Social Responsibility of the Historian* (Providence/Oxford, 1994), p. 87.
3 L. Jordanova, *History in Practice* (London, 2000), p. 171.
4 Some commentators have connected this revival of interest in the facts of history and in demands for restitution as connected to the triumph of liberal democracy, as posed by Francis Fukuyama, to the extent that it reflects the rise of a new international morality; others are dismissive of such optimism. See F. Fukuyama, *The End of History and the Last Man* (New York, 1992); and R. F. Wetzell, 'Commissioning history in the United States, Germany, and Austria: historical commissions, victims, and World War II restitution', *German Historical Institute Bulletin*, 2003 (Spring), 171.

5 O. Dumoulin, *Le rôle social de l'historien* (Paris, 2003).
6 R. J. Evans, 'History, memory, and the law: the historian as expert witness', *History and Theory*, 41 (2002), 326–45.
7 Quoted in Ibid., p. 338. See also H. Rousso, 'Justiz, Geschichte und Erinnerung in Frankreich', in N. Frei, D. van Laak and M. Stolleis, *Geschichte vor Gericht* (Munich, 2000), pp. 141–63.
8 D. Lipstadt, *Denying the Holocaust: the Growing Assault on Truth and Memory* (London, 1994).
9 D. Lipstadt, *History on Trial. My Day in Court with David Irving* (New York, 2005).
10 D. J. Rothman, 'Serving Clio and client: the historian as expert witness', *Bulletin of the History of Medicine*, 77 (2003), 24–44.
11 J. A. Neuenschwander, 'Historians as expert witnesses: the view from the bench', www.oah.org/pubs/nl/2002aug/neuenschwander.html (retrieved 3 February 2005). See also B. W. Martin, 'Working with lawyers: A historian's perspective', www.oah.org/pubs/nl/2002may/Martin.html (retrieved 3 February 2005).
12 www.brown.edu/Research/Slavery_Justice/index.html (retrieved 28 September 2005).
13 Fink, 'A new historian'; Frei, Van Laak and Stolleis, *Geschichte vor Gericht*; J. Torpey, '"Making whole what has been smashed:" reflections on reparations', *The Journal of Modern History*, 73 (2001), 333–58.
14 Wetzell, 'Commissioning history'.
15 H. James, 'Die Bergier-Kommission als Wahrheits-Kommission', in Frei, Van Laak and Stolleis, *Geschichte vor Gericht*, pp. 130–40; *Switzerland: National Socialism and the Second World War, Final Report of the Independent Commission of Experts* (Zürich, 2002).
16 *Schlussbericht der Historikerkommission der Republik Österreich. Vermögensentzug während der NS-Zeit sowie Rückstellungen und Entschädigungen seit 1945 in Österreich. Zusammenfassungen und Einschätzungen* (Vienna, 2003).
17 Commission on Jewish Assets in Sweden at the Time of the Second World War, *Sweden and Jewish Assets: Final Report* (Stockholm, 1999).
18 La documentation Francaise, *Rapport Général. Mission d'étude sur la spoliation des Juifs de France*, présidée par Jean Mattéoli (Paris, 2000). Another ten reports were published at the same time.
19 *US Presidential Commission on Holocaust Assets in the United States*; report available on www.pcha.gov/ (retrieved 30 September 2005).
20 See articles by R. Ludi and J.-M. Dreyfus on Switzerland and France in *Historians as political trouble-shooters: Officially Commissioned Surveys of Holocaust Legacies in France and Switzerland*. Center for European Studies Working Papers Series no. 80, www.ces.fas.harvard.edu/publications/LudiDreyfus.pdf (retrieved 30 September 2005).
21 Ibid.
22 H. M. Clokie and J. William Robinson, *Royal Commissions of Inquiry: the Significance of Investigations in British Politics* (Oxford, 1937); P. Weller, *Royal Commissions and the Making of Public Policy* (Melbourne, 1994).
23 *Große Politik der europäischen Kabinette 1871–1914* (Berlin, 1922–27); *British*

Documents on the Origins of the War (London, 1927–38); and *Documents diplomatiques français 1871–1914* (Paris, 1929–59).
24 See www.usip.org/library/truth.html (retrieved 3 February 2005).
25 See, for example, M. L. Dockrill (ed.), *Europe within the Global System, 1938–1960: Great Britain, France, Italy and Germany, from Great Powers to Regional Powers* (Bochum, 1995).
26 F. Bédarida, 'Temps présent et présence de l'histoire', in F. Bédarida, *Histoire, critique et responsabilité* (Bruxelles, 2003), p. 58.

1

The responsibility of the historian

Peter Mandler

In this chapter I sketch out some general principles that might underpin a definition of the responsibility of the historian.[1] In a liberal profession in a liberal society, there can be no single definition of that responsibility, and no-one is entitled *ex officio* to decide upon it. Any such discussion must be indicative and provisional, and personal. So it ought to begin with a personal statement – who is defining this responsibility and for what reasons?

First, I write not only or even chiefly as a contemporary historian. My own historical work ranges from the eighteenth century to the present, and recently – when, between 1998 and 2002, I was secretary of the principal learned society for history in the United Kingdom, the Royal Historical Society – I have become used to speaking on behalf of 'historians in general', that is, those who study all periods of human history, as if they were a monolithic bloc. They are not; and as this volume demonstrates eloquently, contemporary historians have some special responsibilities and problems that mark them out from other kinds of historians. Nevertheless, I think it may still be useful for me to suggest some ideal-typical notions of what a generic historian's responsibilities may be, and readers can decide for themselves whether contemporary historians deserve special treatment or exemptions.

Second, I write as someone whose professional career has been pursued in the United States and, predominantly, in Britain. I am acutely aware that the political environment in Britain, especially, has shaped my expectations of what a historian should be and can do. This has operated in several different ways. Until recently, in Britain, the university was viewed – for better or worse – as an ivory tower with little connection to the everyday lives (or even the everyday politics) of the mass of the people; even fifteen years ago, only about 15 per cent of 19 year olds were enrolled in higher education, and Britain had fewer students and university teachers as a proportion of its population than practically any nation in Europe. Furthermore, and relatedly, although nearly all academic historians are funded by the state in Britain, they have enjoyed an unusual degree of autonomy. Political affiliations have rarely mattered much in questions of hiring and promotion. Funding for historical research – what little there was in Britain – was channelled very indirectly from the Treasury to universities and from universities to individual scholars, normally through automatic entitlements. There have been no centrally funded research institutions of the kind familiar in France and Germany and elsewhere in Europe, and indeed relatively few full-time (non-teaching) researchers. The Economic and Social Research Council, which supports policy-oriented research, funded few historical projects; and when, recently, an Arts and Humanities Research Board was established, it adopted at first a fully 'responsive' mode of funding, setting no criteria for applications and judging between applications solely on scholarly merit and without reference to a set agenda. This degree of autonomy, of which I largely approve, undoubtedly colours my views on the proper relationship between historians, the public and government, and probably makes me see things as much simpler than in practice they are.[2]

Third, I write as someone in mid-career who has misgivings about the transcendental significance of history. We live at a moment when history does appear to have reached a peak in popular consciousness. In Britain, the number of history titles published annually fluctuated just below or just above 500 for a long period, from 1870 to around 1960. Then, in the early 1960s, the number of annual titles started to grow rapidly, to over 5,000 today. The context was, of course, a growth in the number of titles in all subjects, but this is a relevant context of the rising profile of more serious reading in modern society, and history's relative share grew in this period, too, from 1 per cent to as high as 5 per cent. It would be very interesting to know whether a similar graph could be generated for other European languages; I suspect the recent growth, at least, would feature in many; Klas-Göran Karlsson's chapter in this volume suggests as much for Sweden at least. The number of titles is only one (not very good) indicator; but there are many other indicators which corroborate the view that history has today an unusually strong and vibrant grip on the popular imagination.[3]

But this current peak of popularity ought not to give us delusions of grandeur. We need to think carefully about *why* the public is interested in history and whether its interest is always a good thing. The trough – the low point – of public interest as measured by the number of annual titles came between the start and the aftermath of the two World Wars. This may indicate that interest in history has been inversely correlated with what people construe as 'living through history'. 'Living through history' can engender what the Germans call *Geschichtsmüdigkeit*, a surfeit of eventfulness. Only when the press of current events becomes more remote can people relax enough to take an interest in history – when they can discover that 'history' is more than a catalogue of coups and pogroms. This has its healthy side – it could be a sign of the flourishing of civilised pursuits in time of peace – and also its unhealthy side – it could be a sign of a vicarious, restless, half-guilty revelling in the horrors of the twentieth century only when they have become sufficiently remote no longer to implicate the younger generation. But it does not necessarily mean that people are looking to history to find meaning in life or to solve their problems – or, if they do, that we historians ought to encourage them in this. My own strong feelings about this will probably cause me to err in the opposite direction and to play down too far the significance of historical research in contemporary society.

In that spirit of lowered expectations, I will structure the bulk of my chapter around responsibilities or roles that I think the historian ought *not* to claim, and adopt only at the end a more positive view of the responsibilities or roles I think the historian can legitimately seek.

First, it is not the historian's job to act as society's moral compass, or even to offer moral lessons. Anecdotally, when I ask students what they think history is for, most often they answer, 'to teach lessons'. I am not sure that they believe it; the important thing is, they have learnt that it is at least a respectable answer to a difficult question. Of course they are only repeating the very hackneyed dictum of Santayana that 'those who cannot remember the past are condemned to repeat it'.[4] Santayana's formulation dates from a time when most historians still believed in historicism – in Karl Popper's sense, that history was driven by laws or followed patterns or at the very least that it described a moral arc which could be used not only to judge the past but also to judge the present.[5] Not many historians believe that any longer, although they often still fall back on comfortingly fuzzy formulations – such as 'you can't know where you are or where you're going unless you know where you've been' – which transmit the same message, and the message has been reinforced more recently by contemporary history's fascination with the horrors of the twentieth century and the moral attitudinising that fascination brings with it.

This reinforcing of an outdated historicism is one danger of moralising history. It revives a lot of the popular misconceptions about history that otherwise we are desperate to bury. It suggests that history has an underlying logic or pattern. It implies that history repeats itself, and therefore that remembering the crimes of the past arms us against their recurrence (not just because it trains our moral sense, but because we should be able to 'read the signs', to see the Nazis or the Bolsheviks or even the Jacobins coming back and stamp on them before 1933 or 1917 or 1793 happens again). It promises indeed that history has a practical usefulness which can put it on a par with law or business studies, a tempting argument for historians seeking students, but one which we must resist if we do not really believe it. These arguments will backfire. As Klas-Göran Karlsson says in his chapter, 'how can we use the Holocaust to cope with problems of our own day? Can we reduce current problems of racism and neo-Nazism to problems of information about the Holocaust?' And I will add his implied answer, we cannot use the Holocaust to cope with problems of our own day, and if we try, by reducing current problems of racism and neo-Nazism to problems of information about the Holocaust, we will find we are doing very little to address those current problems of racism and neo-Nazism, and probably engendering, too, cynicism about the Holocaust. Better, as he suggests, to use Holocaust education exclusively to educate about the Holocaust, and to leave open – or to problematise – the question as to what relevance the Holocaust might have to contemporary Swedish society.

Beyond this, moralising history distorts the agenda of historical research. Partly in reaction against the deep ideological and social divisions of the earlier twentieth century, late twentieth-century society developed a set of historical icons to which were attributed transcendent moral authority and thus were elevated above controversy in order to provide points of symbolic unity and self-affirmation. Chief among these is, of course, the Holocaust. Who could deny that the special moral status accorded the Holocaust has diverted scholarly attention and resources to it, and necessarily away from other worthy subjects; directly, in the case of at least one important subject cast into darkness by the shadow of the Holocaust, that is, the fate of Germans in Czech and Polish lands after 1945; but indirectly, in making it more difficult to attract research to other important areas of contemporary history that are made to seem trivial in comparison to the awful majesty of the Holocaust – the impact of mass consumption, or telecommunications and information technology, or even Americanisation and youth culture or changing attitudes to gender and sexuality. It seems absurd to me that the 'Institute of Contemporary History' based at the Wiener Library in London, which publishes the *Journal of Contemporary History*, should still be publishing more work on the Second World War than on all those other subjects put together.

So if, first, it is not the historian's job to provide society with a moral compass, second, relatedly, it is not the historian's job either to be its judge and jury. A number of the chapters in this volume raise this question in very acute and properly situated ways, so I will not dwell upon it. It is pretty well recognised now that the canons of evidence and argument that prevail in the courtroom are different from those that prevail in the classroom, and that as a result historians often come off badly when they are dragged into judicial proceedings. In courtrooms, facts are ascertained and then measured up against the law. In classrooms, facts are ascertained and then interpreted. While superficially similar, these processes are in reality very different. In the courtroom, the law is held to be fixed and resolution is all-important, so that the bulk of the effort is devoted to minute ascertainment of the facts. In the classroom, interpretation is deemed to be fluid and open-ended, and the bulk of the effort may be devoted to interpretation rather than ascertainment of the facts, even though the popular image of historians as fact-grubbers suggests otherwise. This mismatch was evident twenty years ago in a celebrated case that divided feminist historians in America, *EEOC* v. *Sears, Roebuck*. The case hinged on whether Sears, a department store chain, had discriminated against women in their hiring and pay practices. Historians appeared on both sides. The facts (pay disparities) were not in dispute; the winner was the side (Sears) that offered the least interpretation, arguing simply that lower pay reflected the different jobs that women had historically filled. The much more complicated, contextualised explanation offered on behalf of the EEOC, which tried to explain *why* women had historically filled those different (and low-paying) jobs, was the most satisfying to historians, but it was hardly heard in court, as its historian was required to answer most questions with flat yes or no answers.[6] In that case, moral positions were in play on both sides. In other cases, historians' natural inclination to resist moralising makes them even less suited to contributing to judicial proceedings, where guilt or innocence is at stake. The question of guilt or innocence is of course interesting to historians, but it is only a starting point. The next question is *why*. The courtroom is rarely interested in why. To ask why is to indulge in an exercise in situational ethics, which is attractive to historians because historical situation is their subject, but which would paralyse any functioning judicial system and is rightly repugnant to society which looks to the judicial system to decide, not to explain. Elsewhere in this volume Raphaëlle Branche offers a similar case where 'historians were summoned to court to tell the truth in a context that offered no means for the concept of historical interpretation to be considered'.

This is not to say that historians have no place in the courtroom; only that they ought to go in without illusions about their place and authority there. It is no coincidence, it seems to me, that historians have been most successful in courtrooms where they have been asked to pronounce only on historical practice itself – for instance, Richard Evans' demonstration of the poor historical practice of David Irving, or Pierre Vidal-Naquet's defence of his historical practice against the charge of defamation by Jean-Marie Le Pen, or even, as Raphaëlle Branche points out, Jean-Luc Einaudi's defence against the charge of defamation by Maurice Papon, which came to no conclusion about Papon's historical guilt but simply defended Einaudi's right to interpret.

Apart from teaching lessons, my students most frequently inform me that the responsibility of the historian is to tell us 'who we are'. This I consider to be even more misconceived. As with the claim that history teaches lessons, I do not think all that many students actually believe that history tells us 'who we are', that is, that it helps us to secure our individual and collective identities. It may have been true once that history – or its pre-modern analogues, 'custom' and 'tradition' – secured people's identities. But in the developed world at least since the late nineteenth century, the period identified as the seedbed of 'the invention of tradition', the hold of tradition has been weakening to such a degree that authority has needed to invent substitutes. Today, at the beginning of the twenty-first century, we live in a society replete with technologies for constructing, storing and diffusing customs and traditions: books, films, databases, archives, monuments, museums. Furthermore, we are so anxious about the weakening purchase of the past that we now include 'memory' itself among those historical commodities requiring institutionalisation – so we have many more memorials, anniversaries, oral history projects, and new kinds of monuments and museums to capture not 'deep' tradition but simply people's ephemeral memories of the recent past.

Do these things tell us 'who we are'? I do not think so. Like the invention of tradition, the institutionalisation of history and memory is very largely a defensive reaction. Many people feel today that 'progress' is a runaway train; the institutionalisation of history and memory can only put feeble obstacles in its path. What the historian Jose Harris has said about the late nineteenth century is so true of our own time that it is worth quoting at some length:

> [T]he consciousness of living in a new age, in a new material context, and a form of society totally different from anything that had ever occurred before was so widespread as to constitute a genuine and distinctive element in the mental culture of the period ... This sense of the unique dominance of the present time was immensely reinforced by the enormous physical growth in the urban environment, by the exploding of scientific knowledge, and by the political and material Europeanisation of the globe. Such changes ... seemed to many people at the time like a quantum leap into a new era of human existence. Past ages of ignorance, scarcity, and irrationality were deemed, not to be wholly done away with, but to be working themselves out 'like a long-division sum' ... There was a marked decline in a popular sense of continuity with past history, and many contemporaries ... remarked upon the emergence of a new 'race' or 'nation' with no spontaneous memory of past time – a race with an ahistorical mentality ... But throughout the period there were also recurrent echoes of the opposite note ... a lurking grief at the memory of a lost domain – a sense that change was inevitable, and in many respects desirable, but that its gains were being purchased at a terrible price.[7]

Such familiar sentiments! And who could deny that our institutionalisations of history and memory probably represent more that 'lurking grief' than a taking to heart? Worse, as I have already suggested, the fascination with the crimes of the first half of the twentieth century may represent not grief but relief, a half-horrified, half-pleasurable sense that Nazism and Bolshevism are near enough to be experienced in moving pictures and in full colour, but also, despite the injunctions to 'never forget', sufficiently distant not to be threatening.

Far from history providing people with identities, it seems to me that people are more likely to impose their own identities upon history. In a recent poll, which asked British people what were the most important events in British and world history over the past one hundred years, the top responses were the death of Princess Diana in 1997 and the destruction of the World Trade Towers in 2001.[8] In other words, asked to identify significance in history, people searched for significance in their own lives – emotional significance – and projected what they found back on history. We will only encourage that kind of backwards projection if we ourselves promote the idea that history is useful because it builds identity.

Many of the identities nurtured by institutionalised history and memory are in fact not the identities of ordinary people, but rather the self-aggrandised identities of politicians or interest groups. National identities, for example, form the subject-matter of a great deal of recent memorialising efforts, precisely at a time when opinion polls tell us (at least in Britain) that most people's identities are formed more by home, neighbourhood, friends and local community than by the nation. Perhaps this should be a source of consolation to us – do we really wish to be a people whose identities were formed by world wars, genocide, slavery and various other forms of ideological, ethnic or gender oppression?

In view of the other chapters in this volume, particularly those on the Swedish and Finnish experiences, I can see that this British experience is not necessarily closely paralleled elsewhere in Europe. Recently in Scandinavia, and I think in Eastern Europe, too, and for a longer period obviously in Germany, history *has* been used widely and intensively to explore contemporary identity, not only to contrast the 'bad' (earlier) twentieth century with the 'good' present, but also to suggest that the 'bad' (earlier) twentieth century laid rotten foundations upon which the present still sits: eugenics was a foundation for social democracy, collaboration with Nazism a foundation for Christian democracy, collaboration with Stalinism a foundation for social democracy. Or, to take another example closer to my own heart, a great deal of contemporary Jewish education *is* nowadays comprised by study of the Holocaust. Many Jewish parents of the current generation, who are often more anxious to develop their children's Jewish identity than were their own parents but who lack their parents' loyalty to the synagogue, fall eagerly upon the Holocaust to provide their children with a distinctive sense of Jewishness. Personally I find this disturbing: the Holocaust is *not* an adequate substitute either for religion or for ethics or for culture or even for the long and varied history of the Jewish people, to serve as the basis for a twenty-first century Jewish identity. It may be more acceptable to be a victim than a perpetrator, but neither victims nor perpetrators are good role-models for twenty-first century communities.[9]

So even where people do really believe that history tells them 'who they are', therefore, that belief might not be a wholesome one for society – or for history. There is no particular reason, apart from our own professional self-love, to freight contemporary identity with historical reminiscence. And there are good professional reasons not to freight the pursuit of history with these contemporary responsibilities. A historical profession too conscious of its role in valorising contemporary identity would, as with a historical profession too concerned to cater to contemporary moral concerns, follow a severely distorted research agenda. National history would eclipse the histories of other countries and cultures. More than a third of the history titles published in Britain cover British history – quite enough, I think – and it may be a lower proportion than in the past; when David Thomson did a study in 1968 of French (and, more superficially, British and American) history writing, he suggested that writings on their own countries formed 'the great majority' of historical books published. Somewhat counter-intuitively, he concluded, 'Nationalist – even nationalistic – historiography is a highly significant feature of our culture in the 1960s.'[10] If, as I think, that is no longer true today, it is something to be celebrated. One of the advantages of the current obsession with early-to-mid twentieth century history is that the world wars and the dictators at least give students a European and sometimes a genuinely global perspective; in Britain it may even be the case that Stalin and Hitler are better known and understood than Churchill, and certainly better than Lloyd George. But if Stalin and Hitler are more intimately part of your own national history, I think it would be your historians' responsibility to draw more attention to Churchill, or, better still, to Pan-Africanism or the history of Japan and China.

We see in the United States one of the most disturbing consequences of a history developing to serve contemporary identity. As we all know, there has been in the United States over the last twenty-five years a proliferation of academic posts, programmes and departments devoted to the study of identity-groups (based on ethnicity, gender or sexuality). This phenomenon is not in itself a cause for concern; on the contrary, it has helped substantially to broaden the American historical profession's research agenda, and has produced some of the most conceptually original and daring work of the last generation. What disturbs me is the growing insistence – normally conveyed *sotto voce* to young people charting out a career (necessarily *sotto voce*, so as not to run foul of anti-discrimination legislation) – that scholars of these identity-groups be drawn exclusively from these identity-groups. The practical reason for this insistence is that universities want to use identity-group programmes to attract more students from those groups to ensure 'diversity', and for this purpose they need faculty from the same groups who can serve as credible role-models or mentors. (Of course universities also want to ensure 'diversity' amongst their faculty, and these identity-group programmes are useful for that purpose, too.) These are laudable goals – but, as a result, it is difficult for anyone but an African-American to get a job teaching (and thus researching) African-American history; for any straight person to get a job teaching (and thus researching) gay and lesbian history; and so on. Taken to its logical consequence, it would be very difficult for me to get a job teaching my chosen field, British history, as I have poor credentials to serve as a role-model or mentor for any young person seeking to shore up their British national identity. But, then, I do not see my job as being largely (or at all) about telling the British 'who they are'.

I think I would go further and argue that it is not the historian's job even to be a good citizen of the polity and nation in which they work. It used to be common – in some countries it still is common – to share out representation on scholarly bodies amongst the various political parties. This was no doubt an effective device to bridge the deep social and ideological divides that fissured many postwar and Cold War societies. But from the 1950s to the 1980s – and in some cases beyond – it also had the effect of fossilising and distorting the development of the historical profession, and of associating historians with politicians in the public mind. As a result, we got more and more socialist or liberal or conservative history at a time when there were fewer and fewer socialists or liberals or conservatives. I am glad to say that there are many signs that this explicit politicisation of history is waning. At a conference I helped to organise recently, Pieter Lagrou, of the Institut d'Histoire du Temps Présent in Paris, made the point that until recently it would have been impossible to appoint someone like him – young, politically unattached, not even French but Belgian – to what would have been seen as a politically-sensitive post.[11] In his chapter in this volume, Martin Sabrow suggests that the politicisation of the historical profession in Germany inevitably arising from the Wende is already subsiding (although he is not wholly optimistic that this is happening for the right reasons). And at another conference I attended recently, organised by the German Historical Institute in London, historians from across Europe were asked whether there could be common trans-national European 'lieux de mémoire' – and to their own evident surprise found themselves repudiating the idea as the figment of Eurocrats who only wanted from historians the same cultural trappings that national politicians had got in Paris or Berlin or Rome.[12] Perhaps that testifies to the low opinion academics have nowadays of EU governance – but I think it testifies, too, to heightened suspicion of the politicisation of history.

Having bashed the politicians and political control of history several times, and implicitly vaunted the political autonomy of historians in Britain, I ought to add that I do not think either that it is the responsibility of the historian to cater to the fleeting demands of the market. This is the current danger in the British context. For a long time, British universities operated, as I have said, without much outside interference, catering to a relatively small audience. History's place was strong and secure. In the last fifteen years, the higher education system has grown rapidly – it now recruits over 40 per cent of the age cohort – and government has taken more of an interest, not so much in the content of the curriculum as in the costs of the system. It has coped with this by forcing more market behaviour upon universities. Degree programmes and whole departments are now subject to closure if they fail to recruit ever increasing numbers of students. As in Sweden, the growing public interest in history has not been matched by growing numbers of students seeking history qualifications in school or university. Several university history departments have closed as a result in the last few years. Those that remain are under pressure to attract students by offering more attractive courses, responding to the fashions of the day in popular taste. At school level, the resulting 'Nazification' of history has been observable for some time; there are signs that it is now encroaching on the university level as well. The market works its influence in another way, as well. Growing numbers of university-based scholars have been attracted, by the attention and money on offer, into writing popular histories. In my university alone, there are two big blockbusters on the Third Reich in preparation, alleged to have earned already millions of dollars in publishers' advances. I am not sure, by the way, that the market really does want that much history of the Third Reich. The evidence is that the most popular subjects in British schools are medieval subjects, and that students are opting for twentieth-century history at 16 not because it is what they want, but because it is what they know best and thus seems to be the safest option for exam success. Teachers are also reluctant to try to teach subjects in which they have little background, and so they too fall back on the familiar. As far as the readers go, books on the Third Reich are not the bestselling history books either in Britain or in the United States and it seems impossible that the publishers will ever earn back these massive advances. For whatever reason, a kind of stampede is under way that threatens to distort the teaching and writing of history as much as any political diktat.

I hope something positive about the responsibilities of the historian is already apparent in what I have said on the negative side. I do want to make a strong case for defending the autonomy of history from the present – from the politicians, from the immediate demands of the marketplace, from the day-to-day debates of journalism and the mass media. As a number of the chapters in this volume argue, politicians, publishers, journalists, pundits and media moguls are fully capable of doing their own jobs without needing our assistance, and when we join with them we have constantly to be on the watch to ensure that their jobs do not overwhelm ours. This is *not* an argument for history remaining in its ivory tower, detached from society, cultivating a spurious neutrality. Other chapters in this volume make a powerful case for accepting responsibilities from politicians and public opinion, out of general public-spiritedness and out of an understandable desire to show what historians can do. It *is* an argument for history to defend what is unique and peculiar to it, and projecting very vigorously – evangelically – its unique and peculiar values *into* society. We will not be able to do that if we allow others to annex or absorb us, and thus confuse in the public mind the practices of history with the practices of politics and the media.

What are those values and practices? Upon contemporary historians I would want to urge the responsibility of the historian for the whole of the past – not just the last fifty years and not just the history of one's own country. The current fascination amongst politicians and the public for contemporary national history, and especially the history of our own role in the Second World War, is a threat to the discipline as a whole. Large sections of a precious human cultural heritage are at risk – the history of pre-modern Europe, but also the histories of Asia and Africa and the Americas outside the United States which have hardly begun to be explored. The remorseless advance of English as a compulsory second language is making it more and more difficult to train historians of non-English-speaking areas. In Britain modern foreign languages are in a pretty perilous state – even German is vanishing from the curriculum. Historians ought to be leagued with linguists to counter this trend, which they cannot do if they are too focused on the recent history of their own country.

Connected to the pastness of the past is the strangeness of the past. Historians ought to be asserting not the similarities of the recent past and the present, as contemporary history tends to do, but the differences. One of the qualities that distinguishes history from the social sciences is that it preserves the endlessly rich variety of human experiences that are no longer directly accessible today. It is in this way almost an ecological enterprise, like the preservation of endangered species. This, too, is threatened by an orientation which insists that the past is useful to us because it provides a stock of experiences similar to ours from which we can learn immediate lessons. I commend to you the words of the medieval historian Gordon Leff, who wrote in 1969 that 'history's verdict' can only ever be 'a figure of speech'.

> No doubt, in certain situations [he said], parallels with the past can provide a moral boost, as with the parallels drawn in 1950 between Britain's situation then and in 1800. But most of history does not revolve around such comparisons, and

when it does the result is usually history at its most jejune ... history, although it is directed to the past, is essentially about the new. It is read and written as the unfolding of events which by definition have not occurred before. That is the only reason for their having a history. If Hitler's invasion threat in 1940 had been identical with Napoleon's in 1800, no separate study of Hitler's would be needed: we should merely say, 'For Hitler in 1940 see Napoleon 1800.'[13]

Or similarly, I might add, if the threat of racism in 2002 were really identical to the threat of racism in 1940, we should merely say, 'For Haider in 2002 see Hitler 1940'. And in rejecting this line of thinking, we can be proud and positive about the difference of the past.

Because the past is different from the present, history teaches different kinds of lessons, skills and values than do the social sciences that deal with the present. For example, while history ought not to make moral prescriptions, that does not mean it is amoral. Its morality is of a different kind, more democratic, I would say. The distancing that a discussion of moral issues in the past entails allows for a more open and participatory moral debate. The most dangerous and stressful moral issues – mere consideration of which can have terrible consequences in the present – can be considered more carefully and coolly if projected upon the past. Nothing bad will happen to us – or nothing bad ought to happen to us – if we say something speculative or even something slightly irresponsible about moral choices in the past. Our irresponsibilities can be reproved and corrected by interaction with others, without fear of permanent damage having been done by the venture. This is yet another reason to try to persuade the public that history has no direct connection with the present – so long as people in the Balkans contend that moral choices of the fourteenth century still matter today, or people in Northern Ireland still debate the moral choices of the seventeenth century as if they were taken yesterday, then historians will be unable to operate safely in those fields and no real 'lessons' will ever be learnt. The past ought to be something of a refuge, not a battlefield.

The French historian Augustin Thierry said 200 years ago, 'I believe I have found a way to peace in the serious study of history.'

> By this I do not mean that the contemplation of the past and the experience of the ages have led me to write off as a youthful illusion the love of liberty with which I had set out: quite the contrary, I am becoming more and more attached to it. I still cherish liberty, but with a less impatient love ... If our eyes could sweep over that long-travelled road along which we are following our fathers, we would detach ourselves from the quarrels of the day, from the resentments of personal ambition and of partisanship, from petty fears and petty hopes.

Thierry, of course, was a historicist. He still felt that reflection on the past would assist his ideological struggles in the present, by putting them into the longest-term perspective. He went on to say,

> I remind myself that at all times, in all places, many men could be found who felt the same aspirations that I feel, even though their situations and opinions were different from mine, but that most of them died before they could witness the fulfilment of what they had anticipated in thought. The labours of this world are accomplished slowly, and each successive generation merely adds one more stone to the construction of the edifice dreamt of by ardent minds.[14]

Today we are less likely to feel that history is an edifice, and that we are linked to past generations by a common arc of aspirations. But this only makes the past even more capacious – its immediate relevance reduced, its wider and higher relevance enhanced, for it offers us a much freer inquiry into human nature and human possibility if unimpaired by the fleeting moral and political problems of the present.

History is also slower and more painstaking than other disciplines of the human sciences. It gives up its secrets reluctantly, and when we put our hands on those secrets they came in partial and opaque forms, requiring more contextualisation and interpretation than the data of other disciplines. These qualities intrinsic to history give historians a unique set of skills – forensic and investigative, interdisciplinary, evaluative and interpretive. No wonder that journalists and politicians are attracted to us, for we have precisely a patience, a persistence and a thoroughness, and consequently a credibility, that they lack by the very pressurised and volatile nature of their own crafts.

Does this mean, finally, that we ought to resist when politicians and journalists come to us for help? A great deal of what I have said so far might suggest such a resistance – that, for example, the Netherlands Institute for War Documentation ought not to have undertaken its investigation into the fall of Srebrenica, or that Paul Bew ought not to have acted as historical adviser to the Saville Tribunal into the events of Bloody Sunday 1972 in Northern Ireland. But I do not think that is a necessary conclusion even from the extremely high-minded and rather absolutist principles I have been enunciating. For one thing, as Paul Bew says, the kind of material such inquiries can develop, and the privileged access historians can get to that material, is absolutely irresistible. If nothing else, when historians involve themselves in such enterprises, they are doing a service to future historians by ensuring that all the kinds of evidence they want will be available in the form they want it. (For the same reason, my learned society, the Royal Historical Society, provides a service to the UK national archives by advising on how the vast amounts of government records – which cannot all be preserved – should be sampled. At least we can guess at which future historians might like to have.) Beyond this, we do have special skills and values that are useful to such inquiries. The trick, as I have already suggested (and as many of the chapters in this book elaborate in greater detail), is in trying to ensure that historians' involvement does not do damage to history.

Historians have to go into such engagements with politics and journalism making clear what they can do and what they cannot do. They have to try to insist from the outset on the integrity of their own methods, their own pace and their own style – a hazardous business, as the Srebrenica inquiry found, though in their case, in the end, a vital one. They have to try to exert some control over the 'spin' applied to their participation. The application of their unique skills and values does *not* give transcendent moral authority, and any attempts by politicians or interest-groups to claim that the verdicts of historians represent 'the verdict of history' – something quite different – ought to be explicitly repudiated. And sometimes, yes, when the whole enterprise is too polluted by bad faith and politics, historians have to say that they – as scholars and educators – are not the people to turn to. Higher education is not the appropriate venue for a campaign – it is up to the politicians to decide if they are willing to accept a research programme instead of a campaign, and to run the risk (indeed the certainty) that the outcome will not have the clarity or the excitement of a campaign slogan. If we do not resist being drawn into campaigns, then we will put at risk the autonomy, the impartiality and, crucially, the credibility with the public that has been slowly and painfully built up for academic life in Europe over the past century. We will put at risk a lot of the qualities that have caused universities to endure while governments and newspapers have come and gone. Each time a politician or a lobbyist or a journalist comes to us, seeking to borrow our authority, our time and resources for a campaign on the grounds that the public is – today, in the short-term – clamouring for it, we have to try to remember that the greater public interest is in the long term integrity of our craft. There can be no higher responsibility for the historian than to remember the long term.

Notes

1 I am grateful to Mark Mazower and Richard Rathbone, who helped to organise the conference discussed at note 11 below, from which I derived many of the ideas in this chapter; and to the very stimulating discussants at the conference in Stockholm in August 2002 upon which this volume is based. The text of this chapter is, needless to say, entirely my own responsibility.
2 See www.esrc.ac.uk and www.ahrc.ac.uk.
3 P. Mandler, *History and National Life* (London, 2002), especially chapter 4; see also R. Samuel, *Theatres of Memory* (London, 1994). Dr Olaf Blaschke of Trier University is undertaking similar research on the German case.
4 G. Santayana, *The Life of Reason, Vol. I, Reason in Common Sense* (London, 1905), p. 284. But Santayana was speaking here not of *history* but of *memory*, in the most basic and practical sense, that primitive human civilisation was built upon the storing up of experiences. He did *not* believe that 'those who cannot remember history are condemned to repeat it'. In a later volume of *The*

Life of Reason, Santayana in fact criticised the cruder forms of historicism then prevalent.
5   K. R. Popper, *The Poverty of Historicism* (London, 1957).
6   See P. Novick, *That Noble Dream: The 'Objectivity Question' and the American Historical Profession* (Cambridge, 1988), pp. 502–40; also, for competing interpretations of the implications for academic practice, cf. T. Haskell and S. Levinson, 'Academic Freedom and Expert Witnessing: Historians and the *Sears* Case', *Texas Law Review* 66 (1988), 301–31, and A. Kessler-Harris, 'Academic Freedom and Expert Witnessing: A Response to Haskell & Levinson', *Texas Law Review* 67 (1988), 429–40.
7   J. Harris, *Private Lives, Public Spirit: A Social History of Britain 1870–1914* (Oxford, 1993), pp. 32–3, 36.
8   J. Ezard, 'Public Believes History Began on Day Diana Died', *Guardian* (24 August 2002).
9   I ought not to have to say this, because I ought not to need an ethnic credential to make such an argument, but to avoid misunderstanding I should say that I am myself Jewish, the son of a refugee from Hitler, and so I do have a personal stake in contemporary Jewish education, just as I have (along with other professional historians) a personal stake in the complexion of the historical profession.
10 D. Thomson, 'Must History Stay Nationalist?', *Encounter* (June 1968), 22.
11 'Conflicting Loyalties: The Responsibility of the Historian', organised with R. Rathbone and M. Mazower for the Royal Historical Society, School of Oriental and African Studies, University of London, 16 February 2002. A report on this conference by Mark Mazower can be found in the *Royal Historical Society Newsletter*, Spring 2002 (see www.rhs.ac.uk/newsletters.html).
12 'European Lieux de Mémoire', Conference of the German Historical Institute London, Cumberland Lodge, Windsor, 5–7 July 2002.
13 G. Leff, 'The Past and the New', *The Listener* (10 April 1969), 485–7.
14 F. Stern (ed.), *The Varieties of History* (Cleveland, 1956), p. 67.

2

Public uses of history in contemporary Europe

Klas-Göran Karlsson

In Latin, it has been proclaimed that history is the teacher of life, *Historia magister vitae*. But what can we really learn from history? How should we understand the relationship between what we consider as our present situation, our interpretations of the past and our expectations for the future? What are the benefits or values that we, as individuals and members of various collectives, can extract from the historical dimension? How can history be used, and how should it be used? How can the abuse of history be avoided? Twenty years ago professional historians, intellectuals and politicians mostly found such questions devoid of meaning. Today they attract considerable interest all over Europe. Society has regained part of what the American scholar Carl Schorske has defined as the capacity to 'think with history', an expression which he elaborates as 'the employment of the materials of the past and the configurations in which we organise and comprehend them to orient ourselves in the living present'.[1] According to Schorske, this historicist thinking was predominant in nineteenth century Europe, but was eclipsed by twentieth-century modernism.

This chapter focuses on the causes and consequences of the recent return of historicism, borrowing from a typology of different uses of history that was originally elaborated for a study of how history was used to undermine the foundations of the Soviet Union.[2] As a Swede, a historian of East European historiography, and the leader of a large research project on the position of the Holocaust in European historical culture, the illustrations I use will inevitably be influenced by my own experiences. Consider, for example, the intense European interest in the Holocaust at the turn of the millennium.

Holocaust teachings and exports

In June 1997 Swedish Prime Minister Göran Persson initiated a public information campaign on the Holocaust called *Levande historia*, or 'Living

History'. This was justified on the grounds that information about the Nazi genocide of European Jewry could and should prevent genocides from being perpetrated in the future. In fact, the general political-pedagogical idea behind this state-sponsored project, which in 2003 was transformed into a permanent state administrative authority in Sweden, is that history teaches lessons. 'It happened once. It should not have happened, but it did. It must not happen again, but it could',[3] was Göran Persson's urgent warning to the world in his opening address to the Stockholm International Forum on the Holocaust in January 2000. In other words, historical knowledge is the best prescription for recurrent undemocratic social illness, and by extension, the best way to prevent any future genocide.

In Sweden, the leaders of the competing political parties on the right and the left immediately rallied to the support of this initiative, and it was widely admired abroad. Prominent politicians from all over the world came to the Stockholm Forum to express their support for Göran Persson and his Living History initiative. In the years after 1997, the idea was exported to several countries on the eastern shores of the Baltic Sea, among them the Russian Federation. Its main history product, the book *Tell ye your children ...* , was translated into many languages.[4] In this way, the Living History initiative has restored the postwar role of Sweden as a national model to be admired. In a historical-moral sense, the Living History concept of Holocaust education became a new kind of international aid directed mainly towards countries in the former Communist bloc to assist in the transformation processes towards democracy and the rule of law.

It goes without saying that the results of this are hard to measure. The first, general problem has to do with the nature of history. Can information about the premeditated mass murder of large parts of European Jewry in 1941–45 really in itself promote democratic social development? Obviously, current social problems like contempt for democracy and lack of respect for other human beings in some sections of society can hardly be solved by communicating historical information. How is the relationship between the Holocaust and problems in contemporary European society to be understood? A plausible cognitive answer is that there are structural similarities between then and now, such as racist or anti-Semitic ideas that still exist as an undercurrent in society or have recurred lately. In fact, Göran Persson alluded to this continuity of prejudice at the Stockholm Forum:

The evil view of humanity that made the Holocaust possible did not just cease to exist at the end of the Second World War. The ideology of hatred and xenophobia forms the basis for new political parties that are now exploiting the democratic system to gain power. We can see it happening in Sweden. We can see it happening all over Europe.[5]

The problem of such an analysis is that it gives no room for differences and divergences. It is clear, for example, that the ideology of anti-Semitism is much more obscure and discredited today than it was in the inter-war and wartime years. A more emotionally and normatively defined answer is that information about the Holocaust awakens feelings of disgust and repudiation against racism and racial violence, thereby helping to prevent new genocides. But this approach can be simplistic because the story of the Holocaust is often painted in black, as an incomprehensible mess, without sophisticated reflection about the complexities of individual choice that would enable one to make informed decisions today. A third, more qualified answer, using both cognitive and emotional/normative elements, is that Holocaust history, adequately taught, can empower people in their capacity as responsible individual and collective actors in their own lives, by letting them reflect on and value how people acted in the past. Historian Charles Maier has argued convincingly in favour of such an understanding of history: 'The intrusion of history is not only theoretical. It is also a legacy of being an accomplice or a victim, or just an onlooker. In each role, history entails the uncomfortable presence of earlier unresolved roles.'[6]

Obviously, the Living History project cannot be exported successfully without a shared cultural and ideological understanding of the Holocaust, its causes and consequences. In the receiving countries, strong barriers of ready-made, more or less unchangeable conceptions and expostulations sometimes have to be shattered in order to make the project workable. In the Communist period, while great importance was attached to history in general in cultural, educational, political and social life, this did not include the Holocaust, which was totally absent from the East European historical cultures. In the official public history of monopolistic textbooks and socialist-realist monuments, the victims of Nazi aggression were mainly Communists. Jews were not even mentioned, as they were not allowed to compete with the Communists as combined victims, resistance fighters and victors in the public mind.

Likewise, there has been a certain reluctance to acknowledge the victimisation of the Jews during the war in the post-Communist era. There remains a lack of information on the Holocaust in Russian history textbooks, for example. The Communist victims have been replaced by Russian patriots.[7] In nationalistic interpretations of the Nazi war-time atrocities, the martyrdom of one's own national group tends to be emphasised, especially but not solely in East and Central Europe.[8] This tendency is even noticeable in the diaspora of such communities. James Young relates the story of how a local initiative to erect a Babi Yar memorial in Denver, to memorialise the Nazi mass killings of Jews outside Kiev in September 1941, was met with harsh criticism from the local Ukrainian-American community, which accused the initiators of having downplayed the significance of the fact that Ukrainians had also been massacred by the Nazis in Babi Yar.[9]

In addition, the focus on the Holocaust inspired by the Living History initiative has had to compete with a new determination to reveal information about the terror perpetrated in largely the same territories by the Soviet regime and its East European satellites not only against political opponents, but against broad stratas of the population. In independent Ukraine, for example, information about the Soviet 'terror-famine' of 1932–33, in which Ukrainians were unambiguously the victims, have consequently been a more popular subject of historical revelation than the Holocaust, in which Ukrainians also acted as perpetrators.[10] There are no indications that the exporters of Living History have reckoned with such complications that might thwart their efforts to use the lessons of the past to teach horizontal, shared values such as democracy, instead of narrow vertical values which could feed new nationalist movements.

Leaving history behind

Living History was also without precedent in modern Sweden. The context was, however, entirely different from the East European one. The importance of Holocaust education and research, and history teaching in general, was stressed over and over again at the Stockholm Forum. Furthermore, many voices were raised in favour of strengthening a historical consciousness to emphasise that, in Göran Persson's words, 'all of us form the link between a hideous past and a future in which such atrocities as the Holocaust must never be repeated'.[11]

These were radically new political objectives, irrespective of whether we are talking about commitment to learn from the Holocaust specifically, or a commitment to make historically informed choices more generally. No previous Swedish government had shown any marked interest in history for such purposes in the postwar era. History had almost been eliminated as an independent subject in the Swedish general school system, and professional historians had seldom been engaged in public tasks other than writing commemorative publications. The closest that leading politicians came to taking an interest in history was typically when writing memoirs.

Schorske's view of the twentieth century as modernist in its approach was widespread in Sweden, as much among the Social Democrats as among their non-socialist opponents. This involved relating a contemporary situation to what is perceived as a bright future, but leaving history as a dimension inexorably past, allegedly without any relevance for individual or society. Swedish culture could also be defined as 'economistic', oriented towards the production, distribution and consumption of material and social well-being, rather than towards cultural and historical values. It goes without saying that this ideological development has not been unique for postwar Sweden, but was possibly accentuated by the fact that Sweden stood outside the Second World War, and thereby outside many of the emotions and the intellectual debates that kept historical interest alive in the countries that took part in the war. A large research project on Sweden in the Second World War, which was conducted at Stockholm University in the 1970s and resulted in more than twenty doctoral theses, met a most limited public interest.[12]

One reaction to this marginalisation of historians and history teachers was to turn to the allegedly more relevant social sciences for guidance. Consequently, quantitative methods and sociological theories, aiming at nomothetic explanation and prediction, gained a footing among historians in the 1960s. Social history became the predominant strand of historical research.[13] Another reaction was to immunise the profession from participation in contemporary debate. Potential social or state pressure for relevant historical perspectives were met exclusively with references to internal scholarly rules and standards. Among them was the basic idea that a historical phenomenon must be selected for research, explained and understood from its contemporary setting, not from the perspectives, values and demands of later days. It was argued that history has its own inherent logic and no final result. Relevance criteria were seldom openly discussed. From this point of view, any demand that history should teach simple lessons to posterity was rejected from the trivial idiographic argument that history is constant change, and that the future cannot be predicted because it may bring entirely new factors and developments that we cannot anticipate. As a middle position between these extremes, some historians and history teachers endeavoured to combine a respect for the distinctive character of historical phenomena with an interest in connecting history with especially problematic and conflict-ridden aspects of contemporary society, by means of ideas of chronological-genetic developments, of structural, comparative perspectives and of historically framed, 'middle-range' social theories. With another approach, which can be called genealogical, the relation between the present and the past has an emotional rather than an objective character, and is called forth by individuals or identity groups who use history as a means of finding a sense of rootedness in a quickly changing world.[14]

A third reaction, partly related to the latter approach, has been an increased interest in theoretically and 'didactically' analysing the cultural or symbolic terms of interaction between history and society. How was history used in different historical periods and societies? How should historical perspectives be justified and used for different individual and societal purposes, both inside and outside the scholarly community? In more advanced didactic thinking, developed primarily in West Germany/Germany, the obvious solution to the question of the justification and use of history was to reject strictly scholarly ideals. Instead, the concept of historical consciousness, denoting a relationship between an understanding of a current situation, interpretations of the past and expectations for the future, was introduced in order to express an understanding that human beings and various identity groups orient themselves in life and society by making use of history, often in a way that has little to do with a scholarly or educational treatment of the past, but with existential needs, moral indignation, political interests, ideological aspirations and even commercial aims. The concept of 'historical culture' has more recently been developed to denote a wide cultural process and structure in which history is produced, mediated and consumed in a particular society. Also other developments within history scholarship such as new research on memories, monuments and myths, are obviously inspired by this third reaction.[15]

The return of history

This rethinking of the role of history in society is obviously not only due to internal scholarly debate. Developments such as the end of the Cold War, the collapse of Communism in Eastern Europe, and the re-emergence there of pre-Communist and pre-Soviet conflicts, have certainly stimulated historical consciousness since 1990. In Western Europe, the increasing functional problems of the welfare state, and issues surrounding multiculturalism, ethnification, regionalisation and Europeanisation, have also led to historical reflection and reassessment. History has been able to provide adequate answers to many people about who 'we' and who 'they' are, what 'we' have in common with 'them' and what separates 'us' from 'others'. In addition, history has proved to be an extremely efficient weapon for intellectuals and politicians to mobilise large populations for various moral, political and ideological projects.

It goes without saying that the Living History initiative must be analysed from a perspective of political mobilisation. As has been argued elsewhere, the altruistic motive to counteract undemocratic ideas, hinted at above, is not enough to explain the introduction of Living history, why it was introduced precisely in the late 1990s, and why the reception was extremely successful. A more thorough explanation must bring two political arenas to the fore: a national and a European one.[16]

At the time of the introduction of the information campaign, the governing social democracy had been harassed since the early 1990s by accusations that the welfare state had been built not on the sound foundations depicted in the traditional Swedish grand narrative, but on unsound policies such as the forced sterilisation of the 'mentally retarded', the registration of individuals holding radical political opinions, and the confiscation of the property of Swedish Jews who had disappeared during the war. Furthermore, the alleged compliance of the civil service and government – a coalition led by the Social democratic Premier Per Albin Hansson – with Nazi Germany in the first period of the war was severely attacked. In this situation, a Holocaust information campaign can be interpreted as a government strategy to regain the moral-political initiative in national debate.

In the years leading up to Sweden's admission into the European Union on 1 January 1995, the ruling Social Democrats hastily changed their relationship to Europe from a traditionally restrained wait-and-see policy to a more unequivocally positive attitude. The process of Europeanisation has many facets. One, stressed by the British historian Norman Davies, is the endeavour to create a common European identity and foundation of values by calling attention to what he calls 'an Allied scheme of history'. This consists of the ideology of anti-fascism, based on the notion of the Second World War as the triumph of Good over Evil, and a sympathetic attitude towards the victims of the same Evil.[17] Since Davies wrote his book on European history in 1996, the cultural and political idea that the history of the Second World War and the Holocaust can promote a European foundation of values has become still more established. Newcomers into the European Union are requested to submit to these European values by laying bare their national guilt in the Holocaust process. This request is often an aspect of the more general debate over federalism, and the appropriate balance between nation and Europe. The introduction of Living History gave a clear signal that the Swedish government was choosing to promote European values. In this rather unconventional way, Sweden recognised its traditional cultural, economic and political orientation towards Germany, admitted its compliance with Nazi Germany, and acknowledged the guilt of non-participation in the war. Thus, Sweden entered the Second World War in retrospect.

In a broader European perspective, two additional developments in the 1990s, both more or less directly related to the end of the Cold War, probably served to promote an increased interest in the Holocaust. One was the regrettable fact of new genocides perpetrated in different parts of the world, and not only in distant territories such as Rwanda, but also in south-eastern Europe. The Balkan tragedies made it more urgent to develop a cognitive understanding of the general conditions for genocide. In the search for answers, the Holocaust obviously served as an archetype of all genocides, and had already been a focus of historical research. The other development was that ideology, dividing west from east, tended to give way to ethics and 'politics of conscience' with universal claims. In the search for absolute evils, concepts such as 'Auschwitz' replaced the respective antagonists in the Cold War as the expression of the evil.

Uses of history

The account just given proves that history has been frequently used in late twentieth-century Europe. History is made use of when it is activated in a communicative process in order for certain groups in a certain society to satisfy certain needs or look after certain interests. The second part of this chapter is intended to present a more systematic analysis of the mechanisms at work when history is used. What follows is a typology of different ways of using history, produced in order to reach a more general, comparative understanding of the role of history in society. It is based on theoretical links between different needs of history, different uses, different groups and categories of users, and different functions in society. In addition, these uses are thought to possess different degrees of strength and urgency in different European societies and historical periods.[18]

Need	Use	User	Function
Discover Reconstruct	Scholarly-scientific	Professional Historians	Verification Interpretation
Remember Forget	Existential	Everybody	Orientation Stabilisation
Rediscover	Moral	Intellectuals Educated segments	Reconciliation Rehabilitation Restoration
Invent Construct	Ideological	Intellectuals Political élites	Legitimation Rationalisation
Forget Eradicate	Non-use	Intellectuals Political élites	Legitimation Rationalisation
Illustrate Make public Debate	Political-Pedagogical	Intellectuals Political élites Educators	Politisation Instrumentalisation

The scholarly-scientific use of history

The scholarly-scientific use of history is based on relatively strict professional, discipline-specific rules and standards, such as the notion that a historical phenomenon must be understood and explained on the basis of a contemporaneous historical context, not on the basis of latter-day conditions and interests, as well as on an empirical source material. In general, history must be regarded as a prospective movement, in which no final results are given, because history is permanent change. Scholarly-scientific criteria of historical relevance are more often than not determined by internal, scholarly value judgments, which means that the history selected for research or teaching is chosen to illuminate a theoretical position considered fruitful to develop, or to give further empirical evidence to a historical phenomenon or setting that already has been subject to scholarly analysis. Scholarly aims are often cumulative or evolutionary, more seldom revolutionary, but are mainly focused on the discovery of new historical knowledge and on its interpretive reconstruction into two different contexts: the contemporary setting of the phenomenon in question, and the front-line of historical scholarship. This contextualisation of history is often characterised by abstraction, analytical openness and complexity. To be able to carry out a scholarly-scientific intellectual operation of this kind, professional training is normally considered necessary. Part of this ideal self-understanding is often the opinion that it is a scholarly virtue to dissociate oneself from the history interests, needs and requests of the surrounding society.

Quite often, a claim of exclusivity or hierarchy is part of the scholarly-scientific idea of history: one's own professional use of history is legitimate and good, while all non-scholarly uses of history are to be branded as misuse or abuse, or at least judged less outstanding. The scholarly history is thought to 'trickle down' from historians to the larger society, in itself producing intellectual values. This scholarly-scientific use is strongest in liberal Western societies, where scholars are relatively autonomous, and where general prosperity allows for the employment of a group of people occupied solely with the task of safeguarding the 'collective memory'.

The developments since the early 1990s analysed above and in other chapters of this book have rendered the scholarly-scientific position more difficult to maintain. When the state insists that historians should investigate certain topics above others, or urges historians to participate in politically composed history commissions; when non-scholarly, popular history-writers successfully compete with trained historians for the favour of educated readers; when historical fictionalisations are applauded in the media: some professional historians are inevitably tempted to adjust their standards in order to meet these new circumstances. Others may choose to stand even more firmly by their traditional codes of practice. A few have argued for a rethinking of the entire scholarly-scientific concept, questioning the divide between scholarly and non-scholarly uses of history.[19]

In Communist Eastern Europe, professional historians served as an extended arm of the state, mainly performing ideological and fostering tasks. Although often claiming to represent the peak of historical scholarship, scholarly-scientific approaches were normally allowed only when dealing with topics considered situated outside a widely defined political and ideological realm. Consequently, outstanding Soviet scholarly historical works were mostly produced by scholars concentrating on certain aspects of the history of antiquity or the Middle Ages.

With a few notable exceptions (such as the bold reformist Yurii Afanasev, who incessantly asked for 'real' historical truth instead of the political truths – pravda – mediated by Soviet propagandists) historians did not play prominent roles in the critical debates of the glasnost period, but were inhibited by their prolonged and close relationship to Communist power. Even after the fall of Eastern European Communism and the Soviet state, many historians have continued to perform political and ideological roles, nowadays in the service of various nationalist powers. In other East and Central European countries, however, the transition has made it possible to initiate a professionalisation process, often by means of contacts with an international historical community from which they were excluded during the Cold War era.

The existential use of history

The existential use of history is triggered off by the need to remember, or alternatively to forget, in order to uphold or intensify feelings of orientation, and during times of insecurity, pressure or sudden change. Memory has become a central concept in the humanities and the social sciences; it is a retrospective, present-minded mental process in which we confront or integrate reconstructions or representations of the past – normally images of concrete figures, times and places – with our contemporary experiences. Thus, memory can provide a comforting relationship to history, a kind of 'presence of the past', which makes one feel connected to a broad narrative. Consequently, memory fosters identity.

Since the existential use of history often is of a very private nature, it will not be analysed in depth in this context. However, as the American scholars Roy Rosenzwieg and David Thelen have emphasised, an engagement in the 'intimate past', as expressed for example in genealogical trees, diaries and photo-albums, often leads to an interest in larger pasts situated outside the narrow family worlds.[20] It should furthermore be noted that many scholars, following the French sociologist Maurice Halbwachs and historian Pierre Nora, have emphasised that all memories, even the most private ones, are social constructs, predisposed with the cognitive and emotional framework of the social group to which we relate.[21] Therefore, memories can easily be retrieved, manipulated and mobilised on a collective level by those who are able and willing to give utterance to the values and ideals of the social group in question. When that happens, history obviously fulfils other, more politicised and antagonistic social functions. For the same reason, the production and survival of private memories with no political or social sanction is often problematic in totalitarian societies and states.[22]

The existential use of history is normally well developed in societies where the function of memory has been strengthened as a result of conflicts and turbulence, external pressures and/or potent intra-cultural homogenisation. In Russia, for example, interest in 'the Russian idea' related to allegedly non-Communist phenomena, such as the Second World War, the orthodox church and local histories, has palpably increased among individuals and groups in search for new, post-Communist and post-Soviet identities and securities.[23] Existential uses of history, however, may also operate in a post-industrial society which has passed beyond a certain level of material satiation and in which 'post-materialist values', related to belonging, self-expression and the quality of life, are in greater demand.[24]

The moral use of history

The moral use of history is based on indignation at the scant attention given to troubling aspects of history in a society, and on an endeavour to restore or rehabilitate them. Generally, the moral use has proved to be prominent in a situation where a culturally insensitive government, at the head of a totalitarian or a dysfunctional state, is for some reason, such as political-cultural liberalisation or newly gained openness, suddenly exposed to criticism because essential aspects of the past have been concealed from the population. Thus, the point of departure of the moral use of history is often a specific event, such as the introduction of a political reform. However, it may also be the publication of an article, a book or another kind of historical artefact with historical 'exposures' or 'revelations' that meet with a broad social response and, accordingly, achieve a paradigmatic significance.

An example was the policy of openness, or *glasnost*, that the last Soviet state and party leader Mikhail Gorbachev introduced in the years 1986–87. After a short period of a cautious intellectual debate over the 'blank spots' of Soviet history, focused on key-words such as ethics and truth, a broad settlement of historical accounts involving millions of people followed that did not come to an end until the Communist Party was abolished in 1990, and the Soviet Union dissolved a year later. In this process of large-scale, rapidly rising popular indignation and anger, and a resulting delegitimation of Soviet Communist rule, Soviet monuments were destroyed, names of Communist power-holders effectively removed from schools, streets, squares and cities, and monopolistic history text-books taken out of service by the champions of openness. Millions of former Soviet citizens and Communist Party members, who had been dehumanised and killed in the course of several decades of Soviet Communist terror directed against various categories and groups of the Soviet population, were rehabilitated. *Memorial*, the first democratic organisation in the Soviet Union, was created in 1987 with the sole purpose of erecting a monument to the memory of all those who disappeared in the terror machinery. Furthermore, the creation of *Memorial* inspired tens of thousands of Soviet citizens to write letters to *glasnost* newspapers and periodicals containing private narratives of how their lives had been ruined by ruthless Soviet Communist rule. Among the non-Russians in the Soviet state, the publication of documents demonstrating Russian political oppression and imperial attitudes strengthened the feelings of indignation and excitement, collectively experienced on an ethno-national level. Thus the publication of the Molotov-Ribbentrop pact of August–September 1939, which sealed the fate of the independent inter-war Estonian, Latvian and Lithuanian states, caused moral-political turbulence all over the Baltic Soviet Republics.[25]

Another example of a moral use of history, which found less dramatic expressions and had less revolutionary consequences for those in power, was the Swedish history debate mentioned previously. It was less obviously related to political changes, although its outbreak coincided with a governmental change from a Social Democratic to a non-socialist government in the early 1990s. Instead, it was more immediately related to the disclosure of supposed scandals in Swedish twentieth-century history. Symptomatically, these were not written by professional historians, who in several cases had been working on the same issues, but by journalists. One of them was Maria-Pia Boëthius, whose 1991 book *Heder och samvete* (Honour and Conscience) harshly criticised the Swedish war-time political relationship to Nazi Germany from a populist and moralist position; the upper classes and men were indulgent towards Hitler, Nazi demands and Nazism, she argued, while the lower classes and women were not. In two articles published in 1997, another journalist, Maciej Zaremba, writing for the leading Swedish morning newspaper *Dagens Nyheter*, described a policy of forced sterilisations of allegedly inferior citizens, carried out from the 1930s to the 1970s and affecting tens of thousands of Swedes. By revealing a eugenic programme, closely related to contemporary ideas and practices maintained by advocates of Nazism, Zaremba's articles reinforced the position held by Boëthius. The debates surrounding these issues were characterised by a strong moral indignation from critics as well as defenders of the Swedish welfare state.[26]

The ideological use of history

The kind of morally based historical debates discussed above have often been followed by an explicitly ideological use of history. In the case of the Baltic republics, the revelations of the historical existence of the German-Soviet pact started up cultural and gradually more political processes that produced new grand narratives on which to build alternative non-Soviet and post-Soviet national identities. In particular, this work was done in the Baltic Popular Fronts that were organised in the summer of 1988. Baltic histories were provided with new meanings by stressing millennial perspectives of ethnic consciousnesses and national independencies, cultural affiliations to Europe and the Baltic Sea region going back many hundreds of years, and successful state and nation buildings in the inter-war period. By contrast, periods of Russian and Soviet rule over the Baltic area were unambiguously coloured in black.[27]

Ideological uses of history are generally related to attempts to arrange historical elements into a relevant context of meaning, made mainly by groups of intellectuals and politicians in control of public representations. Unlike the scholarly-scientific use of history, this process is not defined by its correspondence to empirical evidence. Instead, what matters is the correspondence to external objectives, or rather the capacity to convince, influence, rationalise, mobilise and authorise with the aid of historical perspectives. Consequently, the focus of the ideological use of history is not on facts, as in the case of the moral use, but rather on the grand narrative, its consistency, pedagogical clarity and capacity to convince and persuade.

The ideological use is intimately connected with the success of those systems of ideas that employ history in order to build up legitimacy and rationalise mistakes and errors in the past by referring to objective necessities or historical laws. In general, ideological history is legitimised by means of absolute chronological boundaries and clear-cut periodisations, black-and-white descriptions, strong continuity lines and perspectives of unproblematic progress. In the Soviet Union, history was used ideologically to prove the supremacy of the Communist system. Sometimes this was done by using a Marxist-Leninist interpretation which depicted historical development through class struggle and revolutionary advance. At other times it was done by applying a nationalistic, so-called Soviet-patriotic perspective of gradual national growth and glorification of the Russian nation. It was the latter perspective that dominated in the protracted Stalinist period of cultural and ideological orthodoxy from the early 1930s to the advent of *glasnost*.

History has proved especially useful for nationalists, whose main interest is to ascertain a special, symbiotic relationship between land and nation, in order to put forward territorial claims. One method is to trace this relationship as far into the past as possible, according to the formula 'the longer back, the more legitimate'. A related method is to claim a more continuous possession of the same territory than any competing national group, while a third position is built less on history than on power. A tragic consequence of such historical claims, clearly noticeable in parts of Eastern Europe since *circa* 1990, has been the ethnic cleansing of groups perceived not to 'belong' to the region they inhabit.

Non-use of history

So far, the moral use of history in Sweden since the early 1990s has not resulted in any clear ideological reconstruction of its grand narrative. In spite of the criticism to which the history of the modern welfare state has been subjected, there appears to remain a broad consensus that it was a positive development. Interestingly, ideological uses of history have been shunned in Sweden. This is rooted in the deliberate adoption by some intellectual and political groups of an attitude according to which history, or some parts of it, should be ignored. Paradoxically, just as is true when ideological uses of history occur, its non-use plays a legitimising function, as a conscious effort is made to rationalise historical misdeeds. The non-use of history is thus in itself an ideological choice.

Generally speaking, the non-use of history is a successful strategy in societies where the legitimacy of the state is not built on history or cultural heritage, but on the belief that social-state relations are especially successful, or that the future looks especially rewarding. One example already mentioned is the official Swedish modernist or 'economistic' notion that history is an object of the past, worthless for the cultivation of a qualitatively new society. Another example is to be found in the early Soviet state, in which a predominant attitude, especially among the influential members of the *Proletkult* organisation, such as the physician Aleksandr Bogdanov and the first Bolshevik Commissar of Enlightenment Anatolii Lunacharskii, was that the new, socialist Soviet society had thrown off the yoke of the past. A socialist society, on its way to reaching the highest level of a Communist ideal society, had nothing to learn from the past, it was argued, but should develop through the everyday interaction between individuals in a society characterised by socialist virtues such as justice, solidarity and love. The *Proletkult* idea was definitively abandoned in the early 1930s, when Stalin decided to use history in a more active ideological way to promote discipline and patriotic emotions.[28]

To this should, however, be added that it is also adequate to talk about a non-use of history in the situation where an aspect of history, traditionally presented as an important or even fundamental one, is passed over in silence. An example of the latter is when the Holocaust is left out of a historical construct by revisionists or deniers of the Nazi genocide.

The political-pedagogical use of history

This last use of history may be characterised as a deliberate comparative, metaphorical or symbolic use in which the transfer effect between 'then' and 'now' is rendered simple and unproblematic, while the scholarly-scientific insistence that history be anchored in the structures of the relevant period is toned down. The main purpose is to summon history as an aid in attacking what are felt to be severe and concrete political and social problems in a later era. A somewhat amusing example occurred in the early days of the new millennium when a Swedish minister, who was having problems reaching an economic agreement with a representative of Norwegian business interests, reacted by publicly designating Norway to be 'the last Soviet state'. Very few Scandinavians were impressed by the minister's intellectual abilities, but the main point is that he was trying to draw attention to his view that the failure to strike a bargain was the Norwegian's fault. This political, comparative use of history, which he would publicly regret later, was most appreciated by Scandinavian journalists.

As an expression of the absolute evil, the Holocaust may be an especially attractive object of comparison for internal or external spokesmen who want to draw attention to the allegedly exposed positions of 'their' historical or present-day social groups in relation to a state or a majority society. As a matter of fact, the Swedish Living History project can obviously be described in terms of a political-pedagogical use of history, since its main point is the transfer of a part of history considered relevant in order to cure maladies considered malign in *fin de siècle* Swedish and European society. The Swedish premier was undoubtedly annoyed by two party colleagues in the Swedish Parliament who argued that 'NATO's bombings of Belgrade are comparable to the Holocaust', at approximately the same time as Persson introduced Living History. The comparison sometimes made between Israeli treatment of the Palestinians and the Holocaust is a particularly troublesome political use of history which often is made to stir up a moral-political debate. As one Swedish writer suggested recently: 'Maybe it is time to stop travelling to Auschwitz with Swedish pupils to teach them the consequences of racism and ethnic cleansing? Maybe we should instead offer them a Christmas journey to Bethlehem, to have a look at what the grandchildren of the Auschwitz victims in their turn do when they engage in ethnic cleansing.'[29] It should, however, be noted that comparison can be a useful scholarly analytical instrument, and that the borderline between a political and a scholarly use is less evident when arguments of a scholarly nature are put forward to relate the Holocaust experience to latter-day processes and events. Consequently, if a scholar maintains that 'the Israeli socio-political psyche is traumatised by the Holocaust experience in ways it neither admits to nor fully understands, but which make its coming to terms on an equal basis with its neighbours – the original population of the Middle East – a problematic if not impossible process',[30] the line of reasoning becomes analytically penetrating. Summing up, history is used politically if its relevance is used to guide political decisions or to assist in securing political advantage.

Conclusion: the abuse of history?

Obviously, these uses of history can overlap. Another objection against the typology, partly touched upon in the first part of the chapter, may be that the scholarly-scientific use cannot be separated from the other uses of history any more. For a historian dealing with aspects of the Holocaust, a detached and balanced account of the kind considered ideal by scholarly-scientific users of history is hard to produce. New areas of scholarly history, in particular the history of categories that were seldom represented in traditional grand narratives, such as women, ethnic groups or homosexuals, are indeed often justified from traditionally non-scholarly positions. Among them are the need to strengthen group identity, the ethical need to incorporate previously hidden aspects into the grand narratives, or the ideological search for a better understanding of subjugation and repression. Such motives are not necessarily incompatible with scholarly approaches. However, it is difficult to reconcile scholarly-scientific methods with the simplistic lessons that characterise the political-pedagogical use of history.

Professional historians, when confronted by these other uses of history, tend to reinforce the virtues of traditional scholarly-scientific history. They are often dismissive of lay history, without seizing the opportunity to engage in a more sophisticated public debate. Historian Peter Novick has argued that old principles and premises of scholarly-scientific history still pervade the professional, scholarly use of history, at least in America, far more than most members of the professional community would admit.[31]

There are other issues not covered by the typology discussed here. The commercial use of history is one example. Today, history is extremely useful to demonstrate that certain commodities are worth buying due to their 'authentic', 'classical', 'original' or 'traditional' values, to name just a few of the most frequent adjectives. There is a need for an analysis of the terms of the legal use of history, in the context of the many commissions and lawsuits that are covered elsewhere in this volume. Even so, the advantage of this typology of historical use is that it may make the historical and comparative analysis easier to perform: after all, it is reasonable to assume that the various uses differ in strength at different times, at different stages of development, and in different geographical spheres, and their shifting interrelations may provide a fruitful object of study.

Another concern is that the concept of 'use' implies that there is also such a thing as 'misuse' or 'abuse' of history. There is no absolute and simple solution to this problem. The professionalisation of history has entailed the danger that the scientific use of history comes to be regarded as the norm and hence as an 'absolute good', whereas any other use is reduced to 'abuse'. This is unjust, not least because historians are like other people in that they may use – and do use – history in non-scholarly ways, both inside and outside their professional lives.

One way of handling the problem is by stressing the user's specific point of view. If we take the position of the professional historian, we could dismiss all uses of history which do not follow professionally acknowledged rules as a misuse of *scholarly* history. However, we do not solve the problematic aspects involved in the other uses of history, which are not guided by the same formal framework of rules and standards. In general, such a position is also hard to accommodate with a history-cultural perspective, since one of its main ideas is that scholarly activities and works are not exclusive in the sense that they are of a higher quality, but rather parts of the wider area of historical culture.

Scholarly-scientific history has, however, a set of virtues that makes this use 'different' from other uses of history, and it is up to the scholars to uphold and communicate these standards and virtues in an open debate about what history is and how it can and ought to be used. No doubt, it is part of the professional historian's responsibility to defend the position that history is not only retrospective and reflective of the present, but must also be judged prospectively in the context of the past. In this sense, history is always subject to double standards. It is equally important that the historian's approach remains open-ended, analytical and critical, not avoiding complexity, and wary of unfounded generalisations. Professional historians have a responsibility to engage in the wider historical debates that include non-professionals because history has no intrinsic value, but gets its *raison d'être* from a dialogic and functional societal context of mediation and use. The use to which history is put cannot be determined solely on scholarly grounds, but involves social and moral judgements from which professional historians should not be isolated.

Notes

1 C. E. Schorske, *Thinking with History: Explorations in the Passage to Modernism* (Princeton, 1998).
2 K.-G. Karlsson, *Historia som vapen. Historiebruk och Sovjetunionens upplösning 1985–1995* (Stockholm, 1999).
3 Opening address by the Prime Minister of Sweden, Göran Persson, at the Ceremonial Opening 26 January 2000, in *The Stockholm International Forum on the Holocaust. Proceedings* (Stockholm, 2000), p. 30.
4 S. Bruchfeld and P. A. Levine, *... om detta må ni berätta ... En bok om Förintelsen i Europa 1933–1945* (Stockholm, 1998).
5 Speech by the Prime Minister of Sweden, Göran Persson, on 27 January 2000, in *The Stockholm International Forum on the Holocaust. Proceedings* (Stockholm, 2000), p. 345.

6   C. S. Maier, *The Unmasterable Past: History, Holocaust, and German National Identity* (Cambridge and London, 1997), p. 160.
7   K.-G. Karlsson, 'The Holocaust and Russian Historical Culture. A Century-Long Perspective', in K.-G. Karlsson and U. Zander (eds), *Echoes of the Holocaust: Historical Cultures in Contemporary Europe* (Lund, 2003), pp. 213–15.
8   P. Lagrou, *The Legacy of Nazi Occupation: Patriotic Memory and National Recovery in Western Europe, 1945–1965* (Cambridge, 2000), p. 251 ff.
9   J. E. Young, *The Texture of Memory: Holocaust Memorials and Meaning* (New Haven and London, 1993), pp. 294–6.
10 J. Öhman, 'From Famine to Forgotten Holocaust. The 1932–1933 Famine in Ukrainian Historical Cultures', in K.-G. Karlsson and U. Zander (eds), *Echoes of the Holocaust: Historical Cultures in Contemporary Europe* (Lund, 2003), pp. 223–53.
11 Speech at the Swedish Parliament by the Prime Minister of Sweden, Göran Persson, on 27 January 2000, in *The Stockholm International Forum on the Holocaust. Proceedings* (Stockholm, 2000), p. 347.
12 The project has been summed up in S. Ekman (ed.), *Stormaktstryck och småstatspolitik: aspekter på svensk politik under andra världskriget* (Stockholm, 1986).
13 One extreme Swedish example of the reaction is found in C. Winberg, *Folkökning och proletarisering: Kring den sociala strukturomvandlingen på Sveriges landsbygd under den agrara revolutionen* (Lund, 1977).
14 Good examples of this second reaction are S. Tägil (ed.), *Regions in Upheaval: Ethnic Conflict and Political Mobilization* (Lund, 1984); S. Tägil (ed.), *Europe – The Return of History* (Lund, 1998).
15 For examples of this third reaction, see for example J. Rüsen, *Historische Orientierung. Über die Arbeit des Geschichtsbewusstseins, sich in der Zeit zurechtzufinden* (Cologne, 1994); K.-G. Karlsson and U. Zander (eds), *Holocaust Heritage: Inquiries into European Historical Cultures* (Malmö, 2005).
16 For a more elaborated analysis, see K.-G. Karlsson, 'History in Swedish Politics – the "Living History" Project', in A. Pók, J. Rüsen and J. Scherrer (eds), *European History: Challenge for a Common Future* (Hamburg, 2000), pp. 148–53.
17 N. Davies, *Europe. A History* (London, 1997), pp. 39–45.
18 The typology is elaborated from Karlsson, *Historia som vapen*, pp. 56–61.
19 See, for example, D. Lowenthal, *The Past is a Foreign Country* (Cambridge, 1985); J. Lukacs, *Historical Consciousness: The Remembered Past* (New Brunswick and London, 1994); R. Samuel, *Theatres of Memory. Volume 1: Past and Present in Contemporary Culture* (London and New York, 1994).
20 R. Rosenzweig and D. Thelen, *The Presence of the Past: Popular Uses of History in American Life* (New York, 1998), chapter 5.
21 See M. Halbwachs, *On Collective Memory* (Chicago and London, 1992); P. Nora, 'General Introduction: Between Memory and History', in P. Nora (ed.), *Realms of Memory: The Construction of the French Past. Volume I: Conflicts and Divisions* (New York, 1992).
22 Modern scholarship has, however, demonstrated that not even the most culturally and ideologically repressive state power can altogether strangle individual,

unsanctioned memories. See R.S. Watson (ed.), *Memory, History and Opposition under State Socialism* (Santa Fe, 1994).

23 See, for example, C. Merridale, *Night of Stone: Death and Memory in Twentieth-Century Russia* (London, 2000); N. Schleifman (ed.), *Russia at a Crossroads: History, Memory and Political Practice* (London and Portland, 1998); N. Tumarkin, *The Living and the Dead: The Rise and Fall of the Cult of World War II in Russia* (New York, 1994).

24 R. Inglehart, *Cultural Shift in Advanced Industrial Society* (Princeton, 1990), pp. 66–103.

25 There is a large literature about this moral use of history, which includes R. W. Davies, *Soviet History in the Gorbachev Revolution* (Houndmills, 1989); R. W. Davies, *Soviet History in the Yeltsin Era* (Houndmills, 1997); Karlsson, *Historia som vapen*; W. Laqueur, *Stalin: The Glasnost Revelations* (London, Sydney and Wellington, 1990); A. Nove, *'Glasnost' in Action: Cultural Renaissance in Russia* (Boston, 1989); D. Remnick, *Lenin's Tomb: The Last Days of the Soviet Empire* (New York, 1994); K. E. Smith, *Remembering Stalin's Victims: Popular Memory and the End of the USSR* (Ithaca and London, 1996).

26 The debates are analysed in U. Zander, *Fornstora dagar, moderna tider. Bruk av och debatter om svensk historia från sekelskifte till sekelskifte* (Glorious Days, Modern Times: Uses of and Debates on Swedish History from the One Turn of the Century to the Other) (Lund, 2001).

27 K.-G. Karlsson, 'Europe's Eastern Outpost? The Meanings of 'Europe' in Baltic Discourses', in M. af Malmborg and B. Stråth (eds), *The Meaning of Europe: Variety and Contention within and among Nations* (Oxford and New York, 2002), pp. 169–90.

28 K.-G. Karlsson, 'History Teaching in Twentieth-Century Russia and the Soviet Union: Classicism and Its Alternatives', in B. Eklof (ed.), *School and Society in Tsarist and Soviet Russia* (New York, 1993), pp. 212–17.

29 K. Mazetti, in *Ordfront Magasin* (December 2002). Translation by the author.

30 H. Bresheeth, S. Hood and L. Jansz, *The Holocaust for Beginners* (Cambridge, 1994), p. 173.

31 P. Novick, *That Noble Dream: The 'Objectivity Question' and the American Historical Profession* (Cambridge, 1988), pp. 2–3.

3

Coming to terms with the (post-)colonial past in Belgium: the inquiry into the assassination of Patrice Lumumba

Georgi Verbeeck

Belgium has no political tradition in establishing parliamentary investigation on aspects of his national history. Its political culture and national consensus is often perceived as too fragile to enable an open debate on painful aspects of its past. This has not only been the case for Belgium's role during the Second World War, but for its politics in colonial Africa also. Notwithstanding the ongoing controversies over the troublesome decolonisation of Belgian Congo, it has taken four decades for the Belgian political establishment to grant a thorough reinvestigation of this episode, which has burdened the relations between the former motherland and its colony for such a long time. This was largely made possible after the transformation of the landscape of political parties in Belgium in the late 1990s. Both the establishment and proceedings of a special parliamentary investigation commission reflected the profound political and ideological cleavages over Belgium's role in the decolonisation of the Congo. The commission showed that the writing of history is closely intertwined with a political agenda. For historians, who were involved in the investigation commission, it was necessary to achieve a balance between academic professionalism and the moral responsibility of revealing a painful past. Historical investigation commissions therefore provide a good example of the public role of historians in a changing political context.

Belgium and its colony in Africa

The process of decolonisation has been a painful enterprise, even for a small country like Belgium with a relatively short-lived experience as a European colonial empire in Africa (1884–1960). The transformation of Congo from a Belgian colony into an independent sovereign state represented a traumatic chapter in the history of the relations between the former mother country and its former colonial vocation. Belgium had shared the position of those European superpowers that had conquered and divided the African continent for many decades, but it had lacked the political, financial and military means and essential tools to prepare its colonial possession for independence. Belgian colonial rule had been characterised by a relatively marginal presence of European settlers (Belgians and others), but rather by a huge involvement of domestic capitalist business circles in the colony's economy and by the spiritual concerns of a highly active missionary church. The Belgian monarchy, capitalist enterprises and the Catholic Church formed the backbone of Belgian rule over its colony. Compared to other European colonies in Africa, primary education, medical services and agricultural cultivation had reached a high standard of quality in Belgian Congo. On the other hand, Belgian colonial rule was deeply characterised by paternalistic, if not racialist views. The Africanisation of the political establishment was a process that was not taken seriously. Political reform and a gradual preparation for sovereignty were never highly placed on the agenda of the Belgian administrators.[1]

Belgium and the Congo were badly prepared for the stormy events that would ultimately lead to the independence of most African states in 1960.[2] It was not until the late 1950s that the call for 'emancipation' became evident in the Belgo-Congolese relations. A first plan for gradual independence – within thirty years – was adopted in 1957 by the Belgian political adviser, Jef Van Bilzen. Belgian Congo could not cope, however, with the rapid 'winds of change' on the African continent. After a sudden upheaval in some Congolese towns and the rapid process of decolonisation in British and French Africa, 30 June 1960 was hastily accepted as day of independence. The transfer of sovereignty was badly prepared and the declaration of independence turned into violence and political turmoil, a chaotic exodus of European citizens, civil war and disintegration of the state, leading finally to foreign intervention.

International invention severely complicated the turbulent decolonisation of Belgian Congo. It was only a few days after independence that some units of the army started a rebellion, largely because of objections to their Belgian commander. In the confusion, the mineral-rich province of Katanga proclaimed secession. Belgium sent in troops, ostensibly to protect Belgian nationals in the disorder. But the Belgian troops landed principally in Katanga, where they sustained the secessionist regime of Moise Tshombe, a long-time enemy of Lumumba. The Congo appealed to the United Nations to expel the Belgians and help them restore internal order. As Prime Minister, Lumumba did what little he could to redress the situation. He had only a weak and poorly trained army at his disposal. The Belgian troops did not evacuate, and the Katanga secession continued. Since the United Nations forces refused or were unable to help suppress the Katangese revolt, Lumumba appealed to the Soviet Union for planes to assist in transporting his troops to Katanga. He asked the independent African states to meet in Léopoldville in August to unite their efforts behind him. His moves alarmed many, particularly the Western powers and the supporters of President Joseph Kasavubu, who pursued a moderate course in the coalition government and favoured some local autonomy in the provinces. The Katanga secession lasted until 1963, when the state was incorporated into the Congolese Republic. Belgium, in the meantime, had substantially lost international credibility due to its support for an illegitimate secessionist regime. In the eyes of many, the Belgian administration had been driven by neo-colonialist ambitions to restore its former empire.

The Congo crisis dominated the agenda of international politics until 1965. Patrice Lumumba was one of the central political figures in this dramatic era.[3] For some he was a national hero representing the hope of the Congolese people for liberation after an age of slavery and colonialism. For others, however, he was an evil enemy in the age of the Cold War, a 'puppet of Moscow'. Lumumba was the first democratically elected Prime Minister of the sovereign Congolese state. His central aim was the maintenance of a unitary, non-tribal state. He had developed into a charismatic and populist leader giving voice to strong anti-colonial feelings among the indigenous people. Pressured by the international constellation of power relations, he slowly drifted towards an anti-Western political agenda. He lost his political power base and was finally killed on 17 January 1961 in extremely suspicious circumstances. Lumumba's death represented a traumatic experience for the international community and represented the tragic failure of a peaceful decolonisation process of Belgian Africa.[4]

Public memory

In post-colonial Belgium the 'loss of our Congo' has never been omnipresent in public memory. A new public consensus emerged, a consensus to forget and neglect the mistakes and horrors of the past, a tendency to ignore the complicity in the failures of the decolonisation. It was only in small radical left-wing circles that the traditions of anti-imperialist and anti-colonial social movements in Congo were cherished.[5] A large part of public opinion was fully convinced that the Belgian authorities had never been involved in the atrocities that took place in Congo following the day of independence. Two central theses were promoted: first, rebellion, chaos and national disintegration were the result of the unorganised withdrawal of the Belgians from their former colony while anti-colonial forces had quickly converted into Moscow orientated clients. Secondly, Belgian responsibility was not at stake, but deeply rooted ethnic rivalries had surfaced leading to bloodshed and barbarism. This view led to a widely accepted perception that the Congo crisis was essentially the result of international pressure and of uncontrollable domestic tensions, ultimately leading to the disintegration of the newly founded state. Belgium was therefore presented as an innocent 'bystander', completely blameless for the atrocities taking place in its former colony and from where it was so brutally pushed out.[6]

In 1999 a book appeared in which this 'innocence thesis' was strongly contested.[7] Ludo De Witte's *The Assassination of Lumumba* strongly contested a previously defended thesis according to which Lumumba had been the victim of his own political and ethnic, enemies at home.[8] He maintained that he had found evidence that the highest echelons of Belgium's political, economic and military establishment – including the Head of State – were involved in plans to kill Lumumba. The assassination of Lumumba was therefore to be seen as nothing less than an officially sanctioned political murder of a democratically elected head of government of a sovereign state, which was aimed at destabilising a newly created state, to maintain foreign dominance and to hamper the necessary process of emancipation. According to De Witte, Lumumba was killed in the service of the political and economic interests of Belgium.[9] Following the controversy over the new study of De Witte, two different conceptions of history emerged.[10] A more traditionalist conception stressed the non-complicity of the official Belgian authorities, emphasising at the same time the responsibility of Congolese political leaders for the chaos in the country following independence. The colonial era was generally seen as a success story, dramatically interrupted by an all too sudden independence. 'Black people were not capable of ruling their own country' was a widespread view. Lumumba was portrayed as a traditional authoritarian ruler with philo-communist sympathies, endangering the valid interests of the West. Military intervention was a necessary response to the killings and dramatic exodus of thousands of Western citizens. The second opinion argued that the Belgian campaign against Lumumba, culminating in his assassination, was proof of Belgium's ongoing ambitions to maintain political, military and economic influence in the Congo. Belgium – both the state and its economic power circles – had acted as an imperialist nation that had brutally sabotaged the liberation process of its former colony. The murder of Lumumba was not an *accident de parcours* with Belgians acting as innocent bystanders, but the result of an intended elimination campaign. The chain of responsibility led to the highest level of the Belgian state, including the monarchy and the government. At stake was the loss of Belgium's national innocence.

The publication of the *The Assassination of Lumumba* provoked a large public debate, both in the media and in politics. The resonance of the debate reached the highest levels of the Belgian state: the government, the Belgian Parliament, the parliamentary Commission for Foreign Relations, and finally a special Parliamentary Inquiry Commission. In Parliament the Minister of Foreign Affairs, Louis Michel, had received many questions about the possible responsibility of the Belgian authorities in this case, but he had stated that he could not assess responsibility based on the findings of a book only. In order to reach a conclusion from an official Belgian instance, and therefore not only based on the findings of one individual scholar, it was decided that the Parliament would create a special Parliamentary Inquiry Commission. The principle of a Parliamentary Inquiry Commission was quickly adopted. It would be granted the authority of an examining magistrate, thereby allowing it free access to the required archives, to call witnesses and to conduct searches. These measures would enable it to undertake a thorough investigation.

Parliamentary investigation

The special Parliamentary Inquiry Commission was set up by a law of 2 February 2000 and started its activities on 23 March 2000.[11] The proposal to set up this inquiry was submitted by a large range of political parties in Parliament excluding the opposition parties. It was an initiative of the liberal and labour parties, green parties and moderate Flemish nationalists. The opposition, both christian democrats and the extreme right-wing Flemish Block, remained relatively reluctant but would ultimately collaborate in a fairly fruitful way. Fifteen commissioners were appointed, reflecting a wide spectrum of political opinions. According to its remit, the Commission was established in order 'to determine the precise circumstances of the assassination of Patrice Lumumba and the possible involvement of Belgian politicians'.[12]

From the very beginning the Commission on the murder of Lumumba had clear political ambitions.[13] It not only intended to instigate a broad debate on colonisation and decolonisation, but also wished to improve the relations with a number of countries in Central Africa, within the changing pattern of political and international constellation after the massacre of 1994 in Rwanda. Official Belgium had to take an initiative in order to restore confidence not only in the newly established regimes in its former colonies, especially Zaire/Congo after the collapse of the Mobutu-regime, but also in Rwanda. It was therefore very clear both for the supporters and critics of the new liberal-labour ('anti-clerical') majority in Parliament that the new Belgian government wished to develop a new foreign policy and an ideological strategy aiming at a closer co-operation with the newly established regimes in Kinshasa and Kigali. The former administrations, dominated by the christian democratic ('clerical') parties, had largely suffered from a reputation of being not critical enough of the old authoritarian and repressive regimes in Central Africa, ignoring the dramatic and all too negative impact of the former Belgian authorities on the process of decolonisation. A new approach towards a painful common past would ultimately reflect the changing political circumstances, both in the former motherland and its former colony. A new political landscape in Belgium and, new political partners in Central Africa had asked for a new interpretation of history, especially in reference to the horrific days and months after the establishment of an independent Congolese state in 1960/61.[14] According to some observers, a critical inquiry into the murder of Lumumba had been entirely impossible under different political circumstances, i.e. if the clerical government had still been in power, or if King Baudouin, who had died in 1993, had still been alive.[15]

The subject under examination was particularly complicated and extremely delicate.[16] Moreover, the period under examination was more than forty years ago. Numerous witnesses were deceased, while others could not or would not accurately relate the facts that they had witnessed. A substantial amount of relevant sources had disappeared in the meantime. It was therefore a question of accurately establishing the facts, in their totality and interdependence, and in precise chronological order. This was not a traditional task for politicians. The assistance of professional historians was therefore required for such a mission. A small committee of experts, consisting of four professional historians, was installed. These experts had to produce a documented research report. It was the politicians' task to draw conclusions and make political recommendations. Four historians worked closely together, assisted by a number of ad-hoc experts in the field of international law, anthropology and from the military intelligence services.

In addition to the scientific research of archives, hearings were organised with witnesses. In total, more than 40 crucial witnesses were heard. As well as relatives of the victims, the authors of the most relevant publications were also heard. All relevant witnesses who where still alive were questioned, for example the Belgian, Congolese and Katangese ministers of that time, the Belgian advisers and diplomats in Brussels, the Congo and Katanga of the time, ex-military and state security employees as well as citizens.

Political debates

The establishment of a special Parliamentary Inquiry Commission and the recruitment of a committee of experts had not been without political risks.[17] At first many observers and politicians had raised serious questions on the usefulness of such an investigation. Moderate right-wing politicians and journalists feared an ideologically motivated manoeuvre against the former conservative governments, led by both christian democrats and liberals.

In their view the investigation commission was a tool in the hands of an anti-clerical government aimed at discrediting Belgium's colonial and post-colonial past. According to some members of the opposition in Parliament, Lumumba had been a cruel and pro-Communist authoritarian leader, to be compared with evil men like Milosevic and Saddam Hussein. Another argument referred to the inefficiency of comparable 'Truth Commissions', as in the South African, East German or Latin American cases.[18] Discussions in Parliament preparing the law to install the special investigation commission reflected old ideological differences of opinion between the new parliamentary majority and the moderate right-wing parties of the opposition. Seen from a wider perspective, one could distinguish between the heirs of an anti-clerical and anti-colonial tradition, embodied by both social democrats and liberals, and a christian democratic, catholic tradition with stronger roots in the colonial experience. The setting up of an investigation commission, however, was approved by a unanimous vote, including the far right, since nobody could seriously oppose this major enterprise which involved coming to terms with an awkward chapter in the nation's past.

Even more interesting from a historiographical standpoint were the debates on the appointment of the four historical experts, whose central goal was to assist the parliamentary commission. Four experts were appointed: strangely enough none of them were well known for their expertise in the field of colonial or African history.[19] None of them had shown a particular interest in this historical episode. Neither a black African historian, nor an African- orientated scholar was invited to take part in the committee.[20] The opposition, however, had strongly favoured the appointment of at least one African expert onto the committee, in a zealous attempt to emphasise the African/Congolese context of the Lumumba drama, and consequently also the responsibility of African leaders for the murder of Lumumba.[21] But according to previous agreements, it was not African responsibility which was at stake, but rather the involvement of the Belgian authorities. The 'Africanist' approach however, was not successful. This led to the installation of a committee of experts in the field of Belgian political history, the theory and methodology of history, and a meticulous evaluation of historical sources.

At first, questions and doubts were raised about the scientific, academic and moral independence and objectivity of professional historians working in close collaboration with political authorities and conducting research under the authority of an official institution. In other words: conducting historical research in the service of the state. By the end of the process however, virtually nobody raised doubts on the fact that the experts had been able to work freely and independently, guaranteeing the scientific objectivity of the parliamentary commission. Although politically and ideo-

Coming to terms with the (post-)colonial past in Belgium 53

logically motivated pressure had played a role in the installation of both the parliamentary commission and the committee of experts, a high degree of scholarly and intellectual independence, in order to carry out the historical research, had been secured.[22]

The committee of historians not only served a political goal, but its work was of paramount importance for the writing of history too. For the first time in decades, a unique opportunity was created to obtain access to important sources of contemporary history, both official documents and a great variety of written and oral sources. Free access to all public and private archives was obtained. Witnesses could be heard in a firm juridical framework, not by the committee of experts, but by the members of the parliamentary commission, leading to new useful insights. The very existence of this investigation commission merited a mention in itself: research into the colonial and post-colonial past in Belgium was still relatively rare.[23]

The role of historians

The Committee of Experts presented its interim report in November 2000[24] and its final report to the parliamentary commission in the summer of 2001.[25] Full conclusions were published in autumn 2001. Both the historical research by the experts and the political conclusions by the members of Parliament exemplified the need for a differentiated and balanced approach towards the historical context and events of winter 1960/61. Political and social circumstances in Belgium were different from now. Belgian politics, institutions, the social and political elite and the media functioned differently from today. The historical investigation also referred to the radically different international constellation during the Cold War. The central obsession was the 'fight against communism', not only in international affairs, but also on the domestic front. During the cold winter of 1960/61, the centrist right-wing government feared a general strike throughout the country as a radical social movement in Wallonia had gained ground. On an international level, the Cold War reached a momentum in Africa, Asia and Latin America. The reports of the national security and intelligence services and also the reports of the council of ministers and the media clearly illustrated this 'fear of communism'. In addition public opinion was traumatised by the written and audiovisual media reports and eye-witness accounts of tragic events and loss of lives during the final days of colonial rule: stories of murder and rape coming from fleeing Belgian refugees forced to abandon all their possessions.[26] Large sections of the population, the media and the political establishment, held one individual responsible for the traumatic outcome of the independence of the Congolese state: Patrice Lumumba.

Also, the entire process of decolonisation had to be examined.[27] The decolonisation process had started on the African continent from the beginning of the 1950s. The Belgian administration at that time had largely underestimated the entire issue. It should be noted that decolonisation of Belgian Congo had not been well prepared nor properly organised. As early as 1955, a first blueprint was published which proposed a gradual process of decolonisation and which would eventually lead to independence after thirty years.[28] It was only after the riots of January 1959, that Congolese independence became a political possibility for the Belgian government. Only five months after the Brussels conference, during which preparations were started for independence, was this realised. The fact that independence was finally granted in great haste, without a thorough consideration of the necessary preparations to ensure a successful process, was undoubtedly the result of growing calls for immediate action stemming from the Congolese leaders themselves, on the one hand, and fear of the economic and human impact of a colonial war on Belgium, on the other. The experiences of France in Algeria and Indo-China certainly influenced the decision in this matter. The Belgian authorities deemed a speedy independence necessary in order to protect Belgian interests against foreign influences. The rapid changes in the Congo and a swift shift from a colonial to a sovereign country did not correspond with a social and psychological development of many Belgians. Many of them remained attached to a colonial outlook on events.

Of crucial importance were of course the conclusions of the investigation commission regarding the so-called 'fight against Lumumba', the campaign by the Belgian authorities against the Congolese Prime Minister.[29] Congo had become an independent and sovereign state on 30 June 1960, but this did not stop Belgium, as well as a number of other countries from intervening directly in its internal affairs. A distinction must be made where the humanitarian actions of the Belgian government to protect its citizens in the Congo immediately after the independence are concerned. Furthermore, due to the Treaty for Friendship, Assistance and Collaboration, a specific relationship continued between the former colony and Belgium even after 30 June. Due to the presence of large numbers of Belgian officials and military personnel a close connection remained. What was more, a large majority of these Belgian citizens felt they were expected to play an important role in the Congo.

The commission clearly demonstrated that there was a Belgian policy to eliminate Lumumba both politically and physically.[30] From the day of independence a fundamental split was growing between Lumumba and the Belgian government. There was growing distrust and many, both in Belgium and the Congo, started campaigning openly to bring about Lumumba's political downfall. Public reaction in Belgium to the events of July 1960 – mutiny in the army, public unrest and a growing exodus of European citizens – supported the Belgian government in its actions, especially where military intervention was concerned. For the Belgian authorities it would be hard to justify a passive *laissez-faire* attitude regarding the tens of thousands of Belgians in the Congo. Officials also worried about the financial and economic losses the Congo crisis could cause. The stakes were high for the Belgian financial groups in the Congo. After the beginning of the Belgian military intervention in July 1960 and the interruption of diplomatic relations, Belgium clearly developed a policy to remove Lumumba. In this campaign, the Belgian support for Katanga and the Tshombe government was an important element. Its purpose was not so much the secession itself, but a confederal reorganisation of the Congo, aimed at removing the economic powerbase from Lumumba and his political movement, the *Mouvement National Congolais*. There was also support for the secession of South Kasaï and these plans for a confederal state must be seen from the same perspective. In order to finance the policy against the Lumumba government, the Belgian government appealed to so-called 'secret funds'. By withdrawing tax money and financing military and paramilitary opposition forces, industrial powers like the *Union Minière* and the *Forminière* also played a crucial role in the campaign against the central government in Leopoldville.[31]

The Belgian actions were only one element in a wider group of opposition forces. Crucial to the final fall of Lumumba was the split between him and the UN Secretary General Hammarskjöld. It forced Lumumba to ask openly for the support of the Soviet Union and thus encouraged the USA to organize active opposition covertly against Lumumba.[32] However, according to the findings of the Commission it was clear that a Belgian or even an American campaign had little or no chance of success without the existence of domestic opposition in Congo itself.[33] Violent opposition against the Lumumba regime became manifest at quite an early stage, ranging from ethnic rivalry, political and syndicalist opposition. The Congo crisis was therefore also to be seen as an internal crisis within a vast but fragmented country, in which all the centrifugal forces gained strength after the colonial administration collapsed and where there were no strong national parties, a solid bureaucracy nor a disciplined army.[34]

On 5 September 1960 Lumumba was deposed and then finally arrested on 10 October. It was the first time that Colonel Mobutu would take action by 'neutralising' both Lumumba and the anti-Lumumba forces in Congo, including the Head of State, Joseph Kasavubu. It was on 6 October that the expression '*élimination définitive*' would be used for the first time by a Belgian minister. This call for a final elimination would turn out to be nothing less than a campaign to eliminate Lumumba physically.[35]

The commission found evidence that there were at least various plans – schemes and unfinished projects – to kill Lumumba.[36] Various secret service agents and members of the military forces were involved in operations aiming at the physical elimination of Lumumba. At least two plans failed however. From a very early stage, two facts are certain. The Belgian government tried to take Lumumba prisoner and transfer him to Katanga, and therefore deliver him to his archenemies. This would mean almost certain death. His arrest, his imprisonment, his second arrest after a failed escape, and his final transfer to Katanga were clearly not in accordance with basic constitutional rules.[37] Lumumba's life was certainly at risk in Katanga. Secondly, the Belgian government showed no signs of concern about the physical safety of the former head of the Congolese government. The Belgian Head of State, King Baudouin, was informed about the very precarious situation of Lumumba, but no actions were taken to rescue his life. Lumumba was finally killed on 17 January 1961 on the orders of the Katangese authorities who had also previously agreed with his transfer. It was a crime that was prepared and executed in a systematic way. The execution took place in the presence of Katangese politicians, members of the police forces (*gendarmes*) and a few Belgian officers. At no time did the Belgian government raise a protest against the unlawful execution of Lumumba and two of his companions, nor did it express its regret or disapproval. Any involvement in the transfer and knowledge of the fate of Lumumba were denied.

Outcomes of the investigations

The conclusions of the investigation commission were widely accepted as a preliminary attempt by Belgium to come to terms with this painful past. According to some critics the conclusions had not been far reaching enough in exposing the responsibilities of leading politicians as well as some industrial and economic interest structures, but in general there was a fairly large positive consensus on the research results of this parliamentary investigation.[38] The impact of this investigation process has been substantial, both on the political as on the historiographical level.

The commission clearly criticised many dysfunctional elements in the political decision-making process.[39] Many actors – ministers, political advisers, military, intelligence and security personnel – had been involved in the destabilisation campaign. On the economic level there has been a wide confusion of private and public interest. Not surprisingly, parliamentary supervision over what occurred and over foreign and African policies in general, was very inadequate. The commission also found a great deal of evidence of both international and domestic laws being violated. The Belgian government was fully aware of the murder of Lumumba. It did nothing to prevent his unlawful and cruel extermination. There was a high degree of direct involvement in this premeditated crime, undoubtedly prepared and executed in a systematic way. Highly contentious in the Belgian political context was the controversial role of the Head of State.⁴⁰ The commission had found evidence that there had been conflict between the Belgian king and the government regarding certain aspects of Congo politics. In certain cases, the king took independent action and obtained important information without informing the government of it. Evidence was found that the king had received an indication that the life of Lumumba was in danger and had taken no action to prevent this crime. King Baudouin's attitude was clearly in violation of the basic principles of a constitutional monarchy, according to which the king has to remain absolutely politically neutral and that there should be a complete consensus of opinion between the Head of State and his government. This accident however represented one of the various examples in the history of the Belgian monarchy, in which the Belgian king undertakes desperate efforts to develop a relatively autonomous and separate foreign policy, especially in Central African affairs.⁴¹

Following the parliamentary investigation, Belgium finally accepted its complicity in the Lumumba assassination and officially offered apologizes to the relatives of Patrice Lumumba and to the entire Congolese people.⁴² Moreover, as a form of reparation, Belgium assisted in establishing a financial fund meant to help the political and social reconstruction of the country devastated after so many years of brutal repression and civil war.⁴³ According to critics, this official gesture of the Belgian state was surely not enough. Commenting on the apology, Colette Braeckman, the Congo expert of the Belgian daily *Le Soir*, said: 'Since democracy was decapitated following Lumumba's assassination in 1961, Congo has become a real disaster, its leaders have become prone to corruption, its people to fend for themselves ... Today, Western appetite for minerals still hamper the birth of a truly democratic, economically giant and prosperous Congo. Instead, they encourage secessions and rebellions ...'. She continued: 'For Congo to stand on its feet again, it must be helped to resume Lumumba's struggle from the point where sabotage and murder interrupted it. In other words, the reconstruction of a unified country whose development could bring peace to the whole region.'⁴⁴

However, radical critics cannot deny that the parliamentary investigation represented a substantial change in official Belgium's attitude towards the post-colonial development in Central Africa. A long political tradition of glorifying the colonial era and neglecting the failures of decolonisation was gradually changed into a critical attitude of Belgium's role in Congo's independence. The new political constellation – both in Brussels after the coalition change and in Kinshasa after the fall of the Mubutu regime and the empowerment of President Kabila – made a re-evaluation of the Lumumba era possible. The end of christian democratic dominance in Belgian politics and the end of Mubutu's dictatorship in Zaïre/Congo opened new perspectives for a more pragmatic policy of bilateral co-operation.[45] The socialist-liberal-green government undertakes attempts to follow new paths in African politics. After many domestic and international scandals, time was appropriate for apologies. A new *excuuscultuur* (culture of apologies) emerged.[46] Prime Minister Guy Verhofstadt agreed to accept Belgium's sins in the 1994 Rwandan tragedy. Time was ready for a comparable gesture towards post-Mobutu Congo.

Conclusion

What do we learn as historians from this historical inquiry?[47] It was the clear intention of the parliamentary commission to establish the involvement of Belgian politicians. Historical research has therefore been confined to the political decision-making process in Belgium. The commission and the historians have shed clear light on the role and responsibilities of the Belgian actors, but this of course was one part of the story. Belgium's responsibility was substantial, but there is no doubt that Belgian actions would remain rather fruitless without the interaction of American interests and with the international constellation in general. Congolese domestic politics played an even more substantial role. The 'traditionalist' approach, which emphasises the responsibilities of Lumumba's internal rivals, is therefore not entirely discredited. The committee of historians has managed to come to a balanced conclusion, trying to combine the (Belgian) 'domestic' with the (African) 'global' approach.[48]

For the broader public, expectations were particularly high. Many were waiting for the final and total exposure of responsible individual leading figures. Some were waiting for the 'smoking gun' to be found on the desk of one of the cabinet's ministers, if not the Prime Minister or the King himself. This is a typical 'intentionalist' approach according to which the result of an action is the logic and inescapable outcome of someone's clearly formulated ambition or intention. Public opinion should be aware of the fact however that historical research is based on the need to be as accurate, fair and balanced as possible. The historical process is never the result of clear intentions, but of a complex combination of conceptions and misconceptions, personal decisions and fixed structures, unfinished projects and miscalculations. The committee of experts clearly favoured a 'structuralist' approach according to which a process of radicalisation, of growing antagonism between the various political actors, ultimately led to this dramatic culmination of events.[49]

The Lumumba inquiry commission represented a unique attempt to come to terms with Belgium's troublesome (post-)colonial past. Politics played a decisive role in the establishment and proceedings of the commission. The role of the historians herein, however, was never seriously contested. A reasonable balance between scholarly professionalism and public duty was obtained. The outcome and empirical findings of the commission were never seriously questioned. After the publication of De Witte's book, the public debate on the Lumumba case was largely closed. This was mainly due to the quality of the commission's work. After the commission no serious attempts were made to reopen or prolong the debate.

Finally, the public use of historical investigation should never be overestimated. History should never serve as a guiding line for political actions. Politics should inspire political actions, not history. The role of the historian is a modest one. One should warn against unrealistic expectations. One of the historians in the committee of experts said: 'The role of an historian is more that of a plougher than of a pearl diver.' The role of historians should never be confused with that of judges.[50]

Notes

1 For a general overview of Belgium's colonial history, see J. Stengers, *Congo: Mythes et Réalitées: 100 ans d'histoire* (Paris, 1989).
2 For a general overview of recent African history, see F. Cooper, *Africa since 1940: The Past of the Present* (Cambridge, 2002).
3 Biographies on Patrice Lumumba include T.R. Kanza, *The Rise and Fall of Patrice Lumumba: Conflict in the Congo* (Boston, 1972); J. T. Omasombo and B. Verhaegen, *Patrice Lumumba: jeunesse et apprentissage politique 1925-1956* (Tervuren/Paris, 1998); T. Turner, *Ethnogenèse et nationalisme en Afrique centrale: aux racines de Patrice Lumumba* (Paris, 2000).
4 Lumumba's life has also often been glorified, as in the documentary movie dedicated to him: *Lumumba* by filmmaker Raoul Peck (1991).
5 Exemplary for the literature produced by Marxist activists: L. Martens, *1958-1968. 10 jaar revolutie in Kongo: de strijd van Patrice Lumumba en Pierre Mulele* (Antwerp, 1988).
6 A highly apologetic view was defended in: J. Brassine, *Enquête sur la mort de Patrice Lumumba* (Brussels, 1990). Brassine's apologetic historiography provoked the critical inquiries on the Lumumba-assassinations ultimately leading to the larger public debates. See also J. Brassinne and J. Kestergat, *Qui a tué Patrice Lumumba?* (Paris/Louvain-la-Neuve, 1991).
7 A thesis referring to the perception of *La Belgique dédouanée*, or the deculpabilisation of Belgium.
8 L. de Witte, *De moord op Lumumba* (Louvain, 1999). De Witte's book is also available in English translation: *The Assassination of Lumumba* (London, 2001). I used the original Dutch version.
9 L. de Witte, *De moord op Lumumba*, pp. 13-30.
10 For a more extensive assessment of the Lumumba-controversy, see my contribution: G. Verbeeck, 'De Lumumba-commissie of een Belgische "Methodenstreit"', *Nieuwste tijd: kwartaalschrift voor eigentijdse geschiedenis*, 1: 1 (2001), 8-23.

11 The findings of the Commission were not available on print at the time when this chapter was written. They are available on the website of the Belgian Parliament, see www1.dekamer.be/commissions/LMB/indexN.html. Summary, introduction and conclusions of the Commission are also available in English, entitled: *Parliamentary Committee of Enquiry in Charge of Determining the Exact Circumstances of the Assassination of Patrice Lumumba and the Possible Involvement of Belgian Politicians* (Brussels, 2001). It was only recently that the final findings were published in L. de Vos et al., *Lumumba: de complotten? De moord* (Louvain, 2004). My contribution, however, is based on previously unpublished material.
12 *Parliamentary Committee of Enquiry. Summary*, pp. 1–2.
13 G. Verbeeck, 'De Lumumba-commissie of een Belgische "Methodenstreit"', 13–17.
14 The proceedings of the Lumumba-commission were extensively covered by the Belgian media. See for example *De Standaard* (26 January 2000).
15 Communication by Emmanuel Gerard to the author.
16 *Parliamentary Committee of Enquiry. Introduction*, pp. 1–2.
17 *De Standaard* (17 December 1999).
18 *De Standaard* (7 January 2000).
19 The members of the college of experts were: Jules Gérard-Libois of the *Centre de Recherche et d'Iinformation Socio-Politique* (CRISP, Brussels), Emmanuel Gerard, Professor of Political History (Catholic University of Leuven), Luc De Vos, Professor of Military History (Royal Military School, Brussels) and Philippe Raxhon, Professor of History (University of Liège). These four key experts were assisted by an additional four ad-hoc experts, covering various scientific expertises: Jean Omasombo (Kinshasa), Eric David (Brussels), Eric Suy (Leuven) and Bart Preneel (Leuven).
20 *De Standaard* (30 May 2000).
21 *De Standaard* (3 May 2000).
22 Special thanks for the many useful insights communicated by Emmanuel Gerard, member of the committee of experts of the commission.
23 *De Standaard* (10 May 2000).
24 *Parlementaire onderzoekscommissie-Lumumba. Nota van de experts 2-11-2000 – 20-11-2000. Interimrapport* (Brussels, 2000).
25 *De Standaard* (7 June 2001).
26 Also the fate of Belgian colonists, victims of violence and forced to flee the country in 1960, is now open for an unapologetic approach. Based on eye-witnesses is: P. Verlinden, *Weg uit Congo: het drama van de kolonialen* (Louvain, 2002).
27 *Parliamentary Committee of Enquiry. Conclusions*, pp. 1–2.
28 Jef Van Bilzen, formerly political adviser of the Belgian Government on the Belgian Congo, published his personal insights in: *Kongo 1945–1965: het einde van een kolonie* (Louvain, 1993).
29 *Parliamentary Committee of Enquiry. Conclusions*, pp. 2–8.
30 Ibid.
31 Ibid., p. 4.

32 On eventual direct involvement of the CIA and US President Dwight D. Eisenhower, see *The Washington Post* (8 August 2000).
33 *Parliamentary Committee of Enquiry. Conclusions*, pp. 2–8.
34 *Parlementaire Onderzoekscommissie Lumumba*, p. 5.
35 Telex by Minister of African Affairs, Count Harold d'Aspremont Lynden, to Ambassador Rothschild in Elisabethville on 6 October 1960.
36 Ibid.
37 *Parliamentary Committee of Enquiry. Conclusions*, p. 10.
38 *De Standaard* (19 October 2001).
39 *Parliamentary Committee of Enquiry. Conclusions*, p. 9.
40 Ibid.
41 *De Standaard* (7 November 2001 and 16 November 2001).
42 *De Standaard* (2 February 2002).
43 A. Lokongo, 'Lumumba apology not enough, but ...', *New African* (March 2002), 405.
44 Ibid.
45 See also De Witte's assessment in *De moord op Lumumba*, p. 20.
46 G. Verbeeck, 'De Lumumba-commissie of een Belgische "Methodenstreit"', 3.
47 Notwithstanding the major public response in Belgium, was the impact on the scholarly debate relatively marginal. Communication by Emmanuel Gerard to the author.
48 G. Verbeeck, 'De Lumumba-commissie of een Belgische "Methodenstreit"', 19.
49 *Parlementaire onderzoekscommissie-Lumumba. Interimrapport*, pp. 7–11.
50 *Parlementaire onderzoekscommissie-Lumumba. Interimrapport*, p. 2.

4

The Bloody Sunday tribunal and the role of the historian

Paul Bew

Why hold a Bloody Sunday tribunal at all? A Labour Prime Minister, James Callaghan, when talking of the occasion in Derry on 30 January 1972 when British soldiers killed thirteen civil rights demonstrators, once implied that these events belonged to history. Indeed, when Tony Blair announced his decision in the House of Commons to hold the inquiry, Mr Gerald Howarth, the Conservative MP for Aldershot, reminded him of Mr Callaghan's words. Prime Minister Blair replied:

> I understand the point that the hon. Gentleman is making. Whether these events should be revisited and whether it will have any effect on the way the armed forces operate on the ground weigh heavily with us. I agree entirely that they have to know that they have the support of their political masters, and they have it one hundred per cent, but it would be a disservice to them to believe that they should have anything to fear from an enquiry that establishes the truth, where people accept that people were killed in circumstances where they should not have been killed. Far from undermining support for our armed services, I believe that by setting up the tribunal of enquiry under a highly respected Law Lord and establishing it in such a way that it can get at the truth, we underline the fact that, unlike the terrorists, we do not have anything to fear from enquiries into the truth.[1]

With these words the Prime Minister entered a brave new world. There were some sceptics in the House of Commons. David Trimble, the then leader of the Ulster Unionists, remarked: 'We are in favour of the truth too. We would like the truth to come out about many things. There will be widespread scepticism about new witnesses. There will also be questions about selectivity in dealing with this incident and not others.'[2] There was no serious attempt to answer Trimble's point about selectivity. For example, the alleged role of the Irish state or sections of it in the establishment of the Provisional IRA remains outside the scope of any official inquiry. But the mood of the times heavily favoured the establishment of the Bloody Sunday Inquiry. On 7 December

1997 Mr Gerry Adams, President of Sinn Fein, had given an interview to the *Independent* which stated: 'One question that's very much in people's minds here is Bloody Sunday. Everybody knows it was a premeditated attack as part of the military-political strategy at that time. You'd think it would be relatively easy to set up an independent inquiry to sort everything out, but to do that the Prime Minister has to challenge all that stuff. That's the test.' It was a test the Prime Minister did not want to flunk at a crucial moment in the peace process, when he was desperate to keep Sinn Fein involved in political dialogue. It is no coincidence that the Prime Minister announced the Bloody Sunday Inquiry at precisely the historical moment when the IRA expressed its anger about the pro-unionist nature of the Heads of Agreement proposals which the two governments published in January 1998. Sinn Fein, in effect, was put on the defensive by the Government's outline plan for the Belfast Agreement, eventually agreed in April 1998, while David Trimble – anxious to pocket the Heads of Agreement – had to swallow the Bloody Sunday Inquiry, which he knew his own constituents would regard as, at best, a remarkable focus of public attention on only one incident of violence during the Troubles which had seen many, many horrendous incidents – the great bulk of them perpetrated not by the state but by paramilitaries.

The Bloody Sunday Tribunal is the most expensive inquiry in British legal history. A total of thirty-six barristers and solicitors from eight firms have been attending the hearings. The inquiry is not now expected to report until 2008.

The inquiry has been led by Lord Saville, a senior British Law Lord, accompanied by two other senior judges. Between 1998 and 2002, the present writer, along with Professor Paul Arthur of the University of Ulster, acted as historical adviser to the Tribunal. We both provided historical background reports for the Tribunal – reports which are available on the Tribunal's website. The Bloody Sunday Inquiry has set the technical standard for future public inquiries. Computer reconstructions, photographs and documents were flashed in front of witnesses and lawyers on personal screens. They also carried livenote, a near simultaneous transcript of proceedings.

On 30 January 1972 thirteen men, all apparently unarmed, were shot dead, and seventeen were wounded by the Parachute Regiment in Derry. Another man died later. The shooting began at the end of a civil rights rally, attended by nearly 10,000 people, when part of the crowd tried to climb over a street barrier and was forced back by the army with rubber bullets and spray from a water cannon. It has not yet been definitely established who fired the first shot: but nationalist Ireland and Irish America is convinced that it was the British army.

In August 1973, the inquest returned an open verdict on those killed by the army. Nevertheless, for nationalists the events of the day were summed up by the coroner, Hubert O'Neill, when he described the killings as amounting to 'sheer unadulterated bloody murder'.

The events of 30 January 1972 created a wave of anger that swept through the Catholic community. In an interview with the Irish broadcasting company RTE the following day, the leader of moderate nationalism, John Hume, captured the mood of the time by saying: 'Many people down here [the Bogside] feel now that it's a united Ireland or nothing'.[3] In a debate in the House of Commons, Bernadette Devlin, speaking of the Home Secretary, Reginald Maudling, said: 'The minister has stood up and lied to the House. Nobody shot at the paratroops, but somebody will shortly ... I have a right, as the only representative in this House who was an eyewitness, to ask a question of that murdering hypocrite'. She then ran across the Chamber, pulled Maudling's hair and slapped his face. Later she said: 'I didn't shoot him in the back, which is what they did to our people'.[4]

Reaction in the Irish Republic was equally hostile, with the *Irish Press* saying: 'If there was an able-bodied man with republican sympathies within the Derry area who was not in the IRA before yesterday's butchery, there will be none tonight'.[5] The Irish Ambassador to Britain was recalled in protest at the events of the previous day, and on 1 February the Irish Minister for Foreign Affairs, Dr Patrick Hillery, arriving in New York on his way to speak to the United Nations, said: 'From now on, my aim is to get Britain out of Ireland'.[6]

The repercussions of the Derry killings continued on 2 February, when, after a series of anti-British demonstrations throughout the day, the British Embassy in Dublin was burned down after it was attacked by a crowd of more than 20,000. Amid the torrent of international criticism of Britain as a result of the killings, Edward Heath announced the setting up of a tribunal of inquiry, to be headed by Lord Chief Justice Widgery. On 18 April 1972 the report of the committee headed by Lord Widgery, investigating events in Derry on 'Bloody Sunday', concluded:

> There would have been no deaths in Londonderry on 30 January if those who organised the illegal march had not thereby created a highly dangerous situation in which a clash between demonstrators and the security forces was almost inevitable ... Each soldier was his own judge of whether he had identified a gunman. Their training made them aggressive and quick in decision, and some showed more restraint in opening fire than others. At the end of the scale, some soldiers showed a high degree of responsibility; at the other ... firing bordered on the reckless ... None of the deceased or wounded is proved to have been shot whilst handling a firearm or bomb.

Nationalist Ireland and Irish America was outraged. Widgery was dismissed as a British establishment 'cover up', despite the reference to 'reckless firing' or the probable innocence of the dead. The British army vigorously defends its disciplinary record in the difficult circumstances of Northern Ireland's bloody conflict; it can point to the striking fact that the IRA and its allies carried out 60 per cent of the killings in the 'Troubles', whilst taking only 13 per cent of the fatal casualties, many of these self-inflicted.[7]

Given the reality that the British army possessed overwhelming firepower, this statistic rather suggests that, in most instances, the British army behaved with self-control and professionalism. But 'Bloody Sunday' is the great apparent exception to this rule. Here the British army is alleged and widely believed to have run amok and slaughtered the innocent. For some writers, downplaying perhaps the fact that the IRA was already in business as a serious killing machine, it is the key moment in generating the thirty-year long conflict by creating popular support for the IRA. Nationalist Ireland and Irish America never accepted the Widgery verdict. Ironically the new documents released by Saville indicate that some senior people in the British army accepted the verdict, but regarded it as rather disturbing – evidence that the army had been responsible for the loss of innocent life. Nonetheless, the bulk of the published commentary has insisted that Widgery was a whitewash. In particular, many books and articles were subsequently published, alleging political responsibility at the level of the British Cabinet.[8] Accompanying these publications were demands for a new 'more independent' inquiry.

Even the Tories felt the need to placate. In a letter to John Hume, the Social Democratic and Labour Party MP for Derry, the Prime Minister John Major, on 21 January 1993, rejected a request for an inquiry into Bloody Sunday, but added: 'The government made clear in 1974 that those who were killed on Bloody Sunday should be regarded as innocent, that they were not shot whilst handling firearms or explosives'.[9]

Immediately following the election of Tony Blair in 1997, John Hume tabled a motion in the House of Commons, calling on the new government to re-open the inquiry into the events of Bloody Sunday in 1972. In early 1998, the New Labour government, anxious to build up nationalist confidence in the peace process, announced there would, indeed, be such an inquiry under Lord Saville. The total cost will be massive; it may very well exceed £200 million.[10] The present writer has acted as one of the historical advisers to the tribunal, appointed late in 1998 and completing his work in 2001.

The Saville Tribunal has raised a fundamental question. Is the heavily legalistic style of work-judges, lawyers, a courtroom method of proceeding actually appropriate to getting at 'the truth' in a case like this? Anyway, who in such a case is engaged in a disinterested search for truth remotely akin to the practice of the average scholarly historian?

Then there is the issue of contemporary political agendas. From the

British Labour government point of view, it may well be considered that the purpose of the inquiry is to allow the offer of a historic apology (Mr Blair has a taste for this sort of thing), and then the 'drawing of a line' under the incident. There was the celebrated Blairite 'Famine' apology of 1997. In this case, the apology was driven by the view of Foreign Office officials in America that this was the best way to placate Irish American political pressure. Similarly, the Foreign Office believed that a Bloody Sunday 'apology' might help to put this issue to rest. New Labour, too, was well aware that any political embarrassment would fall on a Tory government. But, that said, the Ministry of Defence, under all administrations, has a protective role towards the British army. There is certainly some evidence that the Ministry of Defence (MOD) was less than passionately enthusiastic about the inquiry. The West Mercia Constabulary inquiry into the MOD's failure to preserve British army rifles used on Bloody Sunday concluded that rifles were destroyed 'as a result of negligence rather than an overt criminal act'. But the West Mercia report quoted an e-mail between two staff officers at the MOD: 'Here is a good one for a Monday morning. The Bloody Sunday inquiry are [sic] after records (if any) of what happened to the Bloody Sunday weapons! ... On Tuesday the Battle of Hastings inquiry will want to find the long bow which put Harold's eye out!'[11] As for nationalist Ireland, 'Bloody Sunday' now has such iconic significance as a moral illustration – the Irish Sharpeville – that it can hardly accept a report which substantially repeats, perhaps with more detail, the Widgery verdict, even if that is Saville's final conclusion.

The Bloody Sunday Tribunal was set up by a Labour government under Tony Blair. John Major had refused to go down this road. It has been much criticised by the 'forces of conservatism' in British life. But it may be worth recalling that the first great legal inquiry of this sort was set up under radically different circumstances – in this case the initiative came from the Tories. The three-judge special commission of inquiry into Parnellism and crime was established at the behest of the Salisbury government in 1888 to sort out the truth of allegations made by *The Times* against the mainstream leaders of Irish nationalism. By 1888 Parnell, the then respectable leader of the Home Rule Party, was in close alliance with the Gladstonian Liberals, and any proof of a link between Parnellites and the violence of the 1879–82 period would have hurt not only Parnell but his new Liberal allies. In the end, the hearings constituted a victory for Parnell over *The Times*. For *The Times* had foolishly relied on a forged document, attempting to show Parnell's complicity in the Phoenix Park murders of Lord Frederick Cavendish and Thomas Burke in May 1882 – the most infamous political assassinations of the era. But did the special commission get at the whole truth? Recently a long lost British intelligence report has come to light which quotes Patrick

Egan, a key conspirator, as saying that Parnell knew beforehand and neither countenanced nor discountenanced the Phoenix Park murders. It is also possible that Parnell actually joined the Irish Republican Brotherhood on the very eve of the murders; again, the information which allows scholars to say that this is at least possible, came to light many decades later.[12] I have no doubt as to Lord Saville's absolute determination to get at the truth, and I cannot predict what he will judge that truth to be; but like all such verdicts, it can never be entirely authoritative.

These are questions which will trouble any professional historian. We do not like to see the dice loaded in any investigation. We expect that lawyers may have their uses, but what have they to do with getting at historical truth? We suspect the agendas of governments – the British and Irish – as a matter of principle.

But, on the other hand, the Saville Inquiry has made available thousands of documents, which would never have otherwise seen the light of day at this point in history. Perhaps more recently the Hutton Inquiry has inured us to this type of exposure, but there is no doubt as to the risk for government.

For example, some rather tough-minded comments on Derry by a civil servant, Adrian Thorpe, then a 28-year old Foreign Office official, were released. By this time, Mr Thorpe had just concluded his successful Foreign Office career by a stint as Ambassador in Mexico, but in the lead-up to the Good Friday Agreement, he had been an important British official in the Dublin Embassy. He may well have reflected that he only narrowly missed serious embarrassment. But there can be no doubt that the Tribunal has displayed an astounding openness (some would say, insensitively) on such matters, which sets a precedent for all future inquiries.

In the prelude to the opening of the inquiry, large tranches of documents were delivered to my office. These are now all in the public domain, and I can confidently say that, in normal circumstances and going by traditional practice, many would not have seen the light for over fifty years at least.

As one of the Tribunal's historical advisers, I immediately advised on the widest possible disclosure of documents, breaking the normal constraints of the thirty-year rule. In both Britain and Ireland since the mid-1970s, the archives of governments are normally opened after the elapse of thirty years. Particularly sensitive security-related documents are often held back for a longer period. I was, however, genuinely surprised by the scale of the release which followed. To put the matter into perspective, in 1977 I was working on the book that became *The State in Northern Ireland 1921–72*.[13] Whilst I was actually working on some security-related files, they were withdrawn by the Public Record Office. I protested about this at the time in an article in *Index on Censorship*, but I had to admit that there was a defence that the system was in a position to make and did make: that these files might, if published, endanger persons or families still alive. But how much more is true of material released after only thirty years: remember, until recently, the Record Office in London held closed security-related Irish files of the 1880s.[14]

Sifting through these documents, certain key questions arose: what was the role in Bloody Sunday played by the British Cabinet? What was the role played by the Northern Ireland Cabinet? What was the role played by the two wings of the IRA – Provisional or Official? This last question was to be posed even more sharply as a result of the publication during the Tribunal of Liam Clarke and Kathy Johnstone's book *Martin McGuinness: From Guns to Government*.[15]

My main task was to provide a series of introductory reports – some of them quite basic, outlining the chronological context, and one containing an early analysis of some documents. When the principal release came, I prepared a forty-page report,[16] dated January 2000, which constituted my principal work for the Tribunal.

I tried to set Bloody Sunday in a broad historical context. First, there is the nature of the Northern Ireland problem. There can be no dispute as to the sectarian oppression suffered by the Catholic populace of Derry. The city was so gerrymandered that a Catholic majority could not shake Protestant control of local government. Edmund Warnock, a former Ulster Unionist attorney general no less, attested in 1968: 'If ever a community had a right to demonstrate against a denial of civil rights, Derry is the finest example'.[17] But it is important to acknowledge that, unlike the American case, the Northern Ireland civil rights conflict is over-determined by an unresolved issue of national identity and statehood. It is also important to recall that the postwar British welfare state brought material benefits to all the citizens of Northern Ireland, well in excess of the conditions prevailing in the Irish Republic. Northern Ireland is not only a civil rights or equality problem, it is also a 'double minority' problem. Catholics are (or were) a fearful minority in Northern Ireland, while Protestants are a fearful minority on the island of Ireland. They were also a minority in Derry itself. In a famous interview, Eamon McCann, the civil rights radical whose passionate writing on Bloody Sunday is well known, stated in 1969:

> It is perfectly obvious that people do still see themselves as Catholics and Protestants, and the cry 'Get the Protestants' is still very much on the lips of the Catholic working class. Everyone applauds when one says in a speech that we are not sectarian, we are fighting for the rights of all Irish workers, but really that's because they see this as the new way of getting at the Protestants.[18]

Then there is the issue of British 'imperial' interest. In 1993, the Downing Street Declaration asserted famously that Britain had no selfish, economic or strategic interest at stake in Ireland. The striking implication of the

'Bloody Sunday documents' is that Britain felt this way long before 1993. As Eamon McCann has strikingly acknowledged: 'No UK document or minute has emerged advocating a straightforward defence of the realm position or making the preservation of the territorial integrity of the UK a major priority in Northern Ireland policy'.[19]

In particular, on 7 October 1971, the UK Cabinet was told: 'If the priority is to maintain the union', that Northern Ireland should be treated as 'a terrorist problem'. On the other hand, tellingly, another option was considered; if the option of preserving 'the option of creating a united Ireland at some time in the future was to be preserved', then power-sharing was the best option. It is perfectly clear that, to say the least, the UK Cabinet was closer to this second position in late 1971 in the months leading up to Bloody Sunday. Indeed, one CPRS (Central Policy Review Staff, the Government think tank) review document submitted to the Cabinet four months before Bloody Sunday by Burke Trend, the Cabinet Secretary, states: 'The fact that Northern Ireland is constitutionally part of the United Kingdom is no more or less relevant in terms of political realism than the fact that Algeria was part of metropolitan France ... if the six counties ceased to be British, the net saving to public expenditure would be considerable ... Some form of deal with the Irish Republic seems the best option available'.[20] In the light of such language, it is literally impossible to see Bloody Sunday as an exercise of violence, reflecting the broad thrust of an 'imperial' or pro-Unionist British policy in Ireland.

But this raises the question what is the meaning of 'Bloody Sunday'? In line with the destruction of any imperialist agenda, the documents effectively ruled out any possibility of a conspiracy to kill Catholics at the level of British Cabinet or, indeed, the Northern Irish Cabinet at Stormont enjoying the last few months of life before the implementation of direct rule in 1972. There may be an issue for lawyers of 'negligence' – failure to take reasonable steps to prevent a tragedy – but for political historians the facts are more unambiguous: neither the British Cabinet in London nor the Northern Irish Cabinet in Belfast planned Bloody Sunday.

The Heath Cabinet discussed the Derry situation on 11 January 1972. The tone is instructive: 'As to Londonderry, a military operation to impose law and order would require seven battalions ... It would be a major operation, necessarily involving civilian casualties and thereby hardening even further the attitude of the Roman Catholic population'. Heath's own summary of the situation on 11 January was that a military operation to 'reimpose law and order' in Derry might become inevitable, but it should not be undertaken until there was a successful political initiative. This is not the tone of voice of a Prime Minister contemplating a Bloody Sunday massacre within three weeks.

The Northern Irish Unionist Cabinet simply did not have the necessary influence with the British army as to be in a position to plan Bloody Sunday. James Chichester-Clarke's resignation as Prime Minister of Northern Ireland took place on 20 March 1971, precisely because of General Tuzo's refusal to consider security measures which the unionists advocated, including restoration of the Royal Ulster Constabulary (RUC) to 'their rightful role' and the establishment of permanent military bases in a number of nationalist districts to prevent the consolidation of no-go areas.[21] In mid January 1972, Peter Jenkins, then the *dôyen* of the *Guardian*'s political reporters, reported that the most senior British military were tired of dealing with the Stormont apparatus and wanted direct rule.[22] One of the most powerful and compelling witnesses to the tribunal was Robert Ramsey, a senior European Union official, who in 1972 had been an aide to the Unionist Prime Minister Brian Faulkner. Mr Ramsey pointedly recalled how Faulkner had said to him in the aftermath of Bloody Sunday that while he knew his own government was not responsible it would end up taking the blame. In the sense that Bloody Sunday brought forward the implementation of direct rule, Faulkner was proven to be right.

But if we reject the idea of political conspiracy, what about the role of the army? The *Sunday Times* journalist Murray Sayle, who covered the story at the time, has argued that the explanation of Bloody Sunday is clear: the development in the Parachute Regiment of a plan to eliminate the IRA leadership in Londonderry – which as the result 'disgraced the regiment for a very long time to come and presented the IRA with the most resounding moral victory they have had since 1916'.[23] Sayle adds: 'The idea was based ... on the military principle that the way to bring your enemy to battle is to attack something that, for prestige reasons, he will have to defend: the Germans attacking Verdun in the First World War or the same firm attacking Stalingrad. Brought to battle, he will then be annihilated by superior strength.' The civil rights march, the Parachute Regiment reasoned, was just such an objective. The IRA would have to defend the march or lose its popular support in the Bogside – either way, the IRA would be finished.

The documents, unfortunately, do not provide any evidence that such a calculation existed within the army high command. Nor do they suggest – as has been suggested – that the objective was to create a flood of recruits to the IRA and thus make it easier for army intelligence to penetrate. But they do suggest another explanation. In his important study *From Civil Rights to Armalites: Derry and the Birth of the Irish Troubles*, Dr Niall O'Dochartaigh expresses this point with great clarity:

> On numerous occasions over the previous months troops had battled huge crowds in Creggan against a backdrop of gunfire and bombs. On Bloody Sunday there was less violence from the crowd than there had been during

many of these confrontations in Creggan and the Bogside. Thus, to many in Derry, the army appeared to have carried out a calculated massacre of unarmed rioters, deliberately escalating the conflict.[24]

O'Dochartaigh's point is a simple one: why did British army policy change and become so disastrously aggressive? After all, the army had countenanced in September/October 1971 a low key peace policy worked out with local leaders like John Hume, in an effort to de-escalate the conflict.

One very simple observation can be made: in the weeks leading up to 'Bloody Sunday', there is a growing divergence (but one only fully visible with the benefit of hindsight) in the view of the public order security situation in Derry. Local inhabitants and the army were locked into a dangerous asymmetry of perception. The army viewed the situation as increasingly intolerable and one which demanded rectification. For example, the *Summary of Events in Londonderry on Sunday 30 January 1972*, co-authored by Lt Col Overbury and Lt Col Hamilton, contains the key passage:

> In the two weeks prior to the march, the IRA had been particularly active within the city, and the security forces were fired on in 80 separate incidents in which 319 rounds were fired and a total of 84 nail bombs thrown at them. Security force casualties during this period were two killed and two wounded. Two features of the IRA tactics in these attacks were the deliberate use of crowd cover (demonstrations in general public in shopping areas) and the use of the hooligan elements in creating suitable opportunities for attacks against security forces: a reliable and detailed intelligence report received during the week preceding the march, confirmed earlier reports by including the forecast that the IRA could be using the crowd and hooligan technique during the march on 30 January to provoke opportunities for attacks on security forces.[25]

More than any other recent study of Derry, Dr O'Dochartaigh's account is based on a sympathetic understanding of the city's republican and nationalist community – who provided much of his interview material – and it, therefore, has established a right to be taken seriously. But the question he poses has a simple answer: the army felt that their peace initiative of September/October had failed and that they were losing control over public order in Derry.

Let us turn to the unfolding pattern of events. Before the turn of the year, there is every evidence of a military resolve to operate a controlled modulated policy. On 10 November 1971, the local British army Brigadier in Derry, Pat McClellan, wrote:

> The hooligans in Londonderry are particularly youthful, agile and fleet of foot, and any arrest manoeuvre which smacks of ponderousness will not catch them. They must be dispersed by the minimum use of force and arrested by the use of imaginative tactics.

> Commanders are to ensure that the personal standards of conduct of their soldiers do not deteriorate, whatever the provocation. At all costs the soldier must be seen to be impartial, humane and courteous. Similarly, his professional standards must remain high, particularly in the field of fire-disciplined weapon training and alertness.

On 14 December 1971 the General Officer Commanding (GOC) met with the Home Secretary in Lisburn to discuss policy. There is no evidence at this meeting of any major planned initiative to transform the situation in Londonderry: 'The position in Londonderry had reached a point where a choice had to be made between accepting that Creggan and Bogside were areas where the army were not able to go, except on specific information or to mount operations [involving] battalions and which would [involve] some shooting of unarmed civilians'. It became obvious that the army preferred the first course, but wanted to make it clear it entailed accepting, and living with, criticism of 'no-go' areas. The Home Secretary said that he had no doubt that the military judgement was right and that it would be wrong to provoke a major confrontation at this stage. In this meeting with the Home Secretary, General Tuzo was sharply critical of the local security forces: 'He had to say that the RUC high command was flabby and the morale was low'. It is certain that the Home Secretary felt he was being pushed towards 'direct rule by the side door'. The highly detailed ten-page military assessment of options[26] recommends in effect a policy of containment and is consistent with the terms of the military discussion with the Home Secretary. On 20 December 1971 a further document, signed M C CGS (Michael Carver), is in a similar tone:

> The situation here [Derry] is totally different to that in Belfast. The Bogside and Creggan are 'no-go' areas. To change this would need a major military operation, which would demand large numbers of troops, incur a high level of casualties and inflame the situation not only in Londonderry itself, but in the whole of Northern Ireland and particularly in the Republic ... It is clear that the only policy we can sensibly pursue in Londonderry is to maintain a level of military activity which maintains the morale of the Protestants and of our own soldiers, without provoking the Catholic population to an extent which causes us severe casualties, further antagonise them and brings no dividends. Our recent increased activity has tended in this direction, and I recommend, as does the GOC and the Brigade Commander, that we adopt a policy of rather less provocative activity than of recent weeks, although higher than the 'low profile' attitude adopted in September and October.

Nevertheless, it is possible to detect a tone of increasing strain or internal tension in military comment on the situation in Derry. In particular, a concern about the 'radius of anarchy' is beginning to run counter to the concern with impartiality, humanity and courtesy. At the beginning of January, Major General Ford (7 January) reported:

The Londonderry situation is further complicated by one additional ingredient. This is the Derry Young Hooligans. Gangs of tough, teenage youths, permanently unemployed, have developed sophisticated tactics of brick and stone throwing, destruction and arson. Under cover of snipers in nearby buildings, they operate just beyond the hard core areas and extend the radius of anarchy by degrees into additional streets and areas. Against the Derry Young Hooligans – described by the People's Democracy as 'brave fighters in the republican cause' – the army in Londonderry is, for the moment, virtually incapable. This incapacity threatens our ability to deal with the gunmen and bombers and threatens what is left of law and order on the West Bank of the Foyle ...

It is the opinion of the senior commanders in Londonderry that if the march takes place, however good the intentions of the NICRA may be, the Derry Young Hooligans, backed up by the gunmen, will undoubtedly take area control at an early stage.

I was disturbed by the attitude of both the Brigade Commander and the Battalion Commander; also, of course, by Chief Superintendent Lagan. All admitted that the 'front' was gradually moving northwards and, in their view, not only would Great James Street go up in time but also Clarendon Street, unless there was a change in policy. This admission meant that this major shopping centre would, in their opinion, become extinct during the next few months.

I am coming to the conclusion that the minimum force necessary to achieve a restoration of law and order is to shoot selected ring leaders amongst the Derry Young Hooligans after clear warnings have been issued.

These concerns gave us the clue to the selection of the Parachute Regiment for the day's work. The mythic reputation of the tough Paras was believed to be the antidote to Derry's growing lawlessness or expanding radius of anarchy. 'Peace keeping', wrote one officer, was largely a 'confidence trick': the security forces had to instil a 'belief' in the minds of turbulent locals that they meant business. Ultimately, if enough people want to riot and destroy a city, they will succeed. But on 9 August, at a critical moment, the Belfast mob had been intimidated by the Paras – why not try the Paras out in Derry, where they had not been used thus far? The author here talks about giving a paper to the MOD – a paper which, at the time of Bloody Sunday, had not been given – the paper was based on the assumption that 'there was a gap in our armoury which could only be met with a lethal weapon, and that it would be necessary to revert to the hard concept used in counter-insurgency campaigns of warning ringleaders that they would be shot and, if necessary, doing so'. This looks like a growing predisposition to use lethal force in certain violently contested situations, where the army had previously not used that force – but note also the danger of the moment. There has, as yet, been no proper debate at the Ministry of Defence – no proper discussion of the 'downsides'.

Consideration also has to be given to the 'canteen culture' of the Paras. One alleged unpublished memo by a parachute regiment officer was presented to the Tribunal by Colin Wallace. It states: 'Our inner conscience hoped and prayed that if we had to deal with a crowd – it would be a violent one – for this was what we had been trained for'. He quotes a company commander bringing news of the Paras' intended role in Derry the following day: 'We are really going to have a go at them this time. The "hooligan element" would be dealt with'. He describes a captain telling his wife of the plan: 'I can just see the headline,' she said, 'Londonderry's Sharpeville'.

Nevertheless, there is no evidence of a pre-meditated, co-ordinated plan to massacre: on 26 January A. W. Stevens of the Ministry of Defence wrote: 'Once the march is brought to a halt, there will be at least some hooliganism. The GOC, therefore, has in mind to attempt to arrest a fair number of such hooligans and to arrange for a special court sitting on Monday morning, before which they can be brought'.

In these papers, the local command's (conflicting) objectives are clearly outlined: 'Initially we intend to deal with any illegal marches in as low key as possible and for as long as possible'.[27] But on the other hand, it is necessary to note the other aspect: 'IRA terrorist activity to take advantage of the event, to conduct shooting attacks against the security forces, and bombing attacks against businesses, shopping and commercial premises in the city centre'.

It is arguable that there is an obvious tension between the 'concept' of the operation and the assessment of 'threat'. The 'concept' of projected army activity was laid out as

1 lowest possible key;

2 emplacement of barriers at last possible moment;

3 use of CS gas – only when in imminent danger of being overrun;

4 leading members of march will be non-violent.

The threat, however, is defined as:

1 confrontation between the security forces and the marchers;

2 IRA activity to take advantage of event;

3 hooligan reaction – continuing after event;

4 sectarian unrest in Fountain Street area;

There is also a reference to the 'deployment of snipers':

1 legality OK (so long as cleared with Minister of Home Affairs) to deploy to private houses and businesses premises;

2 require details from units;

3 *aim* is to cover troops in rear with counter-sniper fire.

According to Brigadier Pat McClellan:

1 use of force;

2 CS gas is *not* to be used throughout this event, except as a last resort, only if troops are about to be overrun and the rioters can no longer be held off with baton rounds and water cannons.

Yet, at the same time:

1 we expect a hooligan element to accompany the marchers and anticipate an intensification of the normal level of hooliganism during and after the march. Almost certainly, snipers, petrol bombers and nail bombers will support the rioters;

2 bombers may intensify their efforts to destroy business, and shopping premises in the city centre during the event, while the attention of the security forces is directed towards the containment of the march.

This military assessment clearly feeds into the conclusions at the Joint Security Committee meeting, held at Stormont on the eve of the march: 'The operation may well develop into rioting and even a shooting war'.

Enough material has been presented to show that significant segments of the British army approached Bloody Sunday in an angry, frustrated mood. The massive wave of bombing that struck the province on the previous week cannot have helped. The announcement of the death of Major Allers-Hankey – who had been hit in the Derry sniping incident – just as the soldiers went into action, cannot have helped.[28] It does not follow, however, that the British army, without any help from either wing of the IRA, can with certainty be held totally responsible for the tragedy on the day.

The Bloody Sunday files contain an allegation from a Derry IRA informer (code-named Infliction) that Martin McGuinness initiated the tragedy by firing a shot. The Clarke/Johnstone book,[29] relying on different sources, and offering a different account, nonetheless implies that Martin McGuinness has not yet given a full public account of his activities on that day. In the case of the 'Infliction' document, it has been disputed by David Shayler, a former intelligence officer, but implicitly defended by others in the course of the Tribunal.

In June last year, before adjourning the inquiry for the summer, Inquiry Chairman Lord Saville complained that four years after his appointment, he still had little evidence from the Provisional IRA. He then renewed a warning issued the previous year that, if fuller evidence was not provided, he might conclude that the organisation had something to hide.

On 10 July 2003, before rising for the summer's recess, Saville returned to the issue: 'I must also say that there are a number of areas in which evidence that ought to be provided is still absent. At the end of the day, we shall have to reach a judgement on all the evidence that we have heard. But, in reaching that judgement, we may also have to take into account the fact, if it turns out to be one, that people who could have given evidence, have chosen not to, since that fact may have a significance of its own'.[30] Mr. McGuinness, in fact did attend the tribunal and offered a vigorous defence of his own role. It is clear that his public reputation at this stage remains unchanged.

When the oral evidence to the Tribunal was completed in February 2004, there were two broad conclusions to be drawn. The most brilliant of the radical nationalist commentator, Eamon McCann, acknowledged that there was 'no clear evidence ... of a high level plan for a lethal assault on Bloody Sunday'.[31] There had been clear evidence of 'belligerence in senior ranks towards the Bogside'. The evidence of one such British army officer appeared to support that view. The Commander of the Royal Anglians, Col. Roy Jackson, was scathing in evidence about Major General Ford's use of the Paras, declaring that 'arrogance at all levels had characterised the planning of the operation'.

Questions still remained about why exactly the Paras had been employed? Sir David Ramsbotham testified in December 2002 that the commander of one of the resident battalions in Derry, Lt Col. Peter Welsh of the Royal Green Jackets, had phoned him one week before Bloody Sunday to protest about the plan to bring in the Paratroopers. Ramsbotham was principal officer to the Chief of the General Staff, Michael Carver. Ramsbotham felt that it was 'quite certain' that Carver had alerted the Prime Minister about these concerns – especially marked after an angry clash between Paratroopers and marchers at Magilligan the previous weekend. But there is no evidence that the Prime Minister or indeed the Defence Secretary were told of these concerns. In testimony, both Edward Heath and Lord Carrington said they had no memory of such an event.

Then there is the issue of the behaviour of the Paras on the day. Did they disobey orders? Radio logs showed Brigadier Patrick MacLellan, instructing one company of Paras to go through a barrier to 'scoop up ... yobbos', but not to 'conduct a running battle down Rossville Street'. In fact, three companies went in. Lord Saville put it to MacLellan that they then 'disobeyed your orders and went deep into the Bogside ... On one street at least, they started a running battle, precisely contrary to your instructions'. MacLellan replied: 'I accept that'.

There is now little doubt that Saville's treatment of forensic evidence will differ markedly from Widgery. The review of forensic evidence commissioned by Saville from Dr John Lloyd described the forensic evidence accepted by Widgery as 'scientifically unacceptable'. In short, there was no forensic evidence that any of the dead had been handling guns or explosives. Saville, therefore, has an objective basis to reach a different conclusion from that of Widgery: that they were killed as a result of British army malfunction rather than political conspiracy.

Yet, one great problem remains. How does the Tribunal assess the evidence about republican activity on the day? Liam Clarke has pointed out: 'There were signs of orchestration of violence and intimidation of witnesses by the IRA'. There was also evidence of a more or less spontaneous desire by local figures not to say anything which subverted, in any respect, the mainstream nationalist version of the tragedy.[32]

Ivan Cooper, hero of Don Mullan's film about Bloody Sunday, suggested that pages of notes kept in a *Sunday Tribune* archive since 1972 and taken in interviews with a distinguished investigative journalist had been fabricated. It may be so. Nationalist Ireland, since the time of the Casement diaries, has little difficulty in accepting that British intelligence is capable of brilliant and complex forgeries: although it is also so that in the number of the celebrated alleged case – Casement's 'Black Diaries' – a forgery has not actually been proven, despite much investigation and debate.

The key point is this – did the IRA, either Official or Provisional, act in ways which contributed to the tragedy? One might conclude that the soldiers had been at fault in each of the shootings and still want to ask this question. The key point about these alleged activities needs to be understood. In one sense it may change nothing about Bloody Sunday. But nonetheless, these alleged activities are important in the assessment of the 'intelligence' background to the army's behaviour. If there was no reasonable expectation of IRA activity on the day, then it is easier to present the British army as engaging in premeditated slaughter. But if there was a reasonable expectation of IRA activity – of the sort, for example, alleged by Clarke and Johnstone against McGuinness – then the picture is changed to a degree at least. Then we move away from a conspiracy-based interpretation of Bloody Sunday towards one more firmly based on the 'cock-up' principle.

The Bloody Sunday Inquiry has now completed its hearing of the oral evidence. Expensive it has certainly been, but it has also been highly professional. The full truth about Bloody Sunday will never be known, but a lot more now is known. The key question for the British state is this: is its characteristic way of dealing with these problems – by handing them over to lawyers – the only cost-effective way of satisfying the public desire for truth?

At the international round table conference *Contemporary Historians, Professional Standards and the Public use of History*, held at Södertörn University College, Stockholm, on 29–31 August 2002, it was clear that Britain was alone amongst European countries in giving such a big role to judges and lawyers in this type of investigation. In particular the expenditure of hundreds of millions of pounds on legal fees seems to be a real peculiarity of the British. Of course, historical truth and the courtroom are not, in principle, incompatible: see, for example, Richard J. Evans, *Telling Lies about Hitler*,[33] and Adam Nossiter, *Algeria Hotel: France, Memory and the Second World War*.[34] But the fact remains that the bulk of the new knowledge we have up to this point from the Bloody Sunday Tribunal comes from the release of documents, not courtroom confrontations. It is high drama when soldiers and former Prime Ministers are accused of lying, but how many people reading these transcripts are really better informed? The Bloody Sunday Tribunal is part of a struggle for the 'verdict of history' – and the only people who can give you the 'verdict of history' with any remote authority are historians. Historians themselves differ about the verdict of history, but it is their argument which matters, not the confident yet ephemeral rhetoric of barristers. The government has a legacy from the Bloody Sunday Tribunal – not just the heavy financial cost – but also the claims of other victims of the Troubles to have their story respected by the state. It has unfinished business here, and it needs to reflect on the way it has gone about its business thus far. A certain humility is necessary. A consensus now rules which stretches from the anti-revisionist *History Ireland* journal to the most arch revisionist, that in the original Bloody Sunday of November 1920 British armoured cars did not invade the Croke Park stadium as shown in the recent Michael Collins movie, directed by Neil Jordan. Does anyone really believe that a Tribunal of Inquiry which established this fact would actually have changed the intention of the film-maker?

But the fact remains that there is reason to learn the lessons of the Bloody Sunday Inquiry. Future tribunals are in the offing. There will be four more in the wake of the publication of the Cory Report in spring 2004. It is hard to resist the conclusion. Smaller tribunals run on more inquisitorial lines, in which some evidence can be given on camera, and in which people can speak without fear of the consequences, might get closer to the truth.

Notes

1 *New Dialogue News*, 57, February 1998.
2 Ibid.
3 B. White, *John Hume: Statesman of the Troubles* (Belfast, 1984), p. 120; G. Drower, *John Hume: Peacemaker* (London, 1995), p. 60.

4 *Hansard*, 5th series, vol. 830, cols. 37–43.
5 P. Bew and G. Gillespie, *Northern Ireland: A Chronology of the Troubles 1968–1999* (Dublin, 1999), p. 45.
6 Quoted by C. O'Clery, *Phrases make History Here: A Century of Irish Political Quotations, 1886–1986* (Dublin 1986), p. 142.
7 D. McKitterick *et al.*, *Lost Lives* (Edinburgh, 1999), pp. 1474–5.
8 The most detailed and impressive is D. P. J. Walsh, *Bloody Sunday and the Rule of Law in Northern Ireland* (London, 2000). For a deeply emotional and effective see E. McCann, *Bloody Sunday in Derry: What really happened* (Dingle, 2000).
9 *Irish Times* (23 January 1993).
10 *Sunday Times* (23 August 2003).
11 'Bloody Sunday Guns Loss "Careless"', *Sunday Tribune* (11 August 2002).
12 See P. Bew, 'Opening the Bloody Sunday Can of Worms', *The Times* (4 August 2000).
13 P. Bew, *The State in Northern Ireland 1921–72* (Manchester, 1979). Currently in print in revised and extended format as P. Bew, *Northern Ireland 1921–2001: Political Forces and Social Classes* (London, 2002).
14 These relate to issues of alleged criminality and Irish nationalism. See M. O'Callaghan, *British High Politics and a Nationalist Ireland: Criminality, Land and the Law under Forster and Balfour* (Cork, 1994).
15 L. Clarke and K. Johnstone, *Martin McGuinness: From Guns to Government* (Edinburgh and London, 2001).
16 This report is to be found at E7002 on the Tribunal's website.
17 Public Record Office of Northern Ireland, Belfast, CAB 4/140/14, 14 November 1968.
18 *New Left Review*, 55 (May/June) 1969, p. 11.
19 E. McCann, 'Bloody Sunday was no mere British Defence of the Realm', *Sunday Tribune* (29 December 2002). Of all Mr McCann's many striking articles on the work of the Bloody Sunday Tribunal, this is the most serious.
20 *Ibid.*
21 *Sunday Tribune* (31 March 2002).
22 *Guardian* (15 January 1972).
23 M. Sayle and D. Humphrey, 'Bloody Sunday Report', *London Review of Books*, 11 July 2002. Copy filed 3 February 1972.
24 N. O'Dochartaigh, *From Civil Rights to Armalites: Derry and the Birth of the Irish Troubles* (Cork, 1993), p. 261.
25 As pointed out in the preface to my report at E7.00.02, I did not have access to this material, and, therefore, my argument is, to that extent, weakened.
26 *Future Military Policy for Londonderry: An Appreciation of the Situation by CLF: Annexe C.*
27 This document came into the public domain some time ago. See the useful book by D. Hamill, *Pig in the Middle: The Army in Northern Ireland* (London, 1985), p. 87.
28 P. Pringle and P. Jacobson, *Those are Real Bullets Aren't They?* (London, 2000), p. 92.
29 Clarke and Johnstone, *Martin McGuinness*.

30 *Sunday Tribune* (16 and 23 August 2003).
31 'Those Months of Sundays', *Sunday Tribune* (15 February 2004).
32 'Bloody Sunday Truth fails to eclipse the big Derry Myth', *The Sunday Times* (15 February 2004).
33 R. J. Evans, *Telling Lies about Hitler* (London, 2002).
34 A. Nossiter, *Algeria Hotel: France, Memory and the Second World War* (London, 2002).

5

Between scholarship and politics: experiences from the Commission on the Swedish Security Services

Karl Molin

On 25 March 1999, the Swedish Government decided to appoint a commission with the task of presenting an 'overall, exhaustive and definitive survey of the domestic operations of the security services' after 1945. This Commission, which went under the name of the Commission on the Swedish Security Services (SÄKO), appears afterwards as one in a number of critically investigative historical commissions, churned out of the ideological reorientation of the 1990s. These commissions, which all highlight and illustrate various blemishes on Sweden's modern history, expressed the demand of the time for penance and remorse. They were included in a flagellant procession that went through this decade of self-examination, and in this procession, with uncertainty in their steps, but with the whip raised to hit, were the historians.

However, these 'penance commissions' also drew criticism and when the decision to appoint SÄKO was taken, the belief in its suitability as a tool to investigate historical problems had, in reality, begun to wane. Not least, this criticism emerged from academic quarters. Hence, in the following account of SÄKO's prehistory and history, not only will the political conditions be highlighted, but also these critical views of commissions as a mode of work. I will raise the question as to what extent SÄKO's work substantiated the critical views and, at the end, pose the question as to whether there are grounds for testing the same model in the future. The views are purely my own, based on experiences as a university scholar, and as a member of SÄKO for three intensive years.

A time for re-evaluation

Swedish self-understanding and self-esteem has been greatly associated with the welfare state that from the start in the 1930s reached its completion during the non-stop booms of the early postwar decades. The Swedish Model, with a harmonious labour market, social security from the cradle to the grave and a strong public sector, became the focus of international attention and many people wanted to see it as a progressive alternative in the dualistic world of the Cold War, as a Third Way between Communism and Capitalism.

During this period, there was agreement on the fundamental features of the model, and the political opposition's objections were, above all, about the Social Democrats taking all of the credit for its conception and forgetting the important roles that both business and non-Socialist parties had played.

During the 1980s, the model was exposed to severe economic strains. The money was no longer sufficient for the large-scale and generous social insurance systems. People with low or medium incomes were forced to accept a marked deterioration in the standard of living. Instead of competing for credit for the progress, parties began to fight about the responsibility for the deterioration.

In the wake of the crisis, the economic and political thought patterns were transformed. Also in Sweden, monetary logic gained a footing amongst economists, whilst the Keynesian formulas for stimulating economic activity lost credibility. Right-wing currents replaced the left-wing tide.

In foreign policy terms, the Swedish welfare state professed to a strict neutrality policy according to the formula 'non-alignment in peace, aiming at neutrality in war'. The more detailed content of this policy was, however, to remain unknown to the majority of the people. A reason for this was quite simply that important elements of the policy were concealed by military secrecy. This applied, above all, to the extensive preparations Sweden took in order to receive military assistance from the West in the event the Soviet Union were to attack, and to the technical co-operation developed with the West. Sweden, despite this co-operation, could have remained neutral in a future war. Nevertheless, the risk was huge that she would be perceived in the East as a secret NATO member and, hence, military relations with the West were cloaked in great secrecy. This resulted in the foreign policy debate for forty years being conducted within narrow parameters. To this contributed also the notion, fostered by Social Democratic Governments, that the credibility of the neutrality policy would be tainted abroad, if challenged by the domestic political opposition. The impression would be that, if only the opposition won the next election, Sweden would join NATO. Conflicting contributions to the security debate came to be branded as irresponsible, bordering on treasonable.

With the collapse of the Soviet Empire and the end of the Cold War, these restrictions on exchanging views disappeared and the general public was eager to find out what was really hidden under the surface. In the debate, the neutrality policy was referred to as 'the big lie', whilst voices were raised urging neutrality to be scrapped and Sweden to join NATO. Important in this context is that demands for fundamental changes, whether they applied to the state's role in social life or the future of neutrality, were associated with criticism of the country's politics during the last half-century. The result was that the history of the welfare state and of neutrality were subjected to a largely unsystematic, but, nonetheless, close and critical examination.[1] It is in this context that the government commissions come into the picture.

The political role of the commissions

The secret military co-operation between Sweden and the Western powers, the compulsory sterilisation of Swedish citizens for racial or social reasons, trade with Germany during the Second World War (in particular, trade involving stolen Jewish assets), the political and diplomatic handling of the case of Raoul Wallenberg (the businessman and diplomat who, after having led an operation to rescue Jews in Budapest, was captured by the Red Army in January 1945 and since then never heard from); these, aside from the question of the work of the security services, are the leading examples of the subjects dealt with by the retrospective, self-accusatory government commissions of the 1990s.

They all have in common that the Government appointed them, but that it was not the Government who had put the question on the agenda. The appointment of a commission was routinely the Government's answer to a debate that was being conducted in public, often with strongly moralising undertones and with, more or less, accusatory fingers clearly directed at the Government for not wanting to be touched by these blemishes.

To single out a common ideological denominator in these attacks is not easy. Perhaps we can get close to it with the help of one of the great moralists of the nineteenth century, Fjodor Dostojevskij. In *The Brothers Karamazov* he allows the rationalist, Ivan, to confront his empathetic brother, Aljosja, with a critical choice. If you had the fate of mankind in your hands, asked Ivan, and could make people happy and finally make everything all right for them, but only on the condition that you tortured one individual human being, building your construction on the basis of the flowing tears of a human, would you then set to work? The answer was clear: 'No, I would not', said Aljosja slowly.

It would be wrong to claim that the debate of the 1990s assumed Aljosja's uncompromising individualism, or that the moral implications were always fully considered. However, undoubtedly, there was a feeling that the care for the individual's rights compared with the collective needed to be strengthened. It was certainly also the case that, for varying reasons, many regarded that it was now high time to count the tears, upon which the modern Sweden had been based.

That government commissions were given the main responsibility for this pitiful inventory is not surprising given the strong position of the commission system in Swedish political tradition. Its ancestors are part of the bureaucratic reorganisation, which the Swedish Crown, in order to live up to its recently acquired Great Power status, carried out in the middle of the seventeenth century. Special commissions were convened for tasks, which the King's chancery, the administrative departments or the courts of law were unable to perform. They were even invested with sentencing functions and were used, for instance, during witch trials.[2]

The commissions have maintained their importance within the Government Offices, which are still of a modest size, with between 2,000 and 3,000 employees. Approximately 20 per cent of their budget is used to fund ad hoc committees with special terms of reference. The Government determines their directives, and appoints their members.[3]

The purpose of the committees is usually summarised in three points: increasing knowledge within a certain field, creating consensus and drawing up proposals. Major political decisions are regularly prepared by way of a government commission and the committee system is often considered to bear witness to the features that are typical of Swedish political culture: respect for objectivity and scientific expertise, reason and understanding. However, the committee system has during periods been criticised for being long-winded and slow and, above all, serving as a burial ground for questions difficult to manage. In 1982, a reform was carried out cutting the number of committees and limiting their normal life span to two years.[4]

The self-mortifying commissions of the 1990s had, first and foremost, a purpose of acquiring knowledge and were, therefore, not part of the preparation of future government proposals. They were quite simply there to clear up the nation's past, so that those currently in power would not be stained.

Five key problems

The researchers, usually historians and political scientists, who were called on by these historical investigations, were faced with a task that was different from the ones they had come across in their capacity as researchers linked to universities. The problems they faced were reflected partly in the various reports by the commissions and partly in the public debate. The problems are summarised in the following brief five-point account, namely, secrecy, time pressure, lack of competence, demand for compromise and demand for moral criticism.[5]

The problems associated with the use of the Official Secrets Act had been present in conjunction with previous investigations into the work of the security services and had also been brought to the fore by some of the historical commissions of the 1990s, in particular, the Commission on military co-operation with the West. When it came to SÄKO, there were those who took it for granted that the Commission's report would be met with suspicion, not just because it, like all of the commissions, was a product of the Establishment, but also because just a part of the findings was supposed to be published. As will become evident below, there were also features of the Commission's prehistory that could warrant such a gloomy prediction.[6]

A common feature for the historical commissions is that their assignments were broad and the researchers had the feeling that their employer did not understand the strenuous work required for a satisfactory result. The customary two-year deadline had been seen as totally insufficient and, in most cases, had been extended. Nevertheless, several commissions had complained that there had been too little time. The Commission on the handling of Jewish assets noted that, due to time constraint, it had not been able to go into detail and to pursue all intriguing leads.[7]

The problem of the commissions acquiring the right competence was first set out in an article by Olof Ruin, Professor of Political Science, who himself had been a member of one of the historical commissions of the 1990s. He felt that those who were being recruited to the commissions were often extremely busy people who could not devote themselves totally to the research task. Thus, the responsibility for the quality came to rest on the Secretariat, which could hardly assemble the same competence as the academic world could offer.[8]

The fourth point, then, is about compromise. As mentioned, one of the central tasks of the commissions is usually to create consensus on important issues. For a researcher from a traditional academic environment, this is an unfamiliar task. Above all, the researcher wants to develop his originality in the approach and the analysis and is, thus, more interested in stressing differences than finding similarities. Compromise is not a positive word in academic circles. Professor Ruin also pointed out in his aforementioned article that, whilst commission reports were understood to be truths, they bear the stamp of a compromise product. The work is conducted amid a give-and-take between the members in conjunction with the Secretariat, which presents the original text. Referring to his personal experiences, he also mentioned that when differences existed an effort was made, 'in keeping with Swedish political culture', to find formulations, on which everybody could agree. He obviously preferred a system where the individual investigator has a clear personal responsibility for the conclusions.[9]

The fifth problem, the one about employing moral criticism, is undoubtedly the most difficult for an academic to deal with. As the historical commissions played an important role in the critical examination of the near past, pronouncements of moral judgments and the apportioning of blame were seen as an integrated part of their task. An example of this is the Commission on the handling of the Raoul Wallenberg case. The Swedish Government had long been criticised for not having pressed the Soviets energetically and consistently enough. And when the Commission was appointed in October 2001, the Prime Minister had already stated at the beginning of the year that 'a more energetic and purposeful action on the part of Sweden during the 1940s could have led to a more successful outcome for Raoul Wallenberg and his family'. It was also made clear in the Commission's directive that the task was not just to 'investigate', but also to 'evaluate' how cabinet ministers and diplomats acted to free Wallenberg.[10]

In a commentary on the directive, the Commission pointed out that such an evaluation presupposes knowledge of the relevant historical context. For this reason the Commission had sought to map out and understand the conditions under which the Swedish Government and the Ministry for Foreign Affairs operated. This applied both to practical conditions such as the possibility for open communication between the embassies and the ministry and the conditions of a more general nature, such as the security situation in Europe at the time of the collapse of Nazi Germany in May 1945, Sweden's trade and security policy objectives, the overall situation in Swedish-Soviet relations at the time of Wallenberg's disappearance, and also the leading actors' general view of the world.

Still, if the actors are placed in their context, is this not going to look like trying to excuse the mistakes made? The Raoul Wallenberg Commission raised this issue and explained that the purpose in giving an account of the historical context was not to 'hunt for excuses', but only to create a good basis for an assessment and evaluation of the handling of the case. It even says in another passage that 'the premise has been that no circumstances ought to have been able to force the leadership of the Swedish Ministry for Foreign Affairs to abandon its obligations towards one of its citizens'. In other words, the decision-makers of that time were, more or less, prejudged – the question was merely about the nature of the guilt and its extent.[11]

The Commission on the Raoul Wallenberg case was, thus, not alien to passing judgments. The finished report was appropriately named 'A Diplomatic Failure'. And its conclusions were that foreign ministers and leading officials at the Ministry for Foreign Affairs were guilty of a deplorable lack of active interest in the question. They were also criticised for having believed in unreliable information that Wallenberg was dead.[12]

The Commission on Compulsory Sterilisation adopted a more circumspect attitude. When the Commission was appointed in 1997, the Government had, after a stormy debate, already strongly regretted the injustices committed and held out the prospect of financial compensation. Therefore, it was completely logical that the Commission was given the task of 'shedding light' on the question of 'responsibility' for the violations of the individual integrity that had occurred. The investigator found this task difficult to handle. Proving the legal question of responsibility was indeed no major problem. The moral responsibility was a more difficult issue to handle. Already 'shedding light' upon a moral responsibility could be problematic, and even more so was declaring someone morally responsible for decisions based upon values, mindsets and opinions that go back forty to fifty years in time.[13]

In pursuance of its duty, the Commission, nevertheless, gave an assessment of the extent to which the different actors, such as the Government, the Swedish Parliament (*Riksdag*), various authorities, and the medical profession, could be blamed for having violated the integrity of individuals through sterilisation. For instance, it came to the conclusion that it was 'reproachable' that the Government and the Riksdag did not react to the criticism of sterilisation at certain mental hospitals that came to light as early as 1947. The National Board of Health and Welfare is given the same assessment for its reluctance to listen to the views of the relatives.[14]

As to whether also individual doctors should be blamed, the Commission writes: 'If... individual doctors shall be held personally responsible for their actions, or whether they, if anything, shall be regarded as prisoners of the structures and mindsets – this is almost a philosophical question'.[15]

This statement mirrors the uneasiness historians and other researchers experienced when confronted with the task of making moral judgments about the actions of individuals and authorities. Pronouncing damning judgments: could that be done without leaving the sphere of scholarship and entering that of opportunistic moralising?

The prehistory of SÄKO

Thus far, we have discussed the problems SÄKO as a historical commission could anticipate. But how did it happen that a commission on the domestic activities of the Swedish security services came about in the first place? This requires a summary of the historical background.

The first subject of debate in connection with the security services' monitoring of Swedish citizens concerned the registration of political opinions. As early as 1966 a controversial book claimed that the police's register of members of radical political parties and movements threatened the freedom of opinion. The debate resulted in 1969 in the Government forbidding the police to enter anyone in their registers *solely* on the basis that he or she had expressed a political opinion. The next storm of opinion came in 1973, when a couple of young journalists revealed that there was a secret intelligence organisation within the Defence Staff, which went under the name IB. This intelligence organisation's main focus was on gathering foreign intelligence, but it also conducted wide-ranging domestic activities focused on various groups within the New Left. According to the revelations, the monitoring of left-wing groups was conducted in co-operation with the Social Democratic Party.[16]

Following the 1966 and 1973 debates, two questions were raised, which over the next decades would resurface in the public debate at irregular intervals. The first concerned whether the ban on the registration of political opinions, which, in 1973, was incorporated into the Swedish constitution, was being adhered to. The second concerned whether the Social Democrats, virtually the permanent party of government, had carried out spying activities against its political opponents with the help of a government authority, i.e. the Defence Staff.

It would be going too far to recount here the various twists and turns of the debates and commissions over the decades. It will have to suffice with saying that official commissions and reports first denied that the registration of political opinions had taken place. Second, they claimed that, even if the Social Democrats had had a certain degree of co-operation with the Defence Staff, they had consequently not gained any unfair advantages by those means and, third, that the Defence Staff's domestic activities had stopped in 1973 after the revelation. Among engaged debaters and opinion formers, however, there were those who felt that the registration of political opinions had been the rule, that the Social Democrats had instituted the Defence Staff's domestic surveillance and that the aim had been to keep radical opponents within the trade union movement under control.[17]

During the end of the 1990s, both questions returned to the agenda. In 1996, a comprehensive report was published in Norway by a government commission, which had investigated the performance of the Norwegian security services.[18] It disclosed that the Norwegian Labour Party had established extensive co-operation with the Norwegian security police, which, for instance, had resulted in permanent bugging devices being placed in the main building of the Norwegian Labour Movement in central Oslo and for many years used to listen in on the meetings of the Communist Party. In Sweden, the Norwegian report was read with keen interest and the natural question was: did the same intimate co-operation between the Social Democrats and the monitoring authorities take place also in Sweden? It was demanded from several quarters that a similar commission should be appointed in Sweden.[19]

Over the following years, the Swedish security police (SÄPO) released material about a case that had been debated for a long time – the so-called Leander case. Torsten Leander was a carpenter, who, in 1979, obtained a position at the Naval Museum in Karlskrona, but was then requested to leave his job, while waiting for the result of the vetting check. When the result arrived, he was fired. The process contravened labour legislation and, in 1997, Leander received financial compensation from the Swedish Government. The same year parts of the police file on Leander were released. The information in the file was purely about his involvement in various left-wing movements and, therefore, it appeared to be a clear case of registering political opinions. The registration seemed to have been incorrect from the very beginning and it had been wrong to hand over the information to the employer in conjunction with the vetting check.[20]

In the autumn of 1997, yet another minor sensation occurred in the debate about the security services. The cause of this was L.-O. Lampers, a young political scientist, who had written an essay on how a security service officer had planted an agent in a Gothenburg hospital. It was an affair from the mid-1970s, which now reappeared on the agenda. With impeccable accuracy Lampers was able to disclose all details of the planting of the agent. Moreover, it emerged from his dissertation that the Defence Staff's monitoring of Swedish citizens, which the Government stated had stopped in 1973, had in actual fact continued for several years more, and with the Government's consent.[21]

These new details about the security services' methods resulted in the calls for a Swedish 'Truth Commission' growing in strength.[22] Initially, the Government's reply followed a pattern of ready and willing activity that had been established by the earlier historical debates. In November 1997, the Minister for Justice commissioned the so-called 'Registration Committee' (a permanent authority whose main task is to examine SÄPO's handling of registration details) to find out how those looking for work during the years 1969–1996 had been affected by the vetting check. They were given the task of finding out whether there were further instances of unlawful registration and the improper handing over of information to employers.

The next step was more unexpected. The Minister of Justice announced on 20 November 1997 during a parliamentary debate on SÄPO's principles of registration that the Government was to fund wide-ranging, independent research on the military intelligence and security services from 1920 to 1980. On 11 December, the Government formally took the decision to make SEK 20 million available to the Swedish Research Council for research projects in this field.

The Government's decision resulted in the formation of three research groups, with a total of twenty-six researchers, historians, political scientists, historians of ideas, lawyers and sociologists, attending to various aspects of the activities of the security services. Some projects were about the development of the surveillance system in a historical and international perspective, others focused on the groups monitored and the threat perceptions they spawned and, again, others were about the ideological and legal aspects of the security services' activities.

In view of the criticism of the commission system, which had grown during the end of the 1990s you might have expected the university researchers to rejoice at the Government's new policy. However, there were no celebrations. The most obvious reason was probably that scholars had gloomy premonitions regarding access to the archives.

For their completion, many of the planned projects were, of course, wholly dependent on access to the services' archives. The Government was naturally aware of this and, in the public debate, it had promised to instruct the authorities in question to assist the researchers in various ways. If the questions surrounding secrecy were to wind up on the Government's desk, it was going to adopt an open approach.

However, the researchers soon encountered major problems. Even knowing which documents were to be ordered was a considerable problem as the existing archival catalogues were classified. After the order was handed in, there was a long wait for a police official to examine the requested documents and assess their level of secrecy. This process usually entailed many months. Finally, when the order was delivered, some documents might be removed and others incomplete, as they were presented as photocopies of a partially covered original.

The most important reason for these restrictions was the protection of the informants. For the researchers it was difficult to accept that they would not obtain all available information about the services' sources of information. However, they had no interest in publishing names or other information about the informants and suggested that they should be given authorisation with restrictions – i.e. the right to see everything, but not to publish everything. A long drawn-out correspondence between the researchers and the Swedish Research Council on the one hand, and the Government, on the other, ensued.

The services' attitude was intransigent. During the late autumn of 1998, first the military security service and then the police explained that the rules and regulations for handling classified documents could not be disregarded in order to satisfy the researchers. The suggestion that documents should be handed over with restrictions was rejected. Moreover, SÄPO explained that the finding aids to the archive were few and insufficient, and that the lack of staff made long delays unavoidable. Behind this restrictive attitude there was, in all probability, a deep mistrust on the part of the authorities towards the researchers: they quite simply did not trust that restrictions would be respected. Despondency spread amongst the researchers, who had accepted money for assignments that could not be completed. At the beginning of 1999, the newspapers reported that one of the researchers had quit in protest at the impossible conditions. In the press an imminent fiasco was being predicted.

The researchers' problem with secrecy had received massive media attention and had resulted in renewed demands for appointing a 'Truth Commission' with complete access to the archives. Articles were written and public meetings were held, where such a committee was proposed as the way of putting a stop to this eternal debate. Also the Left Party and the Green Party, the two parties supporting the Government in the Riksdag, called for a commission.

Early in 1999, signals were coming from the Government Offices that a change was in the offing. The Prime Minister Göran Persson, explained that he was not planning to take this long drawn-out question with him into the next millennium and on 25 March 1999 he informed that the Government had decided to appoint a commission with far-reaching authority.

SÄKO's task and findings

Thus, the 'normal' procedure had once again found favour. The flagellant procession got a new participant. How did it handle all of the problems that had been associated with the commission system? However, before turning to this question, a short presentation of the Commission, its composition, its working methods and its findings is required.[23]

Gunnar Brodin, Marshal of the Realm, was appointed Chairman and Anders Knutson, former Chairman of the Supreme Court, Vice Chairman. The other members were Ewonne Winblad, journalist and former head of broadcasting for P1, Swedish Radio's talk radio station, as well as Anita Klum, former Secretary General of Amnesty Sweden and now Secretary General of the Voluntary Organisations Fund for Human Rights. It took until August 1999 to appoint two historians: Professor Alf W. Johansson and myself. The Commission's directive stated that it was to document and illuminate, exhaustively and definitively, the Swedish security services' activities to protect the constitution from the end of the Second World War up to present times. In this context, to protect the constitution referred to the security services' surveillance of those Swedish extremist political organisations and groups, which, whether genuinely or potentially, were deemed to constitute a threat to national security and democratic institutions.

The Commission's workload rested to a large extent on the Secretariat, headed by Fredrik von Arnold, Senior District Court Judge and comprising three secretaries and an assistant secretary. Among the secretaries were the aforementioned political scientist L.-O. Lampers, as well as Ulf Eliasson and Magnus Hjort, both History PhD students. Even we senior historians participated at times in the research work and wrote sections of the report, which were published as annexes.

The Commission, according to the directives, could work together with ongoing research projects. That is also what happened, principally by way of a number of project researchers being attached to the Commission either as secretaries or as experts with limited research assignments. By being appointed to the Commission, they were given the necessary access to the services' archives.

On 17 December 2002, the Commission submitted its report including eight annexes, which altogether covered more than 3,000 pages. It provided a detailed and in-depth picture of how the surveillance of Swedish citizens had actually functioned over the last fifty-five years.

The Commission found that, in the 1950s and 1960s, the registration of Communists and Communist sympathisers was particularly widespread. By the end of the 1960s, there were more than 100,000 such persons registered, at times on flimsy grounds. During the last thirty years, there have been at most 5,000 to 10,000 individuals listed in the registers of SÄPO for having had associations with extremist organisations on the Left or Right.

The registration of political opinions in Sweden was formally prohibited by the 1969 Proclamation on the Scrutiny of Personnel. Despite the ban, this practice continued. This was due to, among other factors, the fact that unclear instructions were issued by the National Police Board and the Swedish Government. Thus it became possible to satisfy both political opinion and provide SÄPO with the instruments deemed necessary in light of national security. In the Commission's opinion, the Government's track record represented a clear case of double-talk.

The Commission also found and criticised that SÄPO in its informal working registers, to a great extent, had recorded information in contravention of the ban on registering political opinions. With regards to ongoing practices, the Commission pointed out a palpable risk that this ban could still be violated in connection with the surveillance of individuals active in extremist political organisations.

The Commission also sharply criticised the manner in which telephone wire-tapping rules came to be applied. In practice, not only individuals suspected of involvement in crime against national security but entire political organisations, including the editorial staff of affiliated newspapers, were tapped, an activity, which endangered the very right to conduct legitimate political activities. This concerned, during the 1950s and 1960s, the Swedish Communist Party (now the Left Party) and in the 1970s mainly the leftist parties such as the KFML (Communist Party of Marxist-Leninist Revolutionaries). In the late 1960s and early 1970s, wire-tapping was used against the anti-Vietnam-war FNL (National Front of Liberation) movement. Also the telephones of newspaper offices were tapped, which imperilled the constitutionally guaranteed protection of informants to the press.

The tapping of telephones could go on for years without interruption, in one case almost ten years. The Commission presented a detailed account of how this could happen. It ends up criticising SÄPO for using flimsy and unreliable information when applying for permits to tap, the prosecutor for not having carefully examined the material and for having totally supported SÄPO's judgments and the Courts for not having fulfilled their task of protecting the legal rights of the individual. It also criticised the Attorney General and the Ombudsman (Commissioner for the Judiciary and Civil Administration) for not having reacted against this reprehensible practice.

Wire-tapping was systematically used to gather information also about individuals who were not suspected of any crime. Everyone calling the tapped number had his or her conversation recorded and any piece of it that SÄPO found interesting went into the files. Such 'surplus information' has through the years constituted the greatest single source for registrations in SÄPO's files and has in several cases been made available in connection with security vetting. The Commission observed that this practice lacks legal grounds and that it undermines the legal basis of the system for the vetting of personnel. It concluded that the citizen's right to privacy had been neglected and that the authorities concerned had acted in a manner not acceptable in a state ruled by law.

The Commission also called attention to the fact that SÄPO, on more than thirty occasions, had used bugging devices against extremist organisations. This practice was particularly common at the beginning of the 1950s, and there is even strong evidence to suggest that microphones were permanently installed in a building in central Stockholm for the purpose of monitoring Communist meetings held there.

In spite of all the problems anticipated, the Commission had obviously succeeded in producing a report that gave a comprehensive and detailed picture of how the monitoring actually took place. Nevertheless, the question now is, to what extent, its work was affected by the problems, which the critics of the commission system had put forward. I will begin with the problem that had caused the independent research groups the greatest difficulty – the problem of secrecy.

Secrecy

SÄKO's secrecy problems revolved around two issues: what would the Commission be allowed to see and what would it publish. The first issue was solved radically through a special law for the Commission, which was passed by the Riksdag during the autumn of 1999 and came into effect on 1 January 2000.[24]

With this law, the Commission gained three special powers:

1 Free access to all material, stored by the security services or by other public authorities, which the Commission considered to be of interest for the assignment.

2 The opportunity to study relevant private material, including that which had been handed over to a public archive with a time lock.

3 The possibility to question individuals and impose on them an obligation of truth in the same way as a witness in a court of law.

The first power, i.e. the unrestricted access to the archives, was undoubtedly the most important. This meant that the Commission was spared the lengthy preliminary examination that the research projects were subject to. The various finding aids were set at the Commission's free disposition and we could without restriction make use of the voluminous collections. The co-operation with the archive personnel was excellent.

The second of the Commission's special powers, i.e. the right to break the time lock, met with sharp criticism from leading Swedish archivists. They were concerned that the confidence in the archives' assurances would be jeopardised when it became apparent that the Riksdag could revoke a pledge of secrecy through a simple decision. The consequence could be that owners of private archives would prefer to destroy their material rather than hand it over to a public archive.[25] From the Commission's perspective, we could understand the critical views but, at the same time, we realised that as we were supposed to leave no stone unturned, we could not refuse to make use of this authority. In practice, however, we used it only in two instances and only in one of these cases did we find information that was included in the report.

The third power, to summon for questioning, was made use of more frequently. 75 people were questioned before the Commission and approximately another 350 people were summoned to informal talks to representatives of the Commission's Secretariat. The questioning before the Commission was led by the Vice-Chairman in the capacity of an experienced judge, and was begun with a reminder that an obligation of truth was applicable before the Commission. This reminder hardly had the intended effect. Those questioned generally adopted a very careful attitude. 'I don't remember' was without doubt the most common answer to our questions. The Commission also notes in its report that questioning was a rather inefficient method of investigation 'where the results seldom stood in reasonable proportion to the use of resources'.

Nevertheless, as a whole, it must be noted that the Commission worked under favourable conditions. It had unrestricted access to archive documents and other sources of information, and it received all imaginable support in its search in the archives. But what happened later with the publication of all this information? Would considerable parts of the material remain secret, as the doom-mongers had foreseen?

First of all, it should be noted that no restrictions at all were applied in the drafts and memorandums that were produced within the Commission during the course of the work. Everything, including names of informers, police officers and those monitored, was accounted for openly. This was necessary for the parts of the jigsaw puzzle to slot into place as quickly as possible. When it became time to finalise the texts for publication, it was incumbent on the Commission as an independent authority to be solely responsible for applying the Official Secrets Act.

How this should be dealt with was a topic of much discussion within the Commission. The result was that an expert in this field, the Justice of the Supreme Court, Göran Regner, was appointed to provide assistance to the Commission as regards the secrecy review. His overall judgments served as guidance for the Commission and they were also presented in the report. Without going into legal details, it can be discerned that the fundamental idea is that a restrictive application of the Official Secrets Act would not have been consistent with the task of 'exhaustively and once and for all' charting the activities of the security services. The report would then appear too abstract and diluted to satisfy the task. The Commission chose to 'go as far in information presentation as necessary to be able to fulfil its task'.

In accordance with this liberal basic approach, detailed descriptions of how different coercive measures and investigation methods (e.g. telephone tapping) have been used are given in the reports. Groups and persons monitored were identified. Exceptions from this basic policy were made to protect the identity of confidential informers, decoys and infiltrators. The Commission was also careful as regards presenting names of those monitored. In some cases, the Commission contacted the party concerned to acquire his/her consent. Similarly, names of lower ranking security service employees were protected. Through these restrictions, individual interests of integrity could be protected without losing anything of importance as regards the nature of the activities.

Co-operation with foreign services – with the exception of Nordic co-operation, which was already well known – was protected to the extent that the names of individual countries were not mentioned. Neither did this restriction result in anything of importance being lost regarding domestic monitoring.

In real terms, this means that the original drafts, once objectively motivated changes had been implemented, were only subject to one round of 'anonymising' before they were sent to the printers. In some cases, information about partner countries was also removed. But no other restrictions in relation to the original texts were applied, which was certainly crucial to how the report was received. Those who believed that it would be met with suspicion due to a lack of openness were proved wrong.

Deadlines, competence and compromises

The three problems that can be summarised in the key words: deadlines, lack of competence and forced compromises, were all in different ways also relevant for SÄKO.

Time pressure characterised the Commission's work from the first day to the last. The time frame specified in SÄKO's directive was barely sufficient. The majority of the Commission was appointed in March 1999, the two historians in August 1999 and the special law regulating the Commission's working conditions applied from 1 January 2000. According to the original directives, the report was to be handed over no later than 31 August 2001. This meant that, in practice, the working time did not exceed one and a half years, which from the start appeared to be much too short in relation to the very extensive research task. On request of the Commission the Government postponed the time limit to 31 December 2002.[26]

To the researchers within SÄKO, time seemed too short, even after this extension. Certainly, the Commission – thanks to an overachieving Secretariat – could carry out a careful empirical survey of the services' activities for just over fifty years. More time would not have involved any great changes in this respect. However, the presentation of the findings could have been different. In the original plans, a systematic and collected account of the significance of the findings was included from the perspective highlighted in the title of the report, namely the conflict between national security and personal integrity. Within the Commission, work was also started on a systematic account of to what extent bugging, telephone tapping, shadowing, etc. had actually benefited national security and to what extent those various work methods had violated personal integrity. Information and conclusions now described in different places in the report would have been gathered into a more pedagogic and easily accessible presentation.[27] Time did not allow this account to be completed.

Regarding the issue of SÄKO's competence, it can be noted that even though the members' general qualifications were highly impressive, their particular experience of the domestic security service was to start with not especially extensive. I myself was the only one within the Commission who had earlier carried out empirical research related to its topic. I was also the only one to have been associated with the simultaneously ongoing research projects. When the Commission was appointed and had received its powers, the situation was mainly such that the expert knowledge was found in the research projects, whilst the authority to gain access to the source material resided with the Commission. It appeared to be an all too obvious confirmation that university research could gather greater competence than Governmental commissions.

Most well-known of those not connected to SÄKO was Dennis Töllborg, Professor of Law, who had previously written distinguished pieces about the methods of the security services and the principal problems these lead to. He had also acted as the legal representative for the previously mentioned Torsten Leander and had helped him to obtain redress and financial compensation. His name was not popular within the services. In fact, he came to be the focal point for their mistrust of the research world. He himself did not conceal his discontent with the fact that the Government had overseen his name when appointing the Commission's Chairman and members. He also explained at an early stage that the Commission lacked the necessary competence and most likely would not achieve anything of value.[28]

However, unlike Professor Töllborg, a number of other university researchers came to participate in the work of the Commission. As previously stated, some of them became associated with the Commission, as either secretaries or experts with specific research tasks. They came to play a very important role for the final results, not least as authors of several of the Commission's appendices. The secretaries built up an effective research environment, and in my opinion – which Professor Töllborg will never share – the Commission created a very strong competence within its area.

So, lastly, what are the Commission's experiences of the commission system's culture of compromise? First, it should be pointed out that it is by no means unusual that members of commissions express their own conflicting opinions, e.g. in the form of individual statements. This possibility was never used within SÄKO, which does not mean that unanimity prevailed on all issues. SÄKO's Chairman has on several occasions publicly revealed that within the Commission there had been strong differences of opinion, which, nevertheless, it had been able to be overcome since everyone felt responsible for bringing the task to a successful close. It may sound like a description of continual compromising. In reality, the differences of opinion often took the form of knowledgeable exchanges of information and interpretations that resulted in common standpoints. Furthermore, contrasts in opinion probably had a useful effect in forcing accuracy in argumentation.

An important dividing line concerned the shape of the Commission's end product. Should it be a fairly thin volume, where the results were presented in condensed form without too many details, or should the research performed be presented as completely as possible? Should we choose a slim solution of a couple of hundred pages or a weighty one that would require a couple of thousand pages?

The Commission eventually chose the weighty solution. Besides a main report of over 600 pages, it presented eight appendices totalling approx. 2,500 pages. In this way, another conflict, relating to the actual presentation method, was also solved The historians' ideal of a problem-focused and argumentative presentation stood in contrast to the Principal Secretary's legal technique, where a wide-ranging presentation of facts in the case, is, without colligating argumentation, followed by conclusions and assessments. From the historians' point of view this was an important issue, but as the Commission approached the weighty solution, it became increasingly less dramatic. In the appendices the individual researchers were able to present a fuller analytical line of argument. Thereby, the demands for everything to be said in the main report were reduced.

Still, the Commission won, to a certain extent, its unity at the cost of individual perspectives and assessments. At least, from my point of view, this loss was compensated for by gains in substance and impact.

Moral judgments

Like the majority of historical commissions SÄKO was expected to present evaluating conclusions. According to the Government's, it should 'outline and evaluate' the 'weighing up' done by the political, police and military leadership. Surely, political sentiments surrounding the security services were such that an entirely positive assessment of the services' actions would have caused the Government enormous problems. Such a report would implacably have been greeted with mistrust. Accusations of having hidden or glossed over facts would have come thick and fast and the Government would not have accomplished its primary objective: to have done with it once and for all.

The Commission devoted quite a lot of its meeting time to formulating its assessments of the various actors' actions. The findings, as already mentioned, were often severely critical. The Commission is quite liberal when it comes to appointing culprits. Not only are the security services blamed for having violated personal integrity in a number of ways, but so also are courts and prosecutors accused of having contributed to these violations. The judicial supervisory authorities, the Ombudsman and the Attorney General, are blamed for having sanctioned an unjustifiable practice through their failure to react. The Government and previous commissions are blamed for having given misleading information to the public.

In the eyes of an academic scholar, this might look like a rather unsophisticated variety of history-writing, like using what E.H. Carr called 'the Bad King John theory of history', which maintains that what really matters is the character and behaviour of individuals. Did the Commission miss the point that historical actors always are members of a society and can be understood only in relation to that society? How did SÄKO deal with the question, which the Commission on Compulsory Sterilisation called the 'philosophical' one, namely whether the actors should be made personally responsible for their actions or regarded as 'prisoners of the structures and the mindsets'?

SÄKO did not present its views on this question and it presented no systematic discussion of structural factors such as the social background and the education of the officials or bureaucratic culture and working routines. Nor did it look at contemporary views of the weighing-up between national security and individual rights in any systematic manner. Security threat perceptions in the public debate were touched upon, but not systematically.

However, the Commission did look at one key, structural factor throughout, namely the security services' threat perceptions. It gives an in-depth account of the services' perceptions of threats to national security and democratic institutions. Of little surprise, the Commission shows that the totally dominating elements of those perceptions are the Soviet Union and international Communism. In this, the services mirrored the general perception of Russia and the Soviet Union as the constant enemy. This was a well-integrated part of the majority culture in Western Europe, not least in Sweden, where, for centuries, there was an ingrained fear of the big neighbour in the East, a fear, which in the years after the Second World War was reinforced by intense anti-Communism. That the security services saw the Soviets and their supporters as the main threat seems like an inevitable effect of a general mental structure.

On the other hand, if this question is brought down to an individual level, was it then not the case that the services' staff ought to have been more open-minded when it came to judging individual members of the Swedish Communist Party? Could the officials of the 1950s and 60s not have put into practice the principle of objectivity, which prescribes that information, which benefits a suspect, also ought to be considered? Is this not a principle, which all public authorities must always have in mind? But, then again, what could you expect, when the Minister for Defence informed that Communists were masters of deception and the Prime Minister claimed that it was better with a hundred names too many on the register than one too few?

Therefore, there are reasons to ascribe the authorities concerned a moral responsibility for violations of personal integrity; at the same time there are reasons for preferably laying the blame on 'the spirit of the times' or 'the ideological climate'. However, on these questions the Commission did not offer an opinion. It contented itself with establishing and criticising the disparities between, on the one hand, the moral and legal norms, and the actual actions of the services, on the other. It also gave an account of certain structural factors, above all, threat perceptions, but it never discussed, to what extent such surrounding factors ought to affect the assessment.

Scholarship and politics

Of the various problems that the Commission encountered, the question of moral judgments, which is closely linked with the question about the relationship between the actor and the structure, appears the most difficult one to handle. It is, above all, in this context that the conflict between research and politics became apparent. A short reference to a few elements in the debate following the report's publication can illustrate the problem.

The report was generally described as thorough and exhaustive. Several commentators compared it favourably with earlier similar investigations and concluded that it was time for a shift of focus in the public debate: there was no need any longer to ask what happened but to ask how to avoid that it should happen again in the future.[29]

This was also the general tenor of a parliamentary debate on the Commission's report that took place in February 2003. Representatives of all political parties agreed that 'we now know', and the Government received praise from all quarters for having finally decided on an exhaustive investigation. The report was described as a detailed and in-depth picture of 'Surveillance Sweden', its formation and scope.[30]

But the report was not only regarded as a thorough empirical account. It was also generally described as conveying clear value judgments. 'The [Commission's] judgment on the Security Services' activities to protect the constitution is devastating', said a political columnist in *Dagens Nyheter*, Sweden's largest morning newspaper. Black headlines in a Gothenburg-paper reported on 'Blistering criticism of the Security Police. Also courts and prosecutors criticised by Truth Commission'. Reports on the Commission's findings were consequently marked by indignation. A TV newscaster labelled them the greatest scandal in Swedish domestic politics since the Second World War.[31]

The political reaction to the Commission's findings was not long in coming. Within a few weeks after the report had been submitted, the Minister for Justice explained that the ministry was contemplating the idea of a new ombudsman to act as the advocate for those who SÄPO wanted to wiretap. There was to be a stricter control of registers containing the names of people connected to supervised organisations and legal regulations designed to restrict the use of surplus information obtained through phone tapping.[32]

The main features of this reaction were within the scope of what the members of the Commission might have expected. At the same time, we also presumed that an analysis with stronger emphasis on the mental structures in the surrounding society or bureaucratic cultures, would have been read as a conciliatory and accepting judgment on the actions of the services. When the Commission discarded such an approach, which might have been more scientifically productive, it did so for various reasons. One was the lack of time, another was the hope that other researchers would address those questions, taking our empirical result as their point of departure. But, what is most important in this connection is that at this point we did not act as scholars but as politically concerned citizens. The Commission simply wanted to alert the political leadership to a serious integrity problem and to inspire a debate on how the legal rights of the individual could be strengthened. And we realised that without a strong accusatory note in the report that would not happen.

From the historians' point of view, the root of the problem was that the empirical, fact-finding assignment we accepted involved inescapable political effects. In the long run, accepting this kind of politically inflated assignments will probably end in the scholar being politically branded and the commissions losing a generally trusted investigative resource. So, even if SÄKO, in spite of everything, functioned satisfactorily, it is not a good model for the participation of researchers and scholars in public debate. Historians, political scientists and others should of course not abstain from dealing with politically controversial subjects, but the main rule must be that they do this on their own conditions, i.e. that they independently decide on the approach, contextualisation and the carrying out of the investigation.

If the Government or the Riksdag wants a certain subject to be investigated by academic scholars, the best way seems to be to hand over the assignment and the money to a research council, which makes an agreement with a suitable researcher. Hopefully, such a solution is compatible with the demanding attitude of researchers towards the society, namely that we desire to be both needed and independent and believe ourselves to be capable of convincing everyone that it is precisely by being independent that we are needed.

Notes

1   For an introduction to the Swedish post-Cold War debate on the policy of neutrality see U. Bjereld and A.-M. Ekengren, 'Cold War Historiography in Sweden', in T. B. Olesen (ed.), *The Cold War – and the Nordic Countries: Historiography at a Crossroads* (Odense, 2004), pp. 143–75, and O. Kronvall and M. Petersson, *Svensk säkerhetspolitik i supermakternas skugga 1945–1991* (Stockholm, 2005). For a discussion of how the image of the welfare state has changed, see U. Zander, *Fornstora dagar, moderna tider: Bruk av och debatter om svensk historia från sekelskifte till sekelskifte* (Lund 2001), pp. 407–18 and Å. Linderborg, *Socialdemokraterna skriver historia: historieskrivning som ideologisk maktresurs 1892–2000* (Uppsala, 2001), pp. 409–36.

2 K. Zetterberg, 'Det statliga kommittéväsendet', *Att styra riket* (Departementshistoriekommittén, Stockholm, 1990), pp. 284–309.
3 V. Gunnarsson and M. Lemne, *Kommittéerna och bofinken: kan en kommitté se ut hur som helst?* (Stockholm, 1998), pp. 28–35.
4 Gunnarsson and Lemne, Kommittéerna och bofinken, p. 21; J. Johansson, *Det statliga kommittéväsendet. Kunskap, kontroll, konsensus* (Stockholm, 1992), pp. 9–17.
5 This breakdown is inspired by a newspaper article written by O. Ruin, 'Populism att kräva kommissioner', *Dagens Nyheter* (13 February 1998).
6 C. Jönsson, *Sanning och konsekvens? Erfarenheter från forskningsprogrammet om militär underrättelse- och säkerhetstjänst* (Stockholm, 2000), pp. 36–9; M. Samuelsson, article in *Dagens Forskning*, 2002: 1.
7 *Sverige och judarnas tillgångar: slutrapport* [Sweden and Jewish Assets: final report] (SOU 1999:20), p. 39.
8 Ruin, 'Populism att kräva kommissioner'.
9 Ibid.
10 *Ett diplomatiskt misslyckande: Fallet Raoul Wallenberg och den svenska utrikesledningen* (SOU 2003: 18), pp. 41–2. A similar example is provided by a statement of Prime Minister Göran Persson before appointing the Commission on Sweden and Jewish Assets. In a debate in the Parliament he stated that Swedish authorities had failed to fulfil their obligations and that the Government has to assume full moral and political responsibility for that failure (*Riksdagens snabbprotokoll*, Protokoll 1999/2000: 52, Onsdagen den 19 januari, anförande 36, Göran Persson, www.riksdagen.se).
11 *Ett diplomatiskt misslyckande*, pp. 43, 576.
12 Ibid., pp. 603–12.
13 *Steriliseringsfrågan i Sverige 1935–1975: historisk belysning, kartläggning, intervjuer* (SOU 2000:20), pp. 27–8.
14 *Steriliseringsfrågan i Sverige*, pp. 35–40
15 *Steriliseringsfrågan i Sverige*, p. 41.
16 For an overview of the debate on the police registers, see U. Eliasson, *Politisk övervakning och personalkontroll 1945–1969. Säkerhetspolisens medverkan i den politiska personalkontrollen* (SOU 2002: 28), pp. 129–70. The debate on the Defence Staff's surveillance activities is recounted in L. O. Lampers, *Det grå brödraskapet – en berättelse om IB* (SOU 2002: 92), pp. 25–56.
17 *Rikets säkerhet och den personliga integriteten. De svenska säkerhetstjänsternas författningsskyddande verksamhet sedan år 1945* (SOU 2002: 87), pp. 46–53. For a critical view, see T. Kanger and J. Gummesson, *Kommunistjägarna* (Stockholm, 1990).
18 *Rapport til Stortinget fra kommisjonen som ble nedsatt av Stortinget for å granske påstander om ulovlig overvåking av norske borgere (Lund-rapporten)* (Oslo, 1996).
19 Jönsson, *Sanning och konsekvens*, pp. 7–12.
20 D. Töllborg, 'Appendix. The Leander Case in reflection when we know the true story', in D. Töllborg (ed.), *National Security and the Rule of Law*. (Göteborg, 1997), pp. 179–97; Eliasson, *Politisk övervakning*, pp. 121–4; L. O. Lampers,

'Överskottsinformation från telefonlyssning', *Forskarrapporter till Säkerhetstjänstkommission* (SOU 2002: 95), pp. 325–7.
21 L. O. Lampers, 'Sjukhusaffären i Göteborg 1975', *Forskarrapporter till Säkerhetstjänstkommissionen* (SOU 2002: 95, pp. 193–223) is an expanded version of this essay.
22 For the continued account of the road up to the Government's decision to appoint a Commission on the Security Services, see Jönsson, *Sanning och konsekvens*, pp. 7–44.
23 For the Commission's composition and major results, see its main report *Rikets säkerhet och den personliga integriteten. De svenska säkerhetstjänsternas författningsskyddande verksamhet sedan år 1945* (SOU 2002: 87), pp. 3–44. Eight additional reports were published simultaneously.
24 The law is included as an appendix to *Rikets säkerhet och den personliga integriteten*, pp. 645–8. For a summary of the criticism, see the article by M. Samuelssoon, 'Säkerhetstjänstkommissionen hade rätt bryta datumstämpel', *Dagens Forskning*, 1 (2003).
25 These concerns were discussed at a public seminar arranged by the National Archives of Sweden on 18 May 2000. See article in *Svenska Dagbladet*, 19 May 2000 (Öppenhet oroar arkivarier).
26 *Rikets säkerhet och den personliga integriteten*, p. 4.
27 One expectation is however that such a presentation could be included in a more reader-friendly presentation of the Commission's results that is now being prepared.
28 Interviews with Töllborg in *Expressen* 26 March 1999 ('Nu blev det tokigt igen') and 6 April 1999, ('270 dagar kvar. Hur tänker du fira år 2000?'); I. Cameron and D. Töllborg, 'Internal security in Sweden', in J.-P. Brodeur, P. Gill and D. Töllberg (eds), *Democracy, Law and Security: Internal Security Services in Contemporary Europe* (Aldershot, 2002), pp. 178, 201.
29 U. Bjereld, 'Forskare avslöjar hur IB-agent lurade ...', *Dagens Nyheter* (2 January 2003); J Gummesson, 'Stoppa Carlsson', *Expressen* (14 January 2003); H. Hederberg, 'Studien av inrikesspionaget ett gedige ofentliggörande', *Dagens Forskning* (20–21 January 2003).
30 The debate took place on 29 January 2003. Preliminary minutes from the debates are available at www.riksdagen.se. (*Riksdagens snabbprotokoll*, Protokoll 2002/03: 48 Onsdagen den 29 januari). Satisfaction with the report was expressed in virtually every speech. A minister concluded that two positive things had come out of the Commission's report: we have learnt a lot which we did not know before, and we have come to realise that the legal rights of the individual must be strengthened.
31 C. Friberg, 'Storebror både ser och hör dig', *Dagens Nyheter* (18 December 2003); P.-A. Rehn, 'Svidande kritik mot SÄPO. Även domstolar och åklagare kritiseras av sanningskommissionen', *Göteborgs-Posten* (18 December 2002); SVT 2, Aktuellt 17 December 2003 (Mats Knutsson).
32 Speech by Minister of Law Thomas Bodström in the Parliament 29 January 2003 (*Riksdagens snabbprotokoll*, Protokoll 2002/03: 48 Onsdagen den 29 januari, Speech No. 2 and 18).

6

Historical research where scholarship and politics meet: the case of Srebrenica

J. C. H. (Hans) Blom

On 11 July 1995 the Bosnian-Serb army took control of the Safe Area Srebrenica. During the subsequent days at least 7,500 Muslims were killed in the environs of the enclave. At the time of these events, Dutch troops (Dutchbat) were stationed in that 'safe area' as part of the United Nations Protection Force within the framework of the United Nations peace mission in Bosnia-Herzegovina. The UN presence failed to prevent the fall of Srebrenica and the mass killings. These shocking events led to considerable debate in the Netherlands and elsewhere. During that discussion, questions about precisely what had happened were confused with questions of the responsibility of the troops and politicians involved. The debriefing report by the Dutch Ministry of Defence and a parliamentary debate in December 1995 which was intended to conclude the issue failed to put an end to the controversy. These issues continued to figure prominently in politics and publicity.

In the summer of 1996 the Dutch Cabinet stated that a broadly based international inquiry was called for to obtain a better insight into what had happened. That proposal met with considerable support in Parliament, but the other countries involved and the relevant international organisations turned out not to be very keen on the idea. The Cabinet then looked into the possibilities of holding an inquiry in the Netherlands. For that purpose it established contact with what is now known as the Netherlands Institute for War Documentation (NIOD), an institute in Amsterdam with a strong reputation for independent research on the history of the Second World War. Founded on 8 May 1945, the institute collected sources of different kinds and published a great number of monographs, reports and collections of documents, culminating in the impressive 'official' history of the kingdom of the Netherlands during the Second World War by the first director of the institute, Louis de Jong, in fourteen volumes (in fact twenty-eight books).[1] These publications attracted in most cases a lot of emotional public attention and several were debated quite heatedly because of the strong moral and political aspects of the contents.

The consultations between the Cabinet and the NIOD led in November 1996, after parliamentary approval had been secured, to the issuing of a commission to the NIOD to conduct a scientific historical inquiry into 'the events preceding, during and after the fall of Srebrenica'. In accepting that political assignment at a time when the issue was still very controversial, the NIOD took on a major risk. Not only was it questionable whether such an inquiry could lead to satisfactory results so soon after the events, but the danger that scholarship was or would be harnessed for political ends was not inconceivable either.

After it had proved necessary to postpone the planned publication date several times, the NIOD finally presented an extremely detailed report on 10 April 2002.[2] It attracted a lot of attention from politicians and the media, especially in the Netherlands. From the start that attention was focused more on the political consequences than on the actual contents of the report. That was particularly the case after the Cabinet subscribed to the main findings of the report and tendered its resignation on 16 April (one month before the national election). The Cabinet, and especially Prime Minister W. Kok, explicitly pleaded not guilty, but felt that it bore some responsibility for the complicated process of the intervention in the former Yugoslavia that had so ostensibly failed. Parliament also decided to hold a parliamentary inquiry in the autumn of 2002 on the basis of the NIOD report.

As the director of NIOD since 1996, the author of this chapter was responsible for and intensely involved in all aspects of this immense research-project in which in the end eleven researchers, three research-assistants and an editor participated: the negotiations with the Dutch Cabinet, the organisation of the research, the analytical framework, the format and formulation of the report, the management of public relations, and the response to commentaries on the report. While trying to remain objective but also reflecting upon the experience subjectively, I will especially deal here with issues which emerged right from the start and which are relevant to the relationship between politics and scholarship in the case of an inquiry commissioned by 'the politicians'. Was it wise to accept the assignment? Were the conditions which had been agreed upon in consultation with the Government the right ones, and were they a sufficient basis for scholarly research? What was the effect of the highly charged political and emotional factors during the inquiry? What influence did the political setting have on the nature and contents of the report? What can be said in this light on the publicity aspects of the presentation and on the political consequences? And how did the world of academic historians react to the report? I shall distinguish four stages: that from the request to conduct the research to the acceptance of the assignment; that of the research itself; that of the presentation of the report and its short-term aftermath; and that of the longer-term reactions, including those from the academic world.

The assignment

The decisive factor behind the NIOD's decision in the late summer of 1996 to give a positive response to the Cabinet's request was the conviction that there was a keen desire in society for more clarity on the basis of meticulous and independent research amid the at times highly contradictory flow of information, reports, suspicions and accusations. The desire to know the truth was by no means confined to political circles alone. If the necessary conditions of such an inquiry could be satisfied, the board and directorate of the institute considered at the time, it must fulfil its social obligation of responding to that demand as a scholarly institute. Although the problems certainly did not prove to be less than had been envisaged, I still believe that this was the correct attitude. A refusal to reply to such urgent questions raised by society entails in the long term a relegation of science to what I consider to be a damaging isolation in the ivory tower.

The suggestion that the NIOD accepted the assignment in order to strengthen its alleged uncertain position in the future is unfounded. After all, the decision to continue the institute had just been taken, and an investment had already been made: new premises had been prepared, a reorganisation had just been carried out, a new director had been recruited, and a committee had been formed to advise on the future course of the institute. That situation in fact afforded an outstanding argument *not* to encumber with such a risky, politically charged assignment that would no doubt drain the management of the institute of a lot of energy. That argument was explicitly raised in the internal discussions in 1996, but it was overruled by the social obligation mentioned above.

The attractiveness of the research for the institute thus lay not in the opportunities for strengthening its position. No, its attractiveness lay in the theme itself. If good conditions could be created, there was a fascinating research in the offing. To carry out historical research under relatively favourable conditions on events of such a dramatic nature so soon after they had taken place – certainly was an attractive prospect. In a certain sense it was also a research that was related to the kind of inquiry in which the institute was well experienced: very recent history with a strong political and emotional content and which attracted wide interest (the Second World War, Occupation and Holocaust). The institute did not have any expertise in the field of the history of the Balkans, but that could be brought in from outside.

The conditions for the research that were laid down in the course of a negotiating process lasting several months were concentrated around a few main points.³ First of all, the NIOD would be free to interpret and implement the broadly formulated object of the research and to publish on it as it saw fit. The NIOD itself would determine what was relevant. Secondly, the Cabinet guaranteed unlimited access to Dutch written and oral sources. Only restrictions sanctioned by law (relating to state security or the protection of privacy) could be an argument for restrictions. In the event of irresolvable differences of opinion on the interpretation of these legal provisions, the decision would be taken not by the Cabinet but by an arbitrator. Thirdly, since at the start of the inquiry it was completely unclear exactly what the dimensions of the research were, as well as the fact that the work would have to be carried out in a setting that was changing rapidly, no duration or fixed budget were agreed upon. The duration of the research and the costs would have to emerge in practice.

In retrospect too, those are favourable conditions. Of course, practice would have to show what the result would be. From the start it was evident that the Dutch Cabinet would have hardly any influence (and no say at all) with regard to sources abroad. The failed attempts by the Cabinet to initiate an international inquiry were hardly optimistic signals in this respect. However, that drawback was not a serious enough argument to turn down the assignment.

A different problem emerged, however, during the discussions of the conditions. As stated above, the NIOD was approached when it became clear that the initiative 'with the support of the whole Parliament' to set up an independent international inquiry was doomed to failure. Working on the assumption that this broadly based support would continue to exist, the NIOD decided, after brief but intensive internal consultation, that it was in principle prepared to conduct such an inquiry. A parliamentary inquiry was not on the agenda as an alternative at the time. Besides, there were several good arguments for adopting a different course from a parliamentary inquiry. Such an inquiry would hardly be able to make much headway abroad, and moreover it appeared that Parliament itself had been a not insignificant 'party' in the events under review.

Nevertheless, a section of Parliament turned out to be in favour of a parliamentary inquiry after the NIOD inquiry was announced; or rather, the news leaked out that the Cabinet was in discussion with the NIOD. As a consequence, the NIOD was accused in the public debate of political intervention, or of serving the political interests of the government parties. Although that did not play any part in the argumentation of the NIOD, it did politicise the research even more. In itself that was an argument to reject the assignment after all, but in the new situation such a rejection could also be interpreted as a political intervention (this time in favour of the opposition). There was therefore no alternative but to leave this dimension for what it was.

It increased awareness of the problematical relation between scholarship and politics in this inquiry.

To sum up, optimally favourable conditions could be negotiated for a socially relevant and scholarly fascinating research, though one that was full of pitfalls, without completely removing the problematic relation between the research and politics. A lot would therefore depend on how the research was implemented in practice and whether it would prove possible to keep the political dimension at a certain distance, in terms both of content and of the context in which the research would be carried out.

The inquiry

Of course the NIOD, or rather the researchers of the gradually expanding Srebrenica research team, tried to conduct the inquiry as far as it could as an 'ordinary' contemporary historical research project. I shall pass over the problems connected with that 'ordinary' research as far as possible here. After all, the inquiry was undeniably a very special one too, and I am primarily concerned here with the effects of that. Those effects can be broken down into effects on the formulation of the problem and the approach to the research, effects on the availability and usefulness of the sources, and effects relating to the context of the research (publicity during the research, the need for confidentiality, the pressure of time, etc.).

The key question for the formulation of the problem was above all that of to what extent the burning issues for the politicians and the public should (be allowed to) affect the content of the report. On the one hand, the scholarly dimension of the report made it necessary to provide not only a descriptive reconstruction but also an analytical explanation of the events. The prologue of the report therefore presents a succinct account of which levels of analysis were distinguished and how the research was carried out, based on a conception of the historian's task that places strong emphasis on the explanatory force of the dynamism of successive historical situations.[4] That leads to a mainly chronological approach that attaches considerable importance to shifts of perspective and continually pays implicit (and sometimes explicit) constant attention to the choices – whether deliberate or not – made by all the actors. To a large extent these are characteristics that are to be found in 'ordinary' research too.

But this was no 'ordinary' research assignment. After all, the decisive argument for accepting it, namely social obligation, was itself an indication of the need to respond generously to the 'desire to know' on the part of society. This was to be done, however, not by incorporating the emotional and political motives and tone of the public debate into the research, but – in a situation of uncertainties and rumours – by collecting the most reliable information possible and thereby laying the foundation for the later formation of well-informed opinions in the public debate. From this perspective too, the research would have to be based on the elementary historical questions such as 'what exactly happened?', 'how did it happen?', and 'why did it happen like that?'. In the light of the fact that in 1996 hardly any serious research had been conducted in the loss of a safe area and its consequences, that was a necessity. In many respects the research team had to commence at the most elementary level and reconstruct everything right from the start. This accounts for the very pronounced 'factual' character of the research and, to a large extent, for the large amount of attention that was focused on questions of detail, which were perhaps not all necessary from a purely scholarly point of view. In this connection, it was only natural to pay particular attention to (formal) responsibilities as well.

The Cabinet, and more generally the various Dutch political, civil service and military institutions and individuals have loyally abided by the agreements on access to the sources. They abstained, as far as the research team could see, from attempts to influence the research and lent their assistance when asked to do so. The research in Dutch sources thereby yielded considerably more than would have been possible without these agreements and this assistance. As expected, the situation outside the Netherlands was very different in this respect. The political context of the inquiry acted as a brake there. The problems varied from one country or organisation to another. In the Balkans, for example, where the war was still fresh in the people's minds, the researchers ran up against obstacles of a very different kind to those they encountered in Western countries. Changes – usually improvements – did take place in the course of time. The United Nations in particular lent a large amount of assistance from the moment when it had set up its own inquiry. The opposite case was presented by France, where the government and various individuals involved were strikingly reluctant to assist. More details in this respect can be found in the report.

The problems encountered in trying to obtain access to archival material could be compensated to some extent by interviews. However, many gaps remained in this respect and there is thus every reason to hope that research will continue in the future, especially abroad. All the same, it can be stated that a great deal proved to be possible in the course of time, more than had originally been expected. Investments of time and energy in building up relations of confidence in the diverse circuits (victims, perpetrators, politicians, armed forces, diplomats, etc.) did not always produce the desired results, but taken on the whole they were certainly worth the effort. The large number of interviews outside the Netherlands reflects that. An 'ordinary' problem that featured prominently in this research was the fact that many interviewees had a stake in the outcome of the inquiry. As for the written sources, they often displayed a strong bias too. The answer to this was, as always, a large measure of alertness with regard to the interviews and archival study, a thorough preparation in order to be able to evaluate the reliability better, and a large number of different types of sources and interviewees.

One final problem relating to the sources that has to be mentioned here concerns information that was given in confidence. This was more than usually the case, no doubt connected with the political and emotional dimension of such recent events. In the Balkans in particular, the personal safety of those involved was at risk on more than one occasion. What is more, the research team also managed to build up a strong position of confidence in the circle of intelligence and security operations. Of course, that would have been impossible without the commitment to protect the sources. In short, respect for the confidentiality of the sources of the knowledge acquired in this way had to be observed. In a certain sense this is incompatible with the scholarly principle of verifiability. One possible way out of that problem is not to use the information that is obtained confidentially. However, in a number of cases that would have seriously impaired the value of the research. It was therefore decided to refer to the source of certain information as 'confidential'. The problem is not entirely unknown (for example, it occurs in anthropology or, in a less closely related field, in medical science). So this appeal to trust in the reliability of the researchers is not completely unconventional.

In spite of the dimension of the problems connected with the sources, the researchers were most directly affected by the influence of politics and publicity in the need not to make interim reports on the course of the research. Interim reports could have endangered that part of the research that was still being conducted. There was also the risk that corrections would have to be made later, which would have been extremely unwelcome given the sensitive nature of the issue. Moreover, the coherence between the different aspects might have been relegated to the background or lost from view entirely, with all the problems of distortion that that would entail.

However logical this procedure may have been, it also had its very unfavourable side. It thwarted normal intellectual exchanges with other researchers. It prevented the presentation of partial results or research problems to colleagues. It also led to an undesirable atmosphere of secrecy around the inquiry. In the publicity the interest in everything connected with Srebrenica remained large, with periodical outbursts of very intensive interest (media hypes). It was frustrating not to be able to provide information or to make corrections in this public debate, especially when there was a feeling that it could have been very useful to do so and when there were explicit calls from the media to take part in the debate. The introverted character of the research group which inevitably arose from this was certainly a disadvantage.

The image of the research group (and in its wake possibly of the NIOD as a whole) suffered too, especially as the research continued. In the summer of 1998 such an enormous media attention with the call for revelations provoked political commotion, and once again there was a vociferous clamouring for a parliamentary inquiry. Of course, Parliament was fully entitled to decide on that if it saw fit, but it was striking how the NIOD research was ignored or presented as apparently taking too long and not leading satisfactorily to results. The possibility that the NIOD inquiry might suffer from the further developments was not imaginary. At the time I publicly drew attention to this problem (in an article in a leading Dutch newspaper, *de Volkskrant*, and in a television programme, NOVA).[5] Once again the accusation of political intervention was heard. Though unfounded as a motive, its effect was not entirely groundless.

This experience led to the release of 'procedural progress reports' now and then from the summer of 1998 on. They were empty of contents. The need for silence was still observed, and for good reasons. But presentations of a general kind were given on this particular contemporary historical research and, what is particularly important, statements were made on how long the research was expected to last. This was a reasonable question since some years had passed since the acceptance of the assignment. The argument that it was barely possible to envisage the dimensions of the research and the volume of the source material was still strong in 1996–97, but by 1998 it was no longer convincing. And thus the time pressure, which had been avoided in 1996, entered the research.

That time pressure, which had not been explicitly formulated by the party commissioning the research, but which was powerfully ventilated in politics and publicity, became a major problem. On several occasions it had to be concluded that the expectations which had been raised could not be met. Reasonable argument could be adduced for this. Making use of new research opportunities sounded particularly acceptable, but setbacks in the production of an adequate text, no matter how often it occurs in research, was much less so. However that may be, it was damaging to the image of the inquiry, with all the risks that this might entail for the evaluation of the final result. The research team itself also regarded such delays as undesirable, though it could not be expected to do the impossible. This intensified the external pressure on the team, which had to work under exceptional external conditions anyway. For instance, the intensive contacts with the various categories of those involved, and in particular with the victims and perpetrators, had a substantial emotional effect.

It has to be admitted that there is always a danger that researchers, and historical researchers are by no means exceptional in this respect, may never get to the end unless there are clear-cut deadlines and/or budgetary restrictions. After all, there is always something else to research, and it is always possible to deepen the analysis or to polish the text. So the pressure of time is not necessarily a bad thing. But in this case the negative side was of considerable weight, and this proved to have left its mark on the report where the dotting of the i's and the crossing of the t's was concerned. Fortunately, in my view, this has not affected the main issues or the core content, but it cannot be ruled out, for example, that if there had been more time available, certain parts of the report would have been somewhat more compact and others would have been more strongly elaborated. There can be no denying that in the very last stage (the deadline of 10 April 2002 had to be met) the pressure of time led to infelicities in the editing, with the extremely poor index as the most glaring example (a new one was provided later on).

To sum up, during the research stage the political source of the assignment, the political character of the subject, and the political context in which the research had to be carried out primarily resulted in the presence of a high and continuous level of stress of varying kinds for the research team. In principle a defensible solution, procedure or approach was found for each of the problems, but that did not really cope with that constant stress that accompanied the research all the time. The individual experiences of the researchers and the dynamics of the team as a group were heavily marked by it. It was an important factor, which had been underestimated in the earlier stage of the tender and acceptance of the assignment. It led to many difficulties in the internal management of the research.

The presentation of the report and the short-term aftermath

If the research was affected by its peculiar relation to politics, this was inevitably the case for the report too. I would like to emphasise at this point that the primary ambition of the NIOD and the researchers was to present a solid scholarly historical contribution to the debate. In other words, it is to be read in the first place as a reconstruction of the events that is as precise as possible, and as an explanatory analysis of them, and not as a political or moral (let alone a criminal or labour law) condemnation or appreciation. It was clear from the start that this was and is a problem. After all, the questions from the politicians, media and public were above all politically and morally charged. So it could be expected that the report would be read with those questions in mind.

The authors have tried to anticipate that problem. That was not easy, because every historian, even without being a specialist in the theoretical issues, knows how diffuse the boundary is between a historical judgment and a political or moral judgment, and to what extent numerous non-scientific convictions can indirectly find their way into the scholarly treatises produced by historians. Although there is a world of difference between a historical analytical conclusion on politics in terms of the questions raised and the intentions, on the one hand, and a politico-ideological pronouncement, on the other hand, on a first, superficial reading they often appear to be deceptively close to one another.

There are various ways of dealing with that problem. The easiest is to more or less deny it and to show no concern about mixing the political appreciations with the historical explanatory accounts. This is in fact what most of the politicians and participants in the public debate understandably did. If they recognised the difference at all, they linked the description and analysis of the events so tightly to their own political or moral appreciation of them that the distinction was barely recognisable in their pronouncements any more. Some of the first reactions of professional colleagues directly after the presentation of the report turned out to be of the same nature. Apparently those colleagues reacted mainly as citizens taking part in the public debate on the political and moral aspects of the subject.

On the whole, the NIOD report has been taken to contain two major judgments: it is interpreted as condemnatory of the Dutch decision to send Dutchbat to Srebrenica, but mild on the actions of Dutchbat itself. One can agree with this or dispute it. The question of whether the historical account and analysis contained in the report are accurate has hardly been discussed in the public debate. Nor has it been recognised by most participants in the debate that it is possible to arrive at different political judgments on the basis of the historical accounts contained in the report. The report states clearly in the prologue that the team has wanted to be extremely reticent when it comes to political pronouncements. This cautious formulation follows from the complexity of the issue. The statement that the report does not contain any political pronouncements fails to do justice to this. The intention, however, has been to avoid such pronouncements. Nevertheless, many regard the report as a sort of political judgment by an arbitrator. The apparent need for an authoritative body seems in many cases to have overcome the motivation to pass such judgments independently on the basis of the material that is presented and analysed.

This can be illustrated by a brief comment on one case by way of example. The Dutch decision of 1993 to send Dutchbat is described in great detail, set in context and analysed, because it is one of the factors that explain the situation in which the disasters of July 1995 could (but were not bound to!) take place in and near Srebrenica.[6] That decision was not uncontroversial at the time, even though it met with widespread approval. The problems indicated in the NIOD report were also pointed out at the time. One can draw, but is not bound to draw, the conclusion that it was a foolish and unjustified decision, and that those responsible should preferably be sanctioned. It is also possible to defend it in political terms, and to conclude that the decisive reason to arrive at that decision at the time is also honourable when viewed with hindsight. To have done nothing would have been completely unjustifiable on moral grounds; this was the best of the feasible options. The fall of the enclave and the mass slaughter do not follow directly and unambiguously from that decision. All kinds of intermediate positions, in which the emphasis lies on the conditions which had to be satisfied first, are equally justifiable.

The extent to which the political perspective that is imposed affects the reading of the report can also be seen from the virtual failure in the public debate to pay attention to the main levels of analysis of the report. The report explains with great emphasis that the question of how the fall of Srebrenica and the ensuing mass killings were able to take place is the heart of the matter.[7] And the report continues that the answer can only be found by looking in the first instance at the conflicts in the former Yugoslavia (the most important level of explanatory analysis). Secondly, international intervention in those violent conflicts is also crucial for any understanding of the events (the second most important level of analysis). Seen in these terms, it is thus a pre-eminently non-Dutch affair. Within this historical explanatory framework, the Netherlands is only significant for its role in connection with that international intervention (it is, as it were, no more than a subordinate derivative of the second level of analysis).

In this respect the findings may not have come across properly and were perhaps not unambiguous enough. At any rate, the reaction to the report in the Netherlands has been almost entirely dominated by questions bearing on the Netherlands. Given the nature and background of the research assignment, there was naturally a great deal of material about that in the report. Within the limited context of the Dutch contribution to the UN operation in Bosnia, the two issues mentioned above (the decision to send Dutchbat, and the operations of Dutchbat) certainly are of importance. It is further striking that the greatest commotion has been stirred up by the chapters on what the report called 'the battle for information', but which has been dubbed the 'hushing up scandal' (a term that is explicitly qualified as unsatisfactory in the report) in the public debate.[8] When the report was presented in The Hague on 10 April 2002, I stressed at the end of my speech that Srebrenica represents in the first instance a tragedy in the Balkans, not a scandal in The Hague. That is not what one would suppose from the reactions in The Hague.

It can be noted in this connection that the decision to satisfy the 'desire to know' generously, including those questions that would probably not receive so much attention from a scholarly point of view (for instance, the question of whether or not a roll of film was deliberately destroyed as evidence is of no scholarly interest),[9] has apparently had a negative side-effect. Because there was so much to find in the Dutch sources, in many cases the Dutch topics could be dealt with on a far-reaching level of detail. This was often very satisfying scientifically too (highly detailed, hour-by-hour description often leads to an extra level of insight). Nevertheless, this relatively extensive attention to Dutch topics in terms of number of pages led to a decreased emphasis on the primary importance of the dimension of the history of the Balkans and of the international intervention for the historical explanatory analysis of the main themes of the report (the fall of Srebrenica and the mass killings). To a certain extent it furthered the dominance of reactions to the parts of the report bearing on the Netherlands.

The big gap between the intention of the report and the reactions it provoked may be due, not only to a possible lack of outspokenness in the report, but also to the compelling force of the political setting. It is probably naive and illusory to suppose that a scholarly report could essentially change the nature of the primary reactions in society. The report was commissioned primarily as a result of the political problems regarding the provision of information about Srebrenica in the Netherlands and its potential for becoming a scandal. It is precisely in that context that the most excited reactions can be found in 2002. They have little connection with the core information contained in the report.

To a large extent that is also true of what is at first sight the spectacular result of the research report: the resignation of the Cabinet. In view of the short interval between the presentation of the report and the resignation of the Cabinet, this decision cannot have been the result of in-depth study of the scholarly research. Without for a moment wanting to call into question the integrity of the then Prime Minister Kok – on the contrary – it was nevertheless above all the general confirmation of an extremely unfortunate story, of which Kok must have been aware for much longer, which triggered that resignation. It is the 7,500 killed Muslims who, independently of the report, make the subject such a highly charged one and confer an explosive character on every debate about it. Moreover, the political situation, which was particularly complicated for different reasons, with elections in the offing, played a certain role in the Cabinet's decision to resign. Irrespective of this, it is debatable whether historians would have been pleased if the results of their research had been able to bring about such a profound political effect under their own steam. It could make the profession the target of political influence, which could cause it a good deal of trouble. A direct link (almost a convergence) between politics and scholarship must be avoided.

In the light of this background, one unfortunate aspect of the presentation, which bothered me a lot at first, pales somewhat in significance: the choice of a date close to the election. I had declared my opposition to that in public at one time. Anything of that kind should never be allowed in connection with this subject, of course. There was also a sort of gentleman's agreement with the politicians and Cabinet in particular to avoid it. In spite of the deep conviction I still hold that this was not really correct, it did happen, and I assume full responsibility for that. It can be explained without an apology being made for it at the same time. In 2001 the planning was emphatically to present the report before 1 December. Unfortunately, in the course of the summer setbacks in the production of texts of sufficient quality made this date impossible. The public image this created was very negative, in the first instance for those bunglers at the NIOD who had failed to complete their task again, but also for the Cabinet and above all for Kok, who was suspected – without any grounds – of political manipulation of the date of presentation.

In choosing a new date of presentation, a similar prisoner's dilemma presented itself as the one that had faced us with regard to accepting the assignment. The earliest possible date was about a month before the election, which made it an extremely bad choice and in conflict with the view that I had already made public. But in the given circumstances a date after the election would have been equally difficult to defend. It would have raised the suspicion – once again without any foundation, but difficult to refute – that Kok was manipulating the NIOD in order to postpone the matter until after the election, and that the NIOD was complying. The situation thus forced us to ignore both considerations of a tactical and publicity nature. What seemed practically feasible had to be the target. It had already been going on for too long. We managed to pull it off this time. It is difficult to say how important this choice of a date has been among the environmental factors as a whole. It will not have been decisive; that would be an exaggeration of the importance of decisions taken by scholarly institutes. In actual fact, it did not play any part in the election campaign at all.

To sum up, it can be stated that the particular relation between the political conjuncture and the Srebrenica inquiry did have a major influence on the nature and scope of the report. The aim of the researchers was to come up with a product that was in the first instance academically sound. In addition, the report was intended to be socially relevant by responding to the questions that had arisen in society. It is not for me to decide whether these two objectives were met or not. The issue of scholarly quality was barely raised in the immediate aftermath of the presentation. It was not called into question. The themes that dominated the debate were not primarily determined by the content of the report, but by the questions that had also been dominant at the time of the assignment: in the first instance, questions arising from Dutch politics, in particular those concerning the 'cover up operation', i.e. the provision of information by the Dutch military and civilian authorities. The resignation of the Cabinet within a week of the presentation of the report gave this public debate a very special tone and was also responsible for its relative brevity. The election and above all the political murder of politician Pim Fortuyn in early May 2002 caused interest in the report to diminish rapidly afterwards.

Longer-term reactions

The parliamentary inquiry, which was decided upon, as expected, after the conclusion of the report, was bound to focus on Dutch issues and responsibilities. In principle, such an important instrument of parliamentary politics as this inquiry provided an opportunity to discuss the entire process of forming political judgments, providing information and decision-making in a serious and thorough manner with all of the Dutch parties involved. Moreover, it was able to rise above the level of the day-to-day political struggle precisely because the political settling of accounts had already taken place with the resignation of the Cabinet. The fact that all of the larger parties had shared governmental responsibility and all major decisions had received broad political support in the course of the process since 1991 was also favourable in that perspective. I believe that the inquiry which was actually carried out, the public hearings, and the report issued in January 2003 entitled *Mission without Peace*, missed that opportunity.[10] The hearings were conducted with all the relevant military and political authorities, but no genuine debate got under way. Neither were most of those who were summoned to the hearings subjected to in-depth questioning, with or without the help of the information and analysis contained in the NIOD report. In more than one case they were able to make incorrect statements without being contradicted. Apparently the members of the Parliamentary Inquiry Commission had not properly digested the content of the report, or lacked the political will for such genuinely in-depth self-scrutiny. The conclusions and recommendations of this parliamentary inquiry hardly differed from those of the NIOD investigation, nor did they offer any new perspectives on what had happened or on what was desirable for the future in the light of those events. In so far as the latter question was raised at all, it was to confirm the decisions that had been taken earlier on the procedure for sending troops in the context of peace missions. The report therefore failed to cause much of a stir among politicians or in the media.

When this parliamentary report was presented, the main focus of attention was once again on the so-called 'cover up operation'. In this case part of the explanation offered in the NIOD report was contested. In view of my prime responsibility for the report, it was a curious experience to be summoned to a public 'hearing' by the parliamentary commission that was broadcast live. That hearing completely passed over the main points contained in the report, which were tacitly accepted. Instead, the questions were concentrated almost entirely on whether after the tragedy in Srebrenica the provision of information in the relations between the political leadership of the Ministry of Defence and the Dutch army command was characterised by blunders and communication problems alone (as a brief investigation of the matter by a prestigious former politician had concluded), or whether the blunders had been compounded also by a lack of willingness (as the NIOD report had stated). This hearing turned into a meaningless semantic debate on the meaning of the term 'lack of willingness' that fell on deaf ears.

The NIOD had used this term in the sense of 'lack of good will'.[11] In the public debate it was interpreted as 'sabotage'. That had cost the Commander-in-Chief of the Royal Dutch Army his position in 2002, when he had been forced to resign by the Minister of Defence shortly before the latter and the entire Cabinet resigned. In the light of the Commander-in-Chief's own role (he was Deputy Commander-in-Chief in 1995; the then Commander-in-Chief had retired in the meantime), this was certainly a very severe sanction. In the debate immediately after the presentation of the NIOD report in 2002, I had refrained from intervening in the debate on the consequences that should be drawn. I held (and still hold) that it was not for the researchers to intervene in this debate. That would have unduly confused academic research and politics. This showed just how complex that situation was.

The same could be seen from the attitude of the prestigious former politician referred to above, who took the NIOD report to be a serious personal attack on his integrity. In fact, the report had stated that this accusation, which had been made in the political publicity, was unfounded.[12] The NIOD report also provided a plausible explanation for the difference in insight, which was by no means damaging to the persons concerned. This hair-splitting about an insignificant issue led away from the real issue: Srebrenica. The entire parliamentary inquiry and the treatment of the results demonstrated to what extent the political issue of Srebrenica had lost its urgency in the Netherlands after the presentation of the NIOD report and the resignation of the Cabinet. If Srebrenica came up at all, it no longer led to the public excitement that it had aroused in the past.

The public debate in the main media barely noticed the appearance of two sizeable historical publications in 2003. Both the *Tijdschrift voor Geschiedenis*, the Dutch journal for professional historians, and *Bijdragen en Mededelingen betreffende de Geschiedenis der Nederlanden*, the academic journal for Dutch and Belgian history, published a special issue devoted entirely or almost entirely to the report.[13] In both cases a number of historians published their comments and the researchers of the report were given the right to reply. As bearing prime responsibility for the report, I am called upon to adopt a reticent attitude here. Most of the contributions were characterised by a positive introduction on the report as a whole and considerable understanding of the problems facing the researchers. Nevertheless, with a few exceptions, the dominant tone was a strongly critical one. The most striking feature, in my view, is the fact that those critics only targeted the actual content of the report in a very small number of cases. It is hardly surprising that the researchers were not really convinced by their criticisms. Most of the reactions, however, focused on the questions concerning how the NIOD report had dealt with the political and moral dimensions of the inquiry. It is difficult to sum up these reactions, but generally speaking the report was regarded as unsatisfactory on that point. In particular, the researchers were accused of having incorrectly given the impression of being 'objective' and of having failed to pay proper attention to their own political and moral position and to the way in which this had influenced the investigation and the report. More explicit reflection on that issue would have been welcome. It is no coincidence that several of these critics shared a more 'theoretical' background. The NIOD researchers were rather disappointed by the lack of attention for what they viewed as the core of their research, by what they regarded as a not always correct presentation of what the report had really said on these points, and by what they considered to be the rather unrealistic nature of the demands in the light of the highly unusual problems with which they had been faced.

It is noteworthy that there was one major exception to this pattern, which was also to be found in several more isolated reactions in other academic journals in the Netherlands. The only non-Dutch scholar to contribute to the two major Dutch journals – the Belgian historian, Pieter Lagrou, who was working in France at the time – praised the report in no uncertain terms. In spite of his criticisms, he considered the report 'deserving of unconditional admiration', precisely in the light of the particular problems due to the fact that the inquiry had been initiated only a year after the events that had provoked such feelings of shock and emotion.[14] The inquiry has met with hardly any other published reactions by scholars outside the Netherlands, although there have been many reactions at an informal level, for instance at conferences where researchers from the NIOD Srebrenica team have presented papers, or on websites dealing with former Yugoslavia. The report has also been mentioned in publications.

Finally, both the prosecution and the defence at the Yugoslavia Tribunal in The Hague are reluctant to cite the report explicitly. The researchers are well aware that much of the report is being used, but the way in which the report shows how all of the conflicting parties were guilty of serious acts of violence and the manipulation of information apparently made it less directly useful, if not risky, for the parties involved in the tribunal. The report has not yet received much serious attention in the new states formed in the territory of the former Federal Republic of Yugoslavia, perhaps also because of the language barrier. The political relations between the former warring partners did not offer sufficient opportunities for that either. However, signs are emerging that a more intensive scholarly treatment of the problematic recent past is getting under way there too. A publication of a summary of the report is being prepared in Serbo-Croatian and will no doubt be able to play a role in that debate.

Conclusion

Looking back upon the whole process, it is evident that the NIOD took a big risk when it accepted the political assignment in the fraught circumstances of the time. Nor did the investigation proceed entirely smoothly. At any rate, the final result yielded a large quantity of carefully screened data and a series of analyses that, the researchers considered, helped to clarify what had taken place. Although the report is only three years old (at the time of writing, in 2005), it appears to have stood the test of time so far. The scholarly reactions have been primarily critical of the way in which the report dealt with the political and moral dimensions of the investigation. The political reactions were very intense, and spectacular as a result of the resignation of the Cabinet, but also relatively short-lived. Partly because of the comprehensiveness and thoroughness of the report, the topic rapidly disappeared from the political agenda after its presentation. With regard to content, attention had focused mainly on problems and controversies in the context of Dutch politics (precisely the factors that also played a role in the assignment), in spite of the fact that the report set out to argue that 'Srebrenica' was not primarily a Dutch scandal, but a Balkan tragedy.

All the same, I consider that the investigation has been worthwhile. A remarkable quantity of reliable information has been made available on such recent events. Together with the explanatory analyses by the researchers, the report may still play a role in the future as a basis for further research and as a means of coming to terms with this past in contemporary society. I therefore conclude that, provided the right conditions for such an inquiry are obtained, historians should feel free to accede to requests to conduct investigation into very recent issues with a highly charged moral dimension. In other words, I would do the same again, though with a greater awareness of the problems and with fewer illusions about a high-level public debate afterwards. And I would tackle a number of matters differently. I do not have in mind primarily the main points of criticism from colleagues with a strong interest in theory, but a better organisation to reduce the pressure on the research team as a result of media attention, the political and moral dimension, the pressure of time, working with people who have been involved in extremely violent events (perpetrators, bystanders and victims), and working in a large research team.

Notes

1 L. de Jong, *Het Koninkrijk der Nederlanden in de Tweede Wereldoorlog* (Den Haag, 1979–91).
2 J. C. H. Blom and P. Romijn (*Eindverantwoordelijkheid*) et al., *Srebrenica: Een 'veilig' gebied: Reconstructie, achtergronden en analyses van de val van een 'safe area'* (Amsterdam, 2002). A full translation of this report (of more than 3,000 pages and another 3,000 pages of annexes) is available on www.srebrenica.nl (*Srebrenica: A 'safe' area: Reconstruction, background, consequences and analyses of the fall of a Safe Area*). More details about the aspects discussed in this article can be found in the report. Some passages are even almost literally quoted. The report also contains extensive annotation and surveys of the sources on which it is based (bibliography, lists of archival sources and interviews) including a French parliamentary report and a research-report of the United Nations. For a summarising book in Dutch for the broader public see: P. Bootsma, *Srebrenica: Het officiële NIOD-rapport samengevat* (Amsterdam, 2002). For a comprehensive analytical narrative in English, published just a year after the fall of Srebrenica and the mass murder (and thus before the NIOD investigation started) see: J.W. Honig and N. Both, *Srebrenica: Record of a War Crime* (Penguin Books, 1996).
3 The 'contract' with the Cabinet can be found in Blom and Romijn, *Srebrenica*, pp. 3174–9 [Bijlagen bij de Proloog].
4 Blom and Romijn, *Srebrenica*, pp. 9–31.
5 J. C. H. Blom, 'Politiek rijdt NIOD lelijk in de wielen', in *de Volkskrant*, 28 August 1998; TV programme *NOVA* 28 August 1998; several shorter contributions in radio and TV programmes 28 August 1998.
6 Blom en Romijn, *Srebrenica*, in particular chapters 13, 14 and 15, pp. 1041–63; summary in the epilogue point 3, pp. 3133–6.
7 The fall of the enclave is described and analysed in Part III of the report: Blom and Romijn, *Srebrenica*, pp. 1717–2460; the detailed description of the week before the fall and the fall is discussed in chapters 6 and 7 of this part, pp. 2079–2410; summary in the epilogue points 5–8, pp. 3141–51. The mass murders are described in Part IV, chapters 1 and 2: Blom and Romijn, *Srebrenica*, pp. 2471–577; summary in the epilogue point 10, pp. 3153–56.
8 Blom and Romijn, *Srebrenica*, Part IV, pp. 2777–3076 (chapters 5–8); summary in the epilogue points 13 and 14, pp. 3164–70.
9 Blom and Romijn, *Srebrenica*, Part IV, chapter 8, section 4, pp. 3009–28.
10 *Missie zonder Vrede. Eindrapport Parlementaire Enquêtecommissie Srebrenica* (Den Haag, 2003; Tweede Kamer der Staten-Generaal, vergaderjaar 2002–03, 28506, 3 vols).
11 Explicitly so: Blom and Romijn, *Srebrenica*, pp. 3076 and 3170. For the context see Part IV, chapters 7 and 8, pp. 2933–3076 and epilogue, point 14, pp. 3167–70.

12 Blom en Romijn, *Srebrenica*, p. 3170.
13 *Tijdschrift voor Geschiedenis*, 116, 2 (2003), 187–328 [special issue: 'Het drama Srebrenica. Geschiedtheoretische beschouwingen over het NIOD-rapport'] and *Bijdragen en Mededelingen betreffende de Geschiedenis der Nederlanden*, 118, 3 (2003), 293–357. A theoretical article in English about the NIOD-investigation, published after this article was finished, is: E. Runia, '"Forget about it": "Parallel Processing" in the Srebrenica Report', in *History and Theory. Studies in the Philosophy of History*, 43: 3 (2004), 295–320. The problem with this article, which is interesting from a certain perspective, is that for a factual description of what happened, it is based on unreliable sources. For instance, the author did not try to interview the researchers. This means in my opinion that the basis of this article is fundamentally unsound.
14 Pieter Lagrou, 'Het Srebrenica –rapport en de geschiedenis van het heden', in *Bijdragen*, 325–36; quotation p. 328. See also p. 336.

7

Negotiated history?
Bilateral historical commissions in twentieth-century Europe

Marina Cattaruzza and Sacha Zala

This chapter sets out to describe the various processes and circumstances which led to the establishment of bilateral historical commissions characterised by the participation of historians from two different countries, and to outline their general typology.[1] Because of the limited interest researchers have shown in the matter up until now, we are unable here to deal with the vast case-history involving this type of historical commission. However, we still think it is worth making a start, and bringing a historiographical perspective to bear on this neglected (though far from unimportant) aspect of the organisation of historical knowledge, in which different national traditions come face to face and where the relationship between history and politics is crucial. A nation and its history are inextricably bound together, and this bond can be anything but unproblematic. There is nothing new about the problems bound up with the various national sensibilities: they had already been recognised in the mid-nineteenth century by one of the first great historians to make scientific research on themes of international history. In fact, when publication of his *Englische Geschichte* was about to begin in 1859, the German historian Leopold von Ranke stated cryptically that since he was writing the history of a nation which was not his own, he could not claim to have written a national history, since 'that would be a contradiction in itself'.[2]

Bilateral commissions composed of representatives of historians from two countries with various aims, came into being because of the awareness of the strong national roots of historiographical practice, and in this sense, can be seen as a kind of attempt to redress the balance. At the same time, they were part of a general trend towards the institutionalising of historiographical activity which started in the second half of the nineteenth century. At the multilateral level, the most obvious sign of this process are the international congresses of the historical sciences which began to take place from 1900 onwards (Paris) and the setting up in Geneva of the International Committee of Historical Sciences (ICHS) in 1926.³ At the national level too, the 'corporation' of historians gradually began to organise itself into one or more associations and around certain 'standard' historical journals, tacitly regarded as being 'canonical' of the different national historiographical traditions.

The early years of intellectual co-operation (1919–1938)

The first bilateral historical commissions were established in the 1920s and 1930s, almost concurrently with the publication of impressive editions of contemporary historical sources connected with the outbreak of the First World War, so that those years can be seen as witnessing the beginning of contemporary history as an independent sub-discipline in the field of historical science.⁴ At the multilateral level, a decisive role in the setting up of these commissions was initially played by the League of Nations, in the shape of its Commission Internationale de Coopération Intellectuelle, and various organisations and institutions such as the International Bureau of Education (Geneva), the World Federation of Education Associations (San Francisco), the International Federation of Teachers' Associations (Paris) and above all, the International Institute of Intellectual Co-operation (Paris).⁵ The common aim of these institutions was a teaching of history and geography informed by the values of pacifism, antimilitarism and antichauvinism which could go beyond 'a history of struggles and battles' and arrive at a 'reconstruction of historical facts from the perspective of the development of a single human civilisation'.⁶

The main aim of the bilateral historical commissions was to work together on revising the history textbooks used in the schools of the countries involved, and eliminate statements based on nationalistic and chauvinistic prejudices. More than any other kind of historical writing, textbooks are forced to drastically simplify historiographical data, and condense the historical and political awareness of a given society, its relationship with the international context and how this context is perceived. For this reason, international conferences on textbooks moved in a kind of intellectual no-man's land between aims of a scientific, educational and political nature which were often conflicting.⁷

One of the most active bilateral commissions of the inter-war years was the Franco-Germanic one, established in 1935 by the two countries' respective teachers' associations, with the aim of 'resolving certain contradictions in the historical picture in the textbooks of our two nations'.⁸ The commission convened in Paris in November 1935 and drew up a list of thirty-nine articles with suggestions for revising various judgments expressed in the school textbooks of the two countries. However the outcome was only seemingly positive, since in many cases, the French and German historians simply put forward their own conflicting thesis. The document was published in 1937 and got a favourable reception in France.[9] Although it actually stated that 'the sources do not allow us to attribute to any government or people in 1914 any conscious wish [to start] a European war', it was poorly received in Nazi Germany and got limited circulation.[10] The journal *Vergangenheit und Gegenwart* (the official publication of the national association of German history teachers), was highly critical of the document and the full text was published only in its Berlin edition.[11]

In 1928, the first German-Soviet meeting took place in Leningrad, still in the mood of the 'spirit of Rapallo'.[12] In 1936, two years after the signing of the German-Polish pact of non-aggression, the first German-Polish commission was established for the revision of textbooks, and it met twice, in Breslau and Warsaw.[13] A third meeting was due to take place in Berlin in the spring of 1938, but was cancelled because of the rapidly worsening relations between the two countries.

Reconsideration of national pasts in a European perspective since 1945

The years following the Second World War saw a return to forms of co-operation and communication between historians from countries previously at war with other. These kinds of co-operation were fostered and encouraged in particular by UNESCO and by the Council of Europe. Already at the first sitting of the general conference of UNESCO in Paris in 1946, it was decided to collect documentation regarding history textbooks in general use. In particular, UNESCO wished to encourage bilateral agreements among its member states regarding school textbooks. In the following years, the initiative passed to the national commissions' sub-groups for textbooks, which gave rise to various bilateral meetings, and produced a rich harvest of publications.[14] These initiatives were unofficial in nature and did not involve political representatives of the states concerned. During the Cold War, UNESCO also became the privileged go-between for cultural exchange between the countries belonging the two opposing blocks.

Contacts were re-established between German and French historians, the point of departure being the thirty-nine articles of 1935, republished in 1949 for the first meeting in Speyer.[15] There were two meetings, one in Paris and one in Mainz at the Institut für Europäische Geschichte attended by historians, teachers and representatives from the Internationales Schulbuchinstitut of Braunschweig. The meetings were able to benefit from the enthusiastic participation of Gerhard Ritter, Hans Herzfeld, Pierre Renouvin and Jacques Droz, who took upon themselves the task of reformulating the recommendations of 1935. Gerhard Ritter had an extremely favourable impression of the experience; even with regard to the most delicate subjects, the discussion had stayed objective: 'There is no better way of understanding the other nation's point of view' than bringing together experts rooted in the national tradition of their own country, he concluded. He added, however, that it would be wrong to exaggerate the significance of these experiences: in fact, conflicts between peoples are determined much more by historical myths than by scientific evaluation. To be realistic, Ritter concluded, an enormous effort would be needed to destroy those myths, but the initiative of the French and German historians could be seen as a beginning. On the other hand, the initiative was frowned upon by Ernst Engelberg, the leading light among East Germany's Communist historiographers, who saw it simply as a manipulative measure designed to eliminate possible causes of friction in the process of integrating Federal Germany into Western Europe.[16]

By 1948, Georg Eckert had made the initial contacts for a negotiated revision of textbooks between those parts of Germany occupied by the Western Allies, and other European countries. Eckert had been born in Berlin in 1912, into a family of Social Democrats. In 1933, he had to leave Berlin because of his involvement in the socialist student organisation. He took up his studies again in Bonn, and obtained a doctorate in ethnology in 1935. During the Second World War, he served in the Navy; continuing his research into ancient American civilisations, he obtained his *Habilitation* in 1943. While stationed in Greece, he founded the 'Freies Deutschland' committee for Macedonia and together with his soldiers, surrendered to British troops.[17] In 1946 he became a teacher at the Kant-Hochschule at Braunschweig, and by 1948, had turned his attention once again to revising school textbooks, becoming president of the history teaching commission of the *Arbeitsgemeinschaft deutscher Lehrerverbände*. His wartime role in the military resistance gave him the contacts he needed with the occupying forces, and in 1951 he was able to found the Internationales Schulbuchinstitut in Braunschweig, which was to become the most important centre for studying and revising school textbooks.[18] In the year of its foundation, the institute drew up a plan for collaboration between the association of French history teachers and its German counterpart on the theme of their respective school textbooks, and the immediate result was two initial bilateral conferences, the first in Braunschweig in 1952 and the second in Paris in 1953.[19] From then on, there were regular meetings until 1967, leading to the preparation of a number of 'recommendations' on how to deal with a series of controversial themes. Similar agreements were signed between the Arbeitsgemeinschaft deutscher Lehrerverbände and the British Historical Association, as well as between the National Council for Social Studies in Washington and the Internationales Schulbuchinstitut in Braunschweig.[20] The co-operation with the British Historical Association goes all the way back to the war years, when the association of British historians informed the government of the need for a radical revision of German history textbooks. The work undertaken by the British historians with German teachers is therefore to be see as part of the 're-education' programme mentioned in the final document of the Potsdam Conference.

Alongside the initiatives undertaken by teachers' associations with the enthusiastic support of UNESCO, there were also projects to revise each other's textbooks undertaken in the context of cultural agreements between the different countries. Again, it is worth mentioning the Franco-German agreement of 1954, as well as the Anglo-German one. Article 13 of the Franco-German agreement refers to a mutual commitment to represent events connected to the other country as objectively as possible, and to eliminate from history textbooks value judgments that might encourage negative feelings that threatened neighbourly relationships between the two countries. In 1958, relationships between French and German historiography got a further boost with the founding in Paris of the Centre Allemand de Recherches Historiques, which in 1964 became the Deutsches Historisches Institut. From 1967 to 1980, the activity of the Franco-German commission came to a complete halt, until it was re-launched in 1981, with the explicit aim of picking up again from the work done between 1950 and 1967.[21] This time, analysis of the textbooks of the two countries failed to bring to light evident examples of chauvinism but rather different points of focus and certain omissions. For example, the German textbooks made hardly any mention of the Third Republic, while French textbooks focused almost exclusively on the period of Nazi rule and left out the Republic of Weimar. The results of the Franco-German commission's work were published in 1989 with a conference in Bonn and in 1990 with another conference at the Sorbonne in Paris.[22] In conclusion, in the years immediately following the Second World War, the most intense exchanges with regard to bilateral revision of history textbooks were those between France and Germany, thanks to initiatives undertaken at various levels and supported by various bodies, all of which testify to a strong desire on both sides to go beyond the 'historical enemy' archetype.

Between 1951 and 1953 there were also three meetings between French and Italian historians, organised on the French side by its commission to UNESCO and on the Italian side by a group of historians. A revision of French and Italian history books was agreed upon using the following four criteria: 1) Factual errors; 2) slips, or rather the relative importance given to events in the period studied; 3) biased interpretations; and 4) unfortunate expressions ('mots malheureux') to be eliminated. In 1953, the first Italo-German historical conference took place in Braunschweig.[23]

Historiographical negotiations between the two blocs (1960–1989)

In the early years of its existence, the activity of the Braunschweig institute was limited to the countries of the Western bloc. Between 1961 and 1963, one of the acute phases of the Cold War, the Internationales Schulbuchinstitut came under bitter attack from the Deutsches Pädagogisches Zentralinstitut in East Berlin and the Polish Western Press Agency. Basically, the institute was accused of wanting to impose an official truth in the textbooks in use in Western Europe. In the 1950s, Georg Eckert had managed to establish contact with Polish historians in exile and formulate some recommendations published in 1956 on how German-Polish relations were presented in schoolbooks.[24] A lively discussion ensued between West German historians and Polish historians, both those in exile and those working in Communist Poland. While the attitude of official historians in East Germany remained completely negative, it turned out to be easier to re-establish contact with Yugoslav historians. In fact, the first conference between West Germany and Yugoslavia was held in Braunschweig in 1953, organised by the Internationales Schulbuchinstitut in collaboration with the German and Yugoslav teachers' associations.[25] More than twenty years later, a bilateral Austro-Yugoslav historical commission was set up which held two conferences (1976 at Gösing and 1984 at Otrocec); although the outcome was not particularly significant from the scientific point of view, it did make it possible to keep discussions going between the participants.[26]

In 1964, as president of the West German commission to UNESCO, the indefatigable Georg Eckert presided over the establishment of regular contacts with the historical commissions of the Communist bloc countries; in 1965, a delegation from the West German commission travelled to Warsaw with the aim of continuing talks on textbooks and looking into setting up bilateral historical conferences. Talks resumed in 1969, coinciding with the start of Willy Brandt's *Ostpolitik*, and in Berlin, the pastor Günter Berndt organised a conference entitled 'Poland in the teaching in schools'. Three more conferences followed, one of which was held in Poznan, at the Institute for Research on the Western territories, where Wladislaw Markiewicz was director at the time.[27] Finally, in 1972, the first West German-Polish conference on school textbooks took place in Warsaw, under the patronage of UNESCO, and the bilateral West German-Polish historical commission was set up on that occasion. These meeting were undoubtedly facilitated (if not actually made possible) by the signing of the treaty on 7 December 1970, regulating relations between West Germany and Poland.[28]

In 1972, a second UNESCO conference took place in Braunschweig which proposed a series of first 'recommendations' regarding the school textbooks of both countries. At a subsequent meeting, again in Braunschweig, it was decided that a commission of historians from the two delegations would meet twice a year to scrutinise the school textbooks in use in West Germany and Poland. Moreover, the commission was also to look at the years following 1945, and deal with 'general historical problems and historiographical themes of particular significance for the historiography of both countries'.[29] The work of the commission received further stimulus from the positive conclusion of the work of the Conference for Security and Co-operation in Europe (Helsinki Act, 1975). At the Warsaw conference in October 1975, the commission began to examine the period from 1944 to 1974, which was when there were the most serious differences in interpretation between the historians of the two countries. However, the consensus of opinion over how to assess the crimes committed by the Nazis in Poland during World War II represented a good starting point on which to base further encounters. A series of 'recommendations' was also drawn up in the field of contemporary history.[30] Altogether, from February 1972 to October 1975, eight conferences took place alternately in Warsaw and Braunschweig on the subject of the revision of history textbooks, conferences aimed at formulating the usual 'recommendations'. With the publication of the recommendations in German and Polish, decided at the ninth conference, the first phase of the commission's work was completed.[31] The antagonism between the two blocs to which Poland and West Germany respectively belonged did not represent an obstacle; very wisely, the members of the commission simply took it as a given. For this very reason, the 'recommendations' were basically the result of 'historiographical negotiations', which showed all too clearly just how limited was the Polish historians' room for manoeuvre. There was no mention of the August 1939 pact between Hitler and Stalin, the German occupation of Poland was aimed exclusively at eliminating Polish intelligence, and there was no reference to the Holocaust or the Jews, who were only mentioned indirectly in relation to the Warsaw ghetto uprising. The tricky question of the expulsion of the German population after the war was dealt with using terminology resembling the diplomatic language of art. XIII of the Potsdam Declaration ('Orderly Transfers of German Populations'), thereby managing to avoid the current German term 'Vertreibung'. Conveniently forgotten were also the forced transfers of the Polish population from the old Eastern territories occupied by the Soviet Union to the new Western territories seized from Germany. In West Germany, the commission's twenty-six recommendations came in for some very harsh criticism,[32] and in the course of the next seventeen conferences, until 1994, this commission sifted through and reconsidered the 1976 recommendations.[33]

In the context of a general conference of UNESCO in 1956 in Delhi, a first tentative approach took place between West German and Soviet historians. The initiative was taken by the famous historian Arkadi Jerussalimski, who after a discussion on how to set up a modern universal history, made the following remark to an astonished Karl Dietrich Erdmann: 'It's time the historians of the Soviet Union and West Germany make contact with each other.'[34] In 1965, to celebrate the twentieth anniversary of the victory in the Great Patriotic War, four West German historians were invited to the USSR by the Soviet Academy of Sciences. Informal contacts were made on the sidelines of the international congress of historians held in Moscow in 1970, sometimes by rather unexpected means: once, after a diplomatic reception, the West German historian Karl Otmar Freiherr von Aretin found a message in his pocket asking him to meet a group of Soviet researchers who were obviously dissidents; but these efforts generally came to nothing.[35] However, after the signing of the treaty of Moscow between West Germany and the Soviet Union on 12 August 1970, it was the committee of Soviet historians to take the initiative and propose a conference with their West German colleagues. In June 1972, Karl Dietrich Erdmann, as representative of the ICHS, and von Aretin, representing the Institut für Europäische Geschichte in Mainz, went to Moscow and drew up detailed plans for the organisation of a colloquium in Germany on the history of Germany and Russia in the age of capitalism, 1871–1917. Although the Soviet proposal did not meet with Erdmann's wholehearted approval, the first meeting between West German and Soviet historians took place in 1973 at the Academy of Sciences in Mainz. The conference received a lot of attention in the German press, and was to remain the most productive of all the conferences which followed. In a climate of studied courtesy, the historians from the two delegations debated intensely for four days.[36] There was also a brilliant display of diplomacy, when Werner Conze, president of the association of West German historians, Erdmann and von Aretin drew up a final declaration with three Soviet colleagues, in which it was agreed to exchange school textbooks and continue the colloquiums in the future, as well as to publish the proceedings and open up each other's archives to fellow historians from the other country. At the moment of signing, however, under pressure from the Communist commissar present, the head of the Soviet delegation said he could not sign the closing declaration because the expression under Conze's name, 'Verband der Historiker Deutschlands', would offend the historians of East Germany. A compromise was reached by agreeing to leave out the institutional affiliation below the name of each of the signatories.[37]

The next congress, which took place in Leningrad in 1975, examined the period following the Bolshevik revolution in Russia and the Weimar Republic in Germany. Since the papers presented were now touching on questions to do with the period after the October Revolution, the debate was more heated. It was impossible to reach an agreement on Stalin's assessment of German Social Democrats or on the interpretation of the Treaty of

Rapallo, which for the Soviets represented a way to peace and independence, while on the German side, Andreas Hillgruber stressed the collaboration between the Red Army and the Reichswehr.[38] In the concluding speeches, it was decided that the scholars should have easier access to each other's archives and that there should be consensual revision of textbooks. The two purposes had few practical effects: the access to each other's records came up against the brick wall represented by the Soviet archives, while the agreement about textbooks ran into the impossibility for the German historians to issue any binding directives.

For the following meeting, the Soviet delegation suggested analysing relations between the two nations from 1969 onwards. While this time leap enabled the Soviets to avoid dealing with the insurmountable problem posed by the secret protocol signed by Hitler and Stalin on 23 August 1939, not all the West German historians were keen to take on the question of East Germany. At the international congress of historians in San Francisco in 1975, von Aretin managed to put together an alternative programme, with a theoretical section dedicated to historicism, and a historiographical section, on the period from 1797 to 1815. The third West German-Soviet colloquium took place in Munich in March 1978, and although the Soviet delegation was less prestigious, the discussions were fruitful.[39]

On the other hand, the attempt to organise an international symposium to mark the centenary of the 1878 Congress of Berlin with participants from the Soviet bloc countries, under the auspices of the Association internationale d'histoire contemporaine de l'Europe, was a fiasco. Since together with the programme, there was an exhibition by a foundation called Stiftung Preußischer Kulturbesitz, Moscow boycotted the initiative and also forbade historians from other Warsaw Pact countries to participate.[40] The incident had repercussions on the fourth meeting between German and Soviet historians held in Moscow in October 1981, when relations were still strained because of the boycotting of the Moscow Olympics in 1980, which West Germany had also adhered to. The theme of the congress had to do with the Enlightenment, and aroused little interest in the participants, and perhaps this extinguished any enthusiasm for continuing the meetings.

Establishing historiographical orthodoxy in the Soviet bloc (1955–1989)

The greatest number of bilateral historical commissions were set up in the late 1950s between the various countries of the Soviet bloc, where a dense network of commissions came into being, putting historians from practically every socialist country in touch with each other. When the East German-Soviet commission was set up in 1957, it was seen as a key factor to the success of East German historiography, given the competitive relationship felt by the SED from the very beginning towards the historiography of West Germany.[41] Thanks especially to the work of Martin Sabrow we have a careful reconstruction of the stages by which the SED built a historiography of regime practically from nothing, programmatically subordinated to political power.[42] Contrary to the expectations of the East German historians, who would have liked initially to keep talking to their colleagues from West Germany and perhaps even persuade them of the superiority of the Marxist historical method, they were ordered not to have anything to do with them or take part in their congresses, and to leave the Verband der Historiker Deutschlands. The break was completed in 1958, with the founding of the Deutsche Historiker Gesellschaft as the official association of East German historians.[43] As mentioned above, the East German-Soviet commission came into being on 5 February 1957, at the initiative of the central committees of the two Communist parties involved. The commission was supposed to make the historians of East Germany party to the experiences accumulated by the Soviet historians and place them in a commanding position in that great mission which consisted of building socialism and struggling against imperialism.[44] The protocol of the first meeting defined its aims as follows: 'encourage historians from one country to participate in the scientific meetings, congresses and conferences of the historians of the other country and organise scientific conferences together on questions of mutual interest', 'encourage the co-publication of materials from archives and other sources, and mutual consultation and exchange of views on single chapters and sections of important scientific publications', 'organise the co-operation of German and Soviet historians in the struggle against reactionary history and define their priority tasks', 'formulate proposals for the common treatment of contemporary questions of particular importance', 'propose the translation of research contributions', 'encourage particularly close ties between the scientific institutions and individual researchers of the two countries'.[45] As far as actual contents were concerned, the same set of minutes proposed carrying out 'common research into the history of Germany, the history of the Soviet Union, the economic, political and cultural relations between the two countries, as well as other problems deemed of interest to researchers from our two countries'. Among the research priorities listed were the events leading up to the two world wars, the unmasking of imperialist policy and ideology and the analysis of the progressive traditions of the peoples of the Soviet Union and Germany. Among these, of central importance was the history of the struggle of the working classes of the two countries against imperialism and war. Looking back years later (in 1976), Horst Bartel remarked that dealing with all the various manifestations of bourgeois ideology had been one of most important tasks of the East German-Soviet commission. The attention for the historiography of West Germany, like the almost obsessive treatment of German imperialism and the continuity of Germany's war aims in the First and Second World Wars, can in all likelihood be explained by the reaction of the Communist bloc countries to West Germany's admission to entered NATO.[46] By no mere coincidence, a paper published in 1959 refers to the historians of West Germany as 'NATO-Historiker'.[47]

In the opinion of Walter Schmidt, the author of a detailed, if rather partisan, reconstruction of the gradual independence of East German historiography from the scientific and representative structures of pre-existing German historiography, the aim of the commissions was to give a programmatic dimension to co-operation between the historiographies of the Communist bloc countries. Thanks to this, there was a consequent improvement in the quality of the international co-operation of East Germany's historiography with 'international Marxist-Leninist historical science'. In 1961, the East German-Soviet commission organised a conference on the Nazi invasion of the Soviet Union.[48] In 1964, a meeting of the commission in Moscow analysed the tendencies of West German historiography and its divergences with East German historiography. In 1971, a congress was held on the influence of Engels' thought on the German and international workers' movement.

Of particular interest is the activity of the Polish-East German commission, set up in 1956 in Warsaw with the task of 'preparing contributions which give an account of the progressive and friendly element in the relations between Germans and Poles, in order to explain to the people of the GDR how the history of the Polish people developed'.[49] To do this, it was necessary to make a systematic analysis of the distortion and manipulation of Polish history and German-Polish relations by the forces of German reaction and its ideological accomplices, activities 'pursued today in the West German imperialist state'. The aim of this commission, similarly to that of the East German-Czechoslovakian commission already in existence,[50] was to 'lend a hand in making socialist historians more effective and co-ordinated'.[51] This commission too listed among its aims the co-compilation of textbooks for the two countries. Special attention was paid to the history of the border territories such as Silesia and Pomerania, for which special sub-commissions were instituted. The recommendations published that same year by the Internationales Schulbuchinstitut about relations between the two populations and their representation in school textbooks were given a very hostile reception.[52] There was worried talk of attempts to 'stir up trouble between Poles and Russians in the past and between the people's Poland and the Soviet Union in the present day'. One might even be tempted to suggest that the founding of the commission as early as 1956 might have come about as a reaction to the initiative of the Braunschweig institute. The second conference, held in Berlin, again in 1956, tackled the highly sensitive issue of the 'peace border' along the Oder-Neiße. The task of the historians of Poland and East Germany was summed up as building a common front against the 'revanchists' in Bonn.

In 1959, a weighty volume of 1,000 pages was published on Poland, Germany and the Oder-Neiße line, edited by the Institut für Zeitgeschichte of East Berlin in collaboration with the East German-Polish commission.[53] The following year, the conference was held in Leipzig and was actually accompanied by a joint declaration by the two governments about the urgent need for a historical treatment of the countries giving onto the Baltic Sea. A general outline was drawn up for a study of the history of Pomerania, which was entrusted to a group of historians from the two countries. The Poznan conference of 1958 dealt with the theme of the Polish revolts which had broken out repeatedly in Silesia between 1918 and 1921 with the aim of having the region assigned to Poland.

In Krakow, again in 1958, the theme discussed and subjected to considerable criticism was the *Ostforschung*. To celebrate the tenth anniversary of the founding of the GDR in 1959 and the jubilee of the founding of the Polish state, an itinerant exhibition was organised entitled 'Science at the service of the Drang nach Osten'. The speaker stressed that the exhibition had already been to several Polish cities, reinforcing the idea among the general public that the German *Ostforschung* was a form of shock troops from aggressive German imperialism. The following year, in 1960, at Wroclaw, the theme was 'Poland and Germany before and during the Second World War', where it was emphasised that the Nazi policy towards Poland was being continued by the 'ultras from Bonn'. Later the same year, in Dresden, there was a conference on the rise of popular democracies in both countries, seen as part of the epoch-making transition from capitalism to communism. In 1961, in Danzig, the theme of the conference was the treaties of Versailles, Rapallo and Locarno. The speaker, Gerhard Schilfert, was very pleased to announce that on this difficult theme too, the historians of the two countries had reached a common conclusion, facilitated by the common aim of the struggle for socialism. The Rostock conference of 1962 was completely devoted to analysing and rejecting the recommendations of West German historiography about Polish-German relations. The work concluded with congratulations all round for the historiographical results achieved by throwing into relief the friendly relations between the two peoples and the close collaboration between the historians of the two countries. Finally, in Posnan in 1963, there was an interesting debate on the cultural relationships between the two historiographies during the nineteenth and twentieth centuries.[54]

East Germany also set up bilateral historical commissions with Hungary[55] and Bulgaria.[56] The Polish-Soviet commission tackled the themes of comparative social history, such as the role of the city in the development of Poland and Russia, the history of the rural sections of society, the structure of villages, of peasant communities and of the struggles against feudalism.[57] It would seem that the ideological control over the work of the commissions became much less strict in the 1980s, and it also appears that in 2001, ten years after the collapse of the Soviet Union, a new Polish-Russian commission was set up for the revision of textbooks of history, geography and literature.[58] Co-operation between Soviet and Hungarian historians began as early as 1949, while a mixed historical commission was formed in 1968. In this case too, problems to do with comparative social history prevailed, with a certain amount of attention paid to the relationship between history and ethnology and to questions of historical method.[59] Further evidence of the existence of a variety of commissions between Communist countries can be found for the Czechoslovakian case with bilateral commissions with the Soviet Union,[60] Bulgaria,[61] Hungary,[62] Yugoslavia[63] and Poland.[64]

This list does not aim to be exhaustive with respect to the themes dealt with by the bilateral commissions within the Soviet bloc. However, even these few, incomplete examples give an idea of the vast selection of themes discussed at the commissions' periodic conferences, themes ranging from the workers' movement to international politics, to the history of social classes, to problems connected with Marxist historiography and to the relationship between history and other disciplines. The main emphasis, however, was on the history of the Communist parties and the 'antifascist movement', on polemic against Western historiography (especially that of West Germany) and also on the relations between the various countries.

The enormous efforts made within the socialist bloc to organise this impressive network of commissions shows once again how much importance was attributed to the historical sciences by the Soviet Union and the other Warsaw Pact countries. Historical materialism was the philosophical basis of Marxism, and was endowed with the capacity to predict the future course of history by starting with an analysis of the 'class struggle' in the past. The bilateral structure of the commissions made sure that the Soviet Communist Party could exercise control more easily (every country had a bilateral historical commission in partnership with the Soviet Union) and at the same time, reinforce an awareness of the historical ties uniting the socialist countries. This task was made all the more urgent by the fact that until the pacifying intervention of the Soviet superpower, these countries had shown profound hostility towards each other, mainly because of disputes over borders and over the treatment of minorities. Another priority was to create a historiographical tradition which could compete effectively with that of the West. Interestingly, only the historians of the two Germanies were forbidden to have any scientific relations with each other, obviously because to maintain the previous communications network with colleagues from West Germany would mean jeopardising the creation of a Communist historiography. Contact with historians from other Western countries was not actively discouraged, while invitations to speak at international conferences were seen as opportunities for doing some effective propaganda. However, any contact with West German historians was always subject to careful control by the authorities.[65]

From the data available, the picture that emerges is one of an alternative European history, in which the Warsaw Pact countries represent the culmination of a long historical process. This is the idea behind the mandate, repeated continuously to Communist bloc historians, to scrutinise the past for examples of relationships between the countries involved based on friendship, co-operation and cultural exchange, reserving particular attention to the recent phenomenon of the fight against fascism in the Second World War.

However, these considerations need to be supported by systematic archive work to look closer at the aims of the Soviets at the time when the bilateral commissions were first set up (late 1950s and 1960s) and trace the possible adjustments made over time with regard to the objectives laid down for the commissions themselves. As things stand, we have also been unable to formulate an opinion on the scientific level of the conferences: while some contributions were obviously propagandistic in nature, we cannot exclude the possibility that there were useful and fruitful exchanges of views between historians from the countries involved which led to advancements in the historical knowledge of the themes discussed. In any case, we are sure that this opens up a fascinating area of study into the political uses of history in the Communist bloc countries and the relationship between the various national historiographies and Soviet historiography.

Liquidating controversial pasts in preparation for European enlargement

The fall of the Berlin Wall and the end of the Cold War not only brought about profound changes in the geopolitical map of Europe, but also put an end to the ideological conflicts between the two blocs; we have already seen what a strong influence these conflicts had on historiography. In the wake of political transformation and with astonishing celerity, new bilateral initiatives were launched in 1990 between Germany and Czechoslovakia and between Italy and Yugoslavia to remove the obstacles of a controversial past which the Cold War had for so long made it impossible to deal with. Commissions involving countries from the two opposing blocs which were still functioning (such as the West German-Polish commission), saw their efforts melt away after years of exhausting discussions to try to decide on versions of textbooks which would be politically acceptable for both sides.

One of the biggest political issues which had long weighed upon German-Polish relations was finally resolved on 14 November 1990, with the signing of the treaty which established the permanent nature of the border between the two countries. In spite of this, there were still numerous other problems that needed solving, including the claims of the German refugees, restitution of property and claims for damages for slave labour. On the scientific front, relations between German and Polish historians were relaunched with the opening of the Deutsches Historisches Institut in Warsaw in 1993, which has since organised numerous events.[66] In May 1994, the XXVI German-Polish conference on textbooks was held in Bautzen, and the bilateral work which had extended over seventeen conferences subsequent to the famous 'Recommendations' of 1976 finally drew to a close. For the first time, it was possible to talk about the GDR, tackling issues 'without prejudice and in a mutually free dialogue'.[67] The time of 'recommendations' being negotiated like international treaties was over, as was the time of 'exegesis' of the recommendations, in which historians of the two countries involved cautiously developed their own historiographical points of view. After the end of strict political censorship in Poland, which had long imposed an embarrassed silence on questions such as the secret protocol between Hitler and Stalin, Katyn, and the forced transfer, not only of the German population but also of the Eastern Poles, and of the Bielorussians and the Ukrainians from the territories newly acquired by Poland after the Second World War, the work of the German-Polish commission was resumed and organised on a new, pluralistic basis.[68] Instead of the 'recommendations', members either proposed texts which summarised the various issues, and included considerations of a pedagogical nature and a rich variety of sources, or else simply the conference proceedings.[69]

Unlike the situation with Poland, no bilateral historical commission existed between West Germany and Czechoslovakia prior to the fall of the Berlin Wall. At the initiative of the foreign ministers of the two countries, Hans-Dietrich Genscher and Jiří Dienstbier, a commission was set up and formally instituted in Prague on 16 June 1990.[70] After the separation of the Czech republic from the Slovak one in 1992, the commission was split for juridical purposes into a German-Czech commission and a German-Slovak one. Its aim is to study and evaluate the common history of the three peoples, principally in the twentieth century, placing this in its wider context of co-existence between Czechs, Slovaks, Germans and Jews. As well as on the tragic events connected with the years 1938–1945, the emphasis is on the elements that actually unite these people. On 29 April 1995, on the fiftieth anniversary of World War II, the commission published a six-point declaration touching on a whole series of sore points. Despite the presence of both presidents, Václav Havel and Roman Herzog, at one session of the commission (Dresden, October 1995), the enormous difficulties experienced in drawing up a joint declaration in order to sign the good neighbour treaty in 1992 showed to what extent the past continued to weigh upon German-Czech relations. In 1996, this situation led the commission to publish a brief summary of its work, or rather work in progress,[71] and its decision was praised in the declaration of 21 January 1997.[72] The commission acts independently of political directives and makes its findings public, for example in conferences such as the one on memory held in Brünn in 2001.[73] However, there have been instances of political pressure, for example during the 2002 Berlin conference, when Christoph Zöpel, Secretary of State at the German Foreign Ministry, made the politicians' interest in the so-called 'Benes-decrees' very clear.

The breaking-up of Yugoslavia and the founding of the new independent states created new border relations, especially between Slovenia and the EU countries Austria and Italy. With the creation of bilateral commissions, Slovenia was seeking historiographical links with Europe. Initiatives for a bilateral commission had already been taken in September 1990 by the city council of Trieste, which voted unanimously in favour of setting up a bilateral Italo-Yugoslav commission, entrusted with the task of throwing light on the violence perpetrated against Italians in the border areas of Venezia Giulia in the years 1943–48, a theme which the four Italo-Yugoslav conferences held in the 1960s had not dealt with.[74] The Italian government began talks with the Yugoslav government, which were then suspended after the dissolution of Yugoslavia and resumed in parallel with the new governments of Slovenia and Croatia. In October 1993, the respective foreign ministries instituted two bilateral historico-cultural commissions, one Italo-Slovenian and one Italo-Croatian, each made up of 'seven experts renowned in their own specific field'. In the joint declaration, the two governments emphasised their desire 'to reinforce and extend their friendly bilateral relations on the basis of enhanced mutual understanding and spirit of collaboration' and they gave the commissions the task of 'carrying out an exhaustive study of all the important aspects of bilateral political and cultural relations in the course of this century'. After a first meeting, the Italo-Croatian commission lost momentum and failed to meet again. The Italo-Slovenian commission handed in its final report in July 2000, and this was approved unanimously by its respective foreign ministries. Various factors having to do with political expediency delayed publication of the report, until a series of disclosures in the Slovenian press led to the publication in the daily newspapers of the region concerned of an unofficial version of the text different from the version agreed upon by the commission. Subsequently, the text agreed upon appeared in an unofficial version with an introduction by the Slovenian foreign minister Dimitrj Rupel, and it also appeared in Italy in some journals of contemporary history.[75]

With Austria, on the other hand, Slovenia set up an Austro-Slovenian group of historians and legal experts. Presently it is expected that the commission will publish a bilingual collection of essays.

Conclusions

In view of the vast panorama presented here, it seems reasonable to say that bilateral historical commissions were (as indeed they still are) an important instrument for overcoming an exclusively national vision of historiographical problems, especially on the field of political history. Or rather, the bilateral commissions did help to bring about that 'brotherhood of historians' which often turns out to be more a normative ideal than a culturally operational reality.

On the other hand, they were set up for very specific reasons, in the course of very special political moments in time, with aims and expectations of an extra-scientific nature. Sometimes the political mandate was made more explicit, sometimes less, but it was never completely absent. For this reason, the question of the political mandate of these commissions cannot be reduced to 'free' commissions as opposed to commissions which were mere emanations of governments. It was all about graduality in the relationship between political expectations and free historiographical confrontation. They operated in extremely varied circumstances, in a situation where the forces at play comprised national traditions, 'ecumenical' aspirations and the political and/or civil expectations of their home institutions. As a phenomenon, they are to be placed in the context of other supranational institutions for intellectual co-operation, such as the League of Nations' Commission Internationale de Coopération Intellectuelle or the International Institute of Intellectual Co-operation, which led to the founding in 1945/46 of UNESCO. As regards the importance of what they actually did, this was greater in those periods of transition in the course of which pre-existing historiography was subjected to some kind of trauma and the need was felt for a new *Meistererzählung*. This manifested itself in more drastic terms for the historiography of the Communist bloc countries, which not only had to adhere to the orthodox Marxist-Leninist viewpoint, but was also subordinated to political expediency to a degree unheard of in Western countries. However, after the two world wars, bilateral historical commissions were instituted between European countries which had been at war with each other, with the aim of going beyond historiographical points of view still too coloured by a national perspective. Clearly, although these aims are very laudable in themselves, the risk is that of a trivialisation of history, of adopting a 'compensatory' perspective with historical reconstruction in which historians are tempted to tone down what were real atrocities committed by one side against the other and emphasise the instances of good neighbourliness, sometimes regardless of their true historical relevance. Furthermore, the bilateral work lead in many instances to recommendations for school textbooks where the argumentation was often surreptitious, showing the difficulties of the intellectual exchanges, especially between countries on both sides of the iron curtain. At the same time, as the Western German-Polish paradigmatically shows, the intellectual exchanges were confined practically only to the field of common recommendations for textbooks. Still, even if the countries were not obligated to adopt these recommendations, they created consciousness for open historiographical questions on the bilateral and multilateral level.

In any case, it is surely no coincidence that bilateral historical commissions were particularly active after the two World Wars, and that with the dissolution of the Communist bloc, there has been a mushrooming of bilateral initiatives for the negotiated and consensual rewriting of the history of relations between the countries of Europe in the 'short' twentieth century (1914–89).

Notes

1. The authors should like to thank Judy Moss for the translation of the text.
2. L. von Ranke, *Sämtliche Werke*, vol. 15 (Leipzig, 1870), pp. V–VI.
3. K. D. Erdmann, *Die Ökumene der Historiker. Geschichte der Internationalen Historikerkongresse und des Comité International des Sciences Historiques* (Göttingen, 1987).
4. S. Zala, *Geschichte unter der Schere politischer Zensur. Amtliche Aktensammlungen im internationalen Vergleich* (Munich, 2001), pp. 335–7.
5. League of Nations (ed.), *Handbook of International Organisations* (Geneva, 1929) pp. 77, 87–9, 228–9.
6. M. C. Giuntella, *Cooperazione intellettuale ed educazione alla pace nell'Europa della Società delle Nazioni* (Padova, 2001), pp. 144–52.
7. W. Mertineit, 'Die deutsch-polnische Schulbuchkommission und ihre Empfehlungen zur Zeitgeschichte', *Geschichte in Wissenschaft und Unterricht*, 6 (1976), 329–44. On international initiatives for the revision of textbooks see O.-E. Schüddekopf's well-researched summary, *Zwanzig Jahre Westeuropäischer Schulgeschichtsbuchrevision 1945–1965* (Braunschweig, 1966).
8. G. Ritter, 'Vereinbarung der deutschen und französischen Historiker', *Die Welt als Geschichte*, 12 (1952), 145–8.
9. R. Riemenschneider, 'Transnationale Konfliktbearbeitung. Die deutsch-französischen und die deutsch-polnischen Schulbuchgespräche im Vergleich, 1935–1997', *Internationale Schulbuchforschung*, 20 (1998), 71–9.
10. Ritter, 'Vereinbarung', p. 148.
11. Riemenschneider, 'Transnationale Konfliktbearbeitung', p. 73.
12. K. D. Erdmann, 'Zur Koexistenz der Historiker. Das deutsch-sowjetische

Historikertreffen in Leningrad 1–5 April 1975', *Geschichte in Wissenschaft und Unterricht*, 26 (1975), 442–6.
13 E. Meyer, 'Deutsch-polnische Schulbuchgespräche', *Geschichte in Wissenschaft und Unterricht*, 24 (1973), 35–43.
14 Schüddekopf, *Zwanzig Jahre*, pp. 19–23, 89–118.
15 Ritter, *Vereinbarung*.
16 E. Engelberg, 'NATO-Politik und westdeutsche Historiographie über die Probleme des 19 Jahrhunderts', *Zeitschrift für Geschichtswissenschaft*, 7 (1959), 477–93.
17 H.-P. Harstick, 'Georg Eckert (1912–1974)', in U. A. J. Becher and R. Riemenschneider (eds), *Internationale Verständigung. 25 Jahre Georg-Eckert-Institut für internationale Schulbuchforschung in Braunschweig* (Hannover, 2000), pp. 105–15.
18 R. Rümenapf-Sievers, 'Georg Eckert und die Anfänge des Internationalen Schulbuchinstituts', in Becher and Riemenschneider (eds), *Internationale Verständigung*, pp. 116–28.
19 G. Eckert (ed.), *Deutschland und Frankreich im Spiegel ihrer Schulbücher* (Braunschweig, 1954).
20 Schüddekopf, *Zwanzig Jahre*, pp. 28, 56–7.
21 R. Riemenschneider, 'An der Schwelle zur Wiederaufnahme der deutsch-französischen Schulbuchkonferenzen', *Internationale Schulbuchforschung*, 3 (1981), 72–82.
22 See also R. Riemenschneider, *Vom Erbfeind zur Partner*, in Becher and Riemenschneider (eds), *Verständigung*, pp. 166–79.
23 Schüddekopf, *Zwanzig Jahre*, pp. 43, 104–7.
24 Meyer, 'Deutsch-polnische Schulbuchgespräche'.
25 Schüddekopf, *Zwanzig Jahre*, pp. 62, 107.
26 I. Vilfan-Bruckmüller, 'Zweites Treffen der österreichisch-jugoslawischen Historikerkommission', *Österreichische Osthefte*, 27 (1985), 392–5.
27 Meyer, 'Deutsch-polnische Schulbuchgespräche', p. 38.
28 J. Hackmann, 'Vergangenheitspolitik in der Bundesrepublik Deutschland und das Verhältnis zu Polen', in W. Borodziej and K. Ziemer (eds), *Deutsch-polnische Beziehungen. 1939–1945–1949* (Osnabrück, 2000), pp. 297–327.
29 Meyer, 'Deutsch-polnische Schulbuchgespräche', pp. 37–9.
30 M. Broszat, 'Sechste Deutsch-polnische Schulbuchkonferenz vom 3–7 Oktober 1974 in Warschau', *Vierteljahrshefte für Zeitgeschichte*, 22 (1974), 461–4.
31 Gemeinsame Deutsch-Polnische Schulbuchkommission, *Empfehlungen für die Schulbücher der Geschichte und Geographie in der Bundesrepublik Deutschland und in der Volksrepublik Polen* (Braunschweig, 1995).
32 W. Jacobmeyer (ed.), *Die deutsch-polnischen Schulbuchempfehlungen in der öffentlichen Diskussion der Bundesrepublik Deutschland* (Braunschweig, 1979).
33 A. Reich and R. Maier (eds), *Die lange Nachkriegszeit. Deutschland und Polen von 1945 bis 1991* (Braunschweig, 1995), pp. 183–92.
34 Erdmann, 'Zur Koexistenz der Historiker', p. 442.
35 K. O. von Aretin, 'Die deutsch-sowjetischen Historikerkolloquien in den Jahren 1972–1981', *Jahrbuch für Europäische Geschichte*, 3 (2002), 185–204.

36 K.O. von Aretin and W. Conze (eds), *Deutschland und Russland im Zeitalter des Kapitalismus. 1861-1914. 1. deutsch-sowjetisches Historikertreffen in der Bundesrepublik Deutschland, Mainz, 14-21 Oktober 1973* (Wiesbaden, 1977).
37 Von Aretin, 'Die deutsch-sowjetischen Historikerkolloquien', pp. 186-92.
38 The proceedings were not published.
39 K.O. von Aretin and G.A. Ritter (eds), *Historismus und moderne Geschichtswissenschaft. Europa zwischen Revolution und Restauration 1797-1815. Drittes deutsch-sowjetisches Historikertreffen in der Bundesrepublik Deutschland, München 13-18 März 1978* (Stuttgart, 1987).
40 Von Aretin, 'Die deutsch-sowjetischen Historikerkolloquien', pp. 196-8.
41 H. Bartel, 'Leo Stern und die Entwicklung der wissenschaftlichen Zusammenarbeit zwischen der marxistisch-leninistischen Historiographie der UdSSR un der DDR', *Beiträge zur Universalgeschichte*, 18 (1976), 30-8.
42 M. Sabrow, 'Ökumene als Bedrohung. Die Haltung der DDR-Historiographie gegenüber den deutschen Historikertagen von 1949 bis 1962', *Comparativ*, 6 (1996), 178-202. See also Sabrow, *Das Diktat des Konsenses. Geschichtswissenschaft in der DDR, 1949-1969* (München, 2001).
43 W. Schmidt, 'Die Geschichtswissenschaft der DDR in den fünfziger Jahren', *Zeitschrift für Geschichtswissenschaft*, 31 (1983), 291-312.
44 Taken almost word for word from Bartel, 'Leo Stern', p. 31.
45 Ibid., p. 32.
46 This concern emerges very clearly, for example, in the editorial 'Die Wahrheit ist auf unserer Seite. Zur ersten wissenschaftlichen Tagung der deutsch-sowietischen Historikerkommission', *Zeitschrift für Geschichtswissenschaft*, 6 (1958), 219-30.
47 Engelberg, *NATO-Politik*.
48 'Wissenschaftliche Tagung der deutsch-sowjetischen Historikerkommission über die Rolle des deutschen Imperialismus im Zweiten Weltkrieg', *Zeitschrift für Geschichtswissenschaft*, 7 (1959), 147-51.
49 H. Scheel, 'Gründungstagung der deutsch-polnischen Historikerkommission', *Zeitschrift für Geschichtswissenschaft*, 4 (1956), 805-6.
50 See K. Obermann, 'Die erste Tagung der deutsch-tschechoslowakischen Historikerkommission', *Zeitschrift für Geschichtswissenschaft*, 3 (1955), 628-30.
51 G. Schilfert, 'Zur Tätigkeit der deutsch-polnischen Historikerkommission', *Zeitschrift für Geschichtswissenschaft*, 12 (1964), 297-301.
52 Meyer, 'Deutsch-polnische Schulbuchgespräche', p. 37.
53 Deutsches Institut für Zeitgeschichte (East Berlin) with the collaboration of Deutsch-Polnische Historiker-Kommission (ed.), *Polen, Deutschland und die Oder-Neiße-Grenze* (Berlin, 1959).
54 Schilfert, 'Zur Tätigkeit'.
55 '20. Tagung der Gemischten Kommission der Historiker der Ungarischen Volksrepublik und der Deutschen Demokratischen Republik', *Acta Historica Academiae Scientiarum Hungaricae*, 31 (1985), 191-4.
56 See G. Markov, 'Nauchna Sreshta Na Istoritsite Ot NRB I GDR', *Istoricheski pregled*, 45: 3 (1989), 120-3.

57 'Colloque de la Commission Historique Polono-Soviétique et Soixantenaire des Archives d'Etat à Lublin', *Acta Poloniae Historica*, 11 (1979), 290–2.
58 P. Cheremushkin, 'Russian-Polish Relations. A long way from stereotypes to reconciliation', *Intermarium. On-line Journal*, 5: 3 (2002).
59 A. P. Okladnikov and Z. Pal Pach, 'V Sovetsko-Vengerskoi I Komissii Istorikov (1969–1976 gg.)', *Voprosy Istorii*, 1 (1978), 182–90.
60 V. V. Mar'ina and A. I. Nedorezov, 'V Komissii Istorikov SSSR I CHSSR', *Voprosy Istorii*, 11 (1987), 142–6.
61 S. Purveva, 'Bulgaro-Chekhoslovashka Nauchna Konferentsiia Po Etnokulturnite Protsesi', *Istoricheski Pregled*, 45: 12 (1989), 87–8.
62 J. Vlachovic, 'Zasadenie Ceskoslovensko-Madarskej Historickej Komisie', *Historicky Casopis*, 13 (1965), 303–4.
63 T. Zorn, 'Dvanajsto Zasedanje Jugoslovansko-Ceskoslovaske Zgodovinske Komisije', *Zgodovinski Casopis*, 33 (1979), 327–9.
64 J. Buszko, 'IV Konferencja Komisji Polsko-Czechoslowackiej W Bratyslawie', *Kwartalnik Historyczny*, 68 (1961), 565–6.
65 Sabrow, 'Ökumene als Bedrohung', p. 195.
66 E.g. Borodziej and Ziemer, *Deutsch-polnische Beziehungen*.
67 For the proceedings, see Reich and Maier, *Die lange Nachkriegszeit*, p. 7.
68 See U. A. J. Becher, W. Borodziej and R. Maier (eds), *Deutschland und Polen im zwanzigsten Jahrhundert. Analysen, Quellen, didaktische Hinweise* (Hannover, 2001), pp. 11–15.
69 G. Stöber and R. Maier (eds), *Grenzen und Grenzräume in der deutschen und polnischen Geschichte* (Hannover, 2000).
70 *Berichte zu Staat und Gesellschaft in der Tschechischen und in der Slowakischen Republik*, 3: 2 (1995), 33–6.
71 Gemeinsame deutsch-tschechische Historikerkommission (ed.), *Konfliktgemeinschaft, Katastrophe, Entspannung. Skizze einer Darstellung der deutsch-tschechischen Geschichte seit dem 19. Jahrhundert* (München, 1996).
72 S. Biman, 'Die Deutsch-Tschechische und Deutsch-Slowakische Historikerkommission', in W. Koschmal, M. Nekula and J. Rogall (eds), *Deutsche und Tschechen. Geschichte, Kultur, Politik* (München, 2001), pp. 449–58.
73 A. Wiedemann, 'Öffentliche Erinnerung an Krieg, Diktatur und Vertreibung: Tschechien, die Slowakei und Deutschland seit 1945. Tagung der Deutsch-Tschechischen und Deutsch-Slowakische Historikerkommission am 15. und 16. März 2001 in Brünn', *Zeitschrift für Geschichtswissenschaft*, 49 (2001), 631–3.
74 Schüddekopf, *Zwanzig Jahre*, p. 114.
75 *Slovensko-italijanski odnosi 1880–1956. I rapporti italo-sloveni 1880–1956* (Ljubljana, 2001).

8

The Italo-Slovenian historico-cultural commission

Raoul Pupo

In the second half of the last century, the history of the area around the upper Adriatic (which the Italians call Venezia Giulia) was the subject of heated disputes between Italian historiographers and those from what was then Yugoslavia.[1] It was the bitterness of those disputes and the repercussions they had on relationships between the three countries that led the governments of Italy, Slovenia and Croatia to set up two bilateral historico-cultural commissions at the end of the Cold War to try to re-establish discussions on a fresh footing among the scholars from the three countries. While the Italo-Croatian Commission never really got off the ground, after seven years of work the Italo-Slovenian Commission produced a forty-page Final Report in 1996, which provoked considerable reaction both in Italy and in Slovenia. Controversy surrounded the contents of the Report, on the one hand, which touched upon a series of issues which public opinion in both countries still considered to be very sensitive, and the method used to arrive at the joint document.

The truth is that the historical debate revealed concerns which were more political and ideological in nature than historiographical: this is not really surprising, since the difficulties encountered for decades at the level of *historia rerum gestarum* were simply a reflection of the far more dramatic difficulties encountered at the level of the *res gestae* themselves: the national conflicts which began when the area was still under Austro-Hungarian rule, the bitter border disputes which followed both World Wars, and the persecution of national minorities, first by the Italian fascists and then by the Yugoslav Communists, culminating in the expulsion of almost all the Italians from those territories which had been handed over to Yugoslavia. If we add to all this the fact that in the postwar years, Italy and Yugoslavia belonged to two different worlds, since the break between Tito and Stalin in 1948 made no difference at all to the regime in Belgrade, the underlying reasons for the incommunicability are not difficult to discover.

Two different historiographies

Besides the overlying political reasons, communication between historians was further complicated by the different way historical studies were organised. Italian historiography had a strong tradition of pluralism, whereas Yugoloslav historiography, though not monolithic, was still a regime historiography; certain key issues of the relationship with Italy met with stock responses and any attempt to challenge them was seen as a political provocation. A case in point was the violence visited upon the Italian population in those territories which came under Yugoslav control at the end of the Second World War, including the forced transfer of most of the Italians living in territories which became part of Yugoslavia after the Paris Peace Treaty of 1946 and the London Memorandum in 1954.[2]

Of course, this does not mean that Italian and Yugoslav historians did not talk to each other at all for fifty years: on the contrary, the very presence of various schools of thought in Italian historiography made it possible to identify some common ground for discussion with the Yugoslavs. From the 1960s onwards, the study of Italian fascism, its devastating impact on a pluriethnic territory like Venezia Giulia, and its doomed ambitions of conquest in the Balkans during the Second World War, were the subjects which Italian and Yugoslav historians discussed most frequently and fruitfully.[3] It was a very selective kind of collaboration, however, based largely (though not exclusively) on a certain understanding between Marxist historians which excluded certain themes *a priori*, such as the strained relations between the two resistance movements in the border areas, and even more, the violence to which the Italian population was subjected after the armistice of 8 September 1943 and in the postwar years. Unfortunately, these were precisely the issues which had divided Italian, Slovenian and Croatian local public opinion in these areas, and indeed one of them – the issue of the 'foibe' (deep potholes) into which many Italians were thrown between 1943 and 1945 – had become the symbol of a profound contrast between the Italians of Venezia Giulia and their neighbours to the East which seemed irresolvable.

However, the debate was mostly carried on by people living in the area, almost exclusively in local newspapers, political publications or pamphlets by small interest groups, while from the 1960s onwards, relations between Italy and Yugoslavia had become extremely cordial, and none of the main parties in Italy were remotely interested in raising thorny issues which might recall the worst years of the two country's pasts.[4] The various Italian governments were not interested, since Yugoslavia's international position of 'non-alignment' turned it into a precious buffer-state for Italy, making the christian democrat governments' pro-NATO foreign policy both less risky and less expensive. But the left-wing opposition to those governments was not interested either, because it saw the Tito's federal state as a successful combination of socialism, national independence and original economics, based on self-management. As for the right-wing opposition in Italy, which was the direct descendant of Italian fascism, it had no political influence during the Cold War and any attempt to revive traditional Italian nationalism would have had a seriously destabilising effect on East–West relations. Combined with the cultural limitations of the Italian Right, this also helps to explain why the nationalist historiography concerned with the problems of Venezia Giulia and the Upper Adriatic was almost non-existent, and why, until the 1990s, the political use of border history was delegated to the local level.[5]

At the historiographical level, the history of the Eastern border in the twentieth century suffered for decades from the effects of a whole series of mutual vetos. The underlying reasons for this are quite easy to identify: one was the reaction of antifascist historiography against the nationalist historiography which in the past had made the 'Adriatic Question' one of its battle-cries; another was the guilty conscience of Marxist historians regarding events which the Italian Communist Party (PCI) had been a bit too ambiguous about: Italian Communists had found themselves caught between the principles of the international Communist movement (which between 1944 and 1947 supported Yugoslavia's claims to the detriment of Italy), the defence of Italian national interests upon which much of the PCI's legitimacy was based in the post-fascist political system, and finally Togliatti's 'new party' strategy, which rejected the Yugoslav revolutionary model but was not always understood and accepted by the cadres and the leaders of the party.[6]

Quite apart from this, however, the uneasiness of postwar Italian historiography with regard to the Giulian area (and thus to relations with Yugoslavia) goes back even further, being rooted in the fact that, throughout the twentieth century, the entire history of the Eastern border strongly favoured the creation of political and historiographical myths; at the same time, when properly analysed, it offers the historian all the elements necessary to explode those myths, which in the meantime had become consolidated in Italian political culture. Just think of the myth of the 'mutilated victory' after the Great War, which D'Annunzio and Mussolini helped to cultivate and which contributed so much to the rise of fascism; think too of the extraordinarily successful myth of the 'nice guy' image of the Italian soldier, the humane, merciful occupier so different from those horrible Nazis, which was to be drastically re-assessed thanks to a more critical reappraisal of the Italian occupation of the ex-Yugoslav territories.[7] On the other side, think of the Yugoslav liberation movement, long regarded as a model for all the resistance movements in Europe, but not taken as an example by the Italians

The Italo-Slovenian historico-cultural commission

(unfortunately, according to some), whose image was greatly tarnished by the evidence of the mass violence it used to achieve its goals.[8] Think of the myth of Togliatti as the true defender of Italian interests against any temptation towards international servility, when the sources give the impression (to say the very least) that he was absolutely incapable of saying no to Yugoslavia's annexation plans.[9] Myth-making is an essential element for creating collective, national or political identities, while one of the basic occupations of historical research is showing just how flimsy those myths can be, and this obviously does not make historians very popular, and when a lot of these collision points come together around one particular history, the risk of a general black-out is bound to be very high.

At the end of the 1980s, however, historiography, public opinion and Italian politicians stopped looking the other way and the events of Giulian history finally got some attention. The fall of Communism made it possible to re-examine the history of the Eastern bloc countries and denounce the crimes which had been committed. In the border areas between Italy and Yugoslavia this led to an immediate re-awakening of interest in events such as the foibe and the forced removal of Italians from Istria, seen as a symbol of denied history. Unlike in the previous decades, the change in the political climate meant that the demand to settle up with the past was not restricted to the local level, but was perceived by the national political parties as an essential step before being able to establish a new relationship with countries which (or so it was thought at the time) would rapidly be transformed into democracies. On the other hand, opinions differed as to the best way to do it. From the Right, there were demands for an official parliamentary inquiry to be set up composed of Deputies and Senators with the job of identifying the perpetrators of the massacres (fifty years later) and of basically dragging into the dock not only Tito's regime, but Slovenian and Croatian nationalist policy towards Italy, which had found extremely effective expression under Tito. It is very likely that the reaction on the part of the political class and of public opinion in Slovenia and Croatia (at the time busily engaged in the affirmation of their respective national identities) would have been to close up like a clam and put their national historians to work to show that the foibe were an Italian invention and that anyway the fascists had done a lot worse. The parties of the Centre and of the Left, on the other hand, fearing a revival of nationalist tension, would have probably chosen to depoliticise the question by saying that a historical problem should be solved by historians, and the only way to do that was to compare sources and start a collaboration between experts.

The bilateral commissions

It was the second solution that came to pass. In a surprise vote on 24 September 1990, the City Council of Trieste (the city which was the symbol of the Italo-Yugoslav struggle) gave its unanimous approval (which meant the extreme right too) to a motion asking for a bilateral Italo-Yugoslav Commission to be set up composed of historians from both countries and entrusted with the task of throwing light on the question of the foibe. The Italian government gave its support to the idea, and negotiations began with Belgrade. Progress was rather fitful, since in the middle of talks, Yugoslavia fell apart, but negotiations then continued with the new governments in Ljubljana and Zagreb and concluded successfully. With an exchange of notes between the three governments, in 1993 two mixed historico-cultural commissions were established by the three Foreign Ministries involved, one commission Italo-Slovenian and the other commission Italo-Croatian, with the job of 'carrying out a wide-ranging study and examination of all the important aspects of bilateral political and cultural questions occurring in the twentieth century'.[10] Actually, only the Italo-Slovenian Commission got down to work. The Italo-Croatian Commission never met again after the first preliminary encounter, although it was never officially disbanded. The Italo-Slovenian Commission, on the other hand, worked for over seven years, with various intervals, adopting a method of working which turned out to be rather effective.

The chronological time-span was divided into four periods: 1880–1918; 1919–40; 1941–45; and 1946–56. For each time-period, each of the two delegations produced a basic report, written by one or two of the historians on each side, depending on their specific expertise; these reports were sent to all the members and the plenary sessions of the commission were then devoted to discussing them, on one or more occasions for each period. Once the general discussion was over, four separate work-groups were set up (one for each period), made up once again of one or two scholars on each side, and they were given the task of drawing up a preliminary draft of a common document, which had to take into account the points emerging in the course of the general discussion. The four documents which were produced in this way were submitted to the plenary commission for approval, each one in a different session, and then returned to the groups for the necessary corrections and additions. In the end, the final version of the text was discussed once again in a plenary session, so as to transform them into four chapters of a single document, the Final Report, which was approved, countersigned by all the members of the commission, both Italian and Slovene, and handed over in July 2000 to the Italian and Slovenian foreign ministries. However, the Report had a limited circulation: the fact that there was a general election being fought in Italy at the time, and the coming to power of a Centre-Right government delayed the agreements necessary for its distribution until eventually a series of unofficial leaks in the Slovene press led to it being published in its entirety (but unofficially) in the most important daily papers of Ljubljana and Trieste. It was subsequently published in Italy, again unofficially, by certain journals of contemporary history[11] and in Slovenia by the Ljubljana Institute of Contemporary History in the form of a book containing the two countersigned versions (in Italian and Slovenian), plus an unofficial translation in English.[12] These publications were then followed the one done by the Italo-Slovene association 'Concordia et pax' based in Gorizia and Nova Gorica, a Catholic association which for years has been working on reconciling the Italian and Slovenian communities with the support of the dioceses on both sides of the border.[13] Although some of the members of the commission asked that the preparatory documents and the minutes of the discussion at the sessions should be published in full, in the light of their great historiographical interest, it was decided to keep them secret.

A reading of the final text makes it clear that the task assigned to the commission was performed with a certain degree of flexibility. The mandate to 'concentrate upon the positive elements which unite the two peoples, thereby helping to clarify those events that caused difficulties in their relations in the past', appeared to be too glaringly in contrast with the harsh realities of a period characterised by a multiplication and exasperation of conflicts between Italians and Slovenes. For this reason, the work of the commission (though not disregarding positive aspects and moments) concentrated primarily upon the sources of the conflicts which appeared between the end of the nineteenth century and the mid-1950s. The decision to conclude the analysis with the end of the 1950s, taken early on because of the enormous number of problems that had to be dealt with, in the end made it impossible to take into consideration those last decades of the twentieth century which had in fact been characterised by a significant improvement in bilateral relations. In fact, already from the 1960s onwards, both Italy and Yugoslavia realised that a border so absurd as the one which had emerged from the peace treaty combined with the London Memorandum could only exist between two friendly countries if the entire border zone were not to collapse. There was a shift at the conceptual level, therefore, from the notion of a closed border, a barrier between alternative worlds, to the notion of a 'bridge-border', able to represent a resource in terms of position which could bring advantages to the economic and social structure of the surrounding regions.[14] At the practical level, this led to the setting up of a closely knit system of transborder collaboration, such as that existing from 1978 onwards of the Alpe Adria Working Community, a model of dialogue between regions which at the time were still part of different economic systems and political regimes.¹⁵

The commission also showed little enthusiasm for the request made originally to broaden its sphere of interest to include the cultural history of the area (as its name implied). In fact, despite the presence of non-historians – writers, journalists, and among the Italians, the representative of one of the most important organisations of Giulian-Dalmatian exiles – most of the commission's work focused on political history and its traditional concerns, which also happened to coincide with the expectations of the general public.¹⁶

However, the mandate to carry out a kind of common critical reappraisal of the existing historiography, rather than pointing out new lines of study, was respected. In that sense, the contents of the Report are characterised more by caution than by innovation. There were several reasons for this, but two in particular stand out. First, it was considered a priority to give a balanced judgement on those numerous issues which until then had not only been the object of bitter disputes between historians, but had also provided opportunity for a massive and unprincipled use of history for political purposes. Secondly, there was the problem of the different points of departure on the two sides, since while fascism had been thoroughly examined and processed by Italian historiography, Slovenian historiography was only just beginning to do the same with Communism. Another difficulty had to do with the commission's territorial jurisdiction. While it was natural that the Slovene delegation should want to restrict the field of interest to relations between Italians and Slovenes, it was just as obvious that these relations occurred within very different contexts, depending on the period: first in the sphere of relations between Italy and the Austro-Hungarian Empire, and then between Italy and Yugoslavia. Therefore, when dealing with the so-called 'Adriatic Question', which involved more than simply those territories inhabited by Slovenians, the primary interlocutors of the Italian government had initially been Vienna and subsequently Belgrade, but certainly not Ljubljana; for this reason, it was by no means an easy task to link together the dimensions of region, nation and state.

On the Italian side, for example, Venezia Giulia had always been treated as a single entity, and so Italian historians had dealt with the problems posed by the fascist policies directed against the Slav populations living there as a single issue (without distinguishing between Slovenes and Croats) in the same way as they dealt with the subsequent question of Yugoslav treatment of the Italian population. Slovenian historians, on the hand, felt under no obligation to start a discussion about as the political decisions made by the Yugoslav authorities, except inasmuch as these decisions affected Slovenians, and the same applied to the situation which had arisen in the postwar years when most of Istria was annexed to Croatia. Consequently, it became completely impossible to make general assessment of a phenomenon such as the mass flight of the Italians from Istria (also from areas handed over to the Slovenians, though to a lesser extent). It was just as difficult to make a common historical judgment on the consequences of the 1946 peace treaty: for Italy, it was catastrophic because most of Venezia Giulia was handed over to Yugoslavia, while among Slovenian historiographers there an opinion going round according to the annexation of Istria to Croatia was in a certain sense 'paid for' by the Slovenes with their having to give up Trieste.[17]

After long discussions, the problems were solved in a fairly balanced manner, but given the above-mentioned premises, it should come as no surprise that the main aim of the commission was to find some common language and a modicum of common ground, and try to sweep away that accumulation of prejudices and commonplaces that had built up over time regarding relations between Italians and Slovenians, an accumulation that had produced a whole series of stereotyped, incommunicable reconstructions. The centrality of this aim is undeniable, given the crucial role played by these heavily stereotyped narratives in the past (and today) in shaping daily intercourse between the national groups, and in influencing political debate in the border areas, and indeed relations between the two governments. By way of example, almost half a century later, the local Triestine press, both in Italian and Slovene, still contains letters and articles almost every day (often highly polemical in tone) about problems to do with Italo-Slav relations, and the main newspapers in Slovenia often discuss similar matters: in both countries, the question of the apologies demanded on both sides for the crimes of the past is raised periodically by political groups, re-proposing mutually incommunicable readings of history, and this actually interfered with Slovenia's process of adhesion to the European Union; the thorny issue of the restitution of the abandoned property of Italian exiles, or rather of compensation for them, has still not been solved fifty years later, and fuels further polemic about the history of Istria; the foiba of Basovizza (a village near Trieste where several hundred Italians are thought to have been killed) has become the symbol of the violence inflicted by the Yugoslavs in 1945 and a site commemorating a divided, conflicting memory; the Italian press and leading political figures – and not just on the right wing – continue unrepentant to repeat estimates of the total number of victims of Yugoslav violence (and of the number of exiles from Istria), which have no bearing on reality.[18]

When explaining historical processes, the commission was equally careful to steer well clear of using those monocausal models so popular in the past. To give a concrete example, there was unanimous agreement among members of the enormous responsibilities of the fascist regime for its attempts to destroy the national identity of the Slovenes and Croats living in Venezia Giulia and of the long-term political destabilisation policy adopted with regard to the Kingdom of Yugoslavia; but that was not taken mechanistically to be the 'prime cause' of a vortex of violence and acts of reprisal which subsequently ensued for decades. The commission's Final Report combined a consideration of the often unbearable weight of the past with an exploration of the autonomous dynamics of domination and violence which accompanied the Communist takeover after the war and the regime's consolidation.

Compared to those questions of general approach, the treatment of the most sensitive issues (the foibe and the flight from Istria) presented fewer problems. The explanation for this is that there were historians present in the commission (Italians and Slovenes), who were involved in those same years in looking for a fresh approach to these questions through a fertile exchange of material and opinions.[19] In this case then, the commission was able to make use of the most up-to-date research findings, and the formulation made in the Final Report is an effective summary of these.

As for the main limitations of the method adopted, these can be said to consist firstly in a tendency to over-simplify, arising from what was felt as an imperative to express common historical judgements on subjects traditionally considered explosive; secondly, in a reluctance to give summary opinions on more than a century of relations between Italians and Slovenes, and a preference for a more detailed analysis single moments; thirdly, in a clear prevalence of institutional and political history over social history, mainly in deference to the wishes and expectations of a wider audience (meaning not only our governments, but also our respective public opinions).

Nevertheless, it would be too reductive to assess the work achieved only on the basis of the Final Report, because perhaps the most important aspect of the experience was the method adopted, and its implications for the relationship between the two historiographies. In the first place, the creation of the commission set in motion a process of opening up of the archives which benefited all scholars. In the second place, the very existence of the commission at an extremely delicate time, when Slovenian historiography was being re-invented, provided historians from the two countries with an open, receptive and stimulating forum for discussion. What came out of this was a willingness to compare and collaborate which would have been absolutely out of the question just a few years earlier, and this can represent the basis, not only for ongoing relations between historiographies, but also for marking out more innovative lines of investigation. The stark contrast between the state of Italo-Slovene relations and the state of Italo-Croatian ones, from the point of view of historical studies, is revealing in itself. In the former case, the mutual collaboration which began with the commission continues, not only in personal relations between individual scholars, but also in joint research projects involving scientific institutions from both countries: one example is the project entitled 'Forced transfer of population and social transformation in the province of Trieste and district of Capodistria in the twentieth century' already set up by the Department of Geography and History of the University of Trieste in collaboration with the Centre for Scientific Research of the Republic of Slovenia, Capodistria, while a second project entitled 'From divided land to bridge-border. Laceration and collaboration in the border zones between Italy and Yugoslavia in the postwar years (1945–1965)' was set up by numerous Italian and Slovenian research institutes.[20] In the second case, the fact that the commission never got off the ground, which was principally due to Croatia's much more difficult transition to democracy, presents a mirror image of how the historiography of the new central-European republic closed in upon itself; in fact, relations between Italian and Croatian scholars of contemporary history are almost non-existent, and there are still problems gaining access to the archives in Croatia.

Conclusions

The ability of the Italo-Slovene Commission to arrive at a result, even though it took some years of work, met with considerable surprise, especially on the part of the governments who had commissioned the enterprise. Perhaps they thought the problem would be safely out of the way for a good number of years, and when things turned out differently, their embarrassment was evident. Some of the commissioners too, knowing the difficulties involved, had never been over-optimistic about the chances of producing a common document, and one which would be written without having to sacrifice their own professional principles to external requirements for compromise. No particular pressure was put on the commission by the diplomats, either with regard to the time taken or to the content of the work sessions. For their part, the nationalist circles in the two countries naturally could not wait to accuse their respective national delegation: already in the course of proceedings, one of the members of the Slovene delegation resigned and promptly published an article reiterating all the traditional tenets of patriotic historiography, and once the Final Report was published, the Slovene members were often accused of having sold national interests down the river in exchange for getting their work published in Italian journals; the Italian members, on the other hand, were accused of 'justifying' Slovenian claims to Trieste.[21] This kind of reaction had been expected, however, and if anything indicates that the commission went to great pains to avoid those historiographical clichés still all too commonplace in Italy and Slovenia, and not just among ordinary people, but also in political and cultural circles.

More serious consideration should be given to the concern expressed by many that the Final Report might be treated a sort of 'official history', agreed upon at the diplomatic level so as to favour good relations between Italy and Slovenia on the eve of Slovenia's accession to the European Union. Subsequent events have shown that this was not the case, however, and not only because the members of the commission were very careful to stress the fact that the conclusive document was no more than a starting-point for discussion for all historians. Much more important is the fact that it has become far more difficult to talk about Italian and Slovene historiography as two neatly separate entities, and no longer so difficult to talk of a group of scholars, each with his or her own sensitivities and preferences, and not necessarily any closer to his/her own compatriots from a scientific point of view than to historians from any other country. From this point of view, the experience of the bilateral commission should be seen as the conclusion of a traditional way of writing frontier history, rather than the beginning of a new era. In fact, particularly among the younger generations of scholars, there is a growing need for a post-national history. By this is meant not only a way of reconstructing the past which takes into account the point of view of all those involved (which every good historian should do) but rather the ability to move freely and without mental constraints in the diverse contexts in which Giulian events unfolded at different moments. This is probably the only approach that can hope to reconstruct the dynamics of an area like Venezia Giulia and the Eastern Adriatic where, during the last two centuries, different forces became interwoven in a way incomprehensible when seen from within the single national histories. For example, between the nineteenth and twentieth centuries, Trieste, Istria and Dalmazia were crucial sites of the national 'risorgimenti' of Italy, Slovenia and Croatia, while during the Second World War, these places saw encounters, confrontations and collisions not just between very different organisations, but between very different models of resistance: the Italian model, characterised by party pluralism and committed to establishing a liberal-democratic system after the Liberation – and the Yugoslav one, founded on Communist hegemony and committed to transforming Yugoslavia into a socialist country after the war, whatever the cost. Of course, it is this constant overlapping of contexts and imperatives, not unlike what happened in other territories belonging to the great pluriethnic empires before the First World War, that gives significance to the history of the Giulian area: in order to do it justice, a reconstruction of the facts cannot be divorced from a constant willingness to question again and again those interpretative categories upon which the national historiographies have erected their monumental but fragile constructions. In the future, this will probably be the major challenge for Italian and Slovenian historians alike (and hopefully for Croatian ones too).[22]

Notes

1. The term 'Venezia Giulia' was coined in 1863 by the Gorizian glottologist Graziadio Isaia Ascoli to unite under a single name all the territories belonging to the Habsburg Empire which Italy was claiming along its eastern border, divided at the time into various administrative constituencies but unified, in Italian eyes, by the presence of populations speaking dialects which were of Veneto origin. In this perspective, the presence of Slav populations in the same areas seemed quite unimportant, and even more so, any distinction between Slovenians and Croatians, usually ignored by the Italians present in the areas. On the Yugoslav side, after 1918 and above all during the peace conferences, the term *Julijska Krajina* was used, or more often, the French term *Marche Julienne*. Obviously, Yugoslav historiography and even more so Slovenian and Croatian historiographers distinguish between the 'Slovenian Coastal Area' (meaning alternatively the strip of coastline around Trieste, or the border area as far as the Friuli plains) from that part of Istria considered to be Croatian.
2. For an overview of the mass atrocities commonly described as 'the Giulian foibe' ('foibe' is the name of the deep holes occurring in the Karst rock formations throughout the border areas between Italy, Slovenia and Croatia into which many of the victims were thrown), as well as a look at the historiographical debate and the political use of the issue, see R. Pupo and R. Spazzali, *Foibe* (Milan, 2003). On the subject of the expulsion of the Italians from Dalmatia and Istria, see C. Columni, L. Ferrari, G. Nassisi and G. Trani, *Storia di un esodo. Istria 1945–1956* (Trieste, 1980); for an up-to-date synthesis see M. Cattaruzza, 'L' esodo istriano: questioni interpretative', *Ricerche di storia politica*, 2: 1 (1999), 27–48; R. Pupo, 'Gli esodi e la realtà politica dal dopoguerra ad oggi', in *Storia d'Italia. Le regioni. Friuli–Venezia Giulia* (Torino, 2002); for a comparative perspective see M. Cattaruzza, M. Dogo and R. Pupo (eds), *Esodi. Trasferimenti forzati di popolazione nel Novecento europeo* (Napoli, 2000); for a social history approach see G. Nemec, *Un paese perfetto. Storia e memoria di una comunità in esilio. Grisgnana d'Istria 1930–1960* (Gorizia, 1998); see also, by the same author, 'The re-definition of gender roles and family structures among Istrian peasant families faced with urban society in Trieste (1954–1964)', *Journal of Modern Italy*, Special Issue *Gender and the Private Sphere in Italy since 1945*, 9: 1 (2004). For a re-reading of the conflicting memories of Italians, Slovenes and Croats in anthropological terms, see P. Ballinger, *History in Exile. Memory and Identity at the Borders of the Balkans* (Princeton and Oxford, 2003).
3. On the Italian side, the prime mover in Italo-Yugoslav collaboration was the network of institutes for the History of the Liberation Movement, and in particular the Regional Institute for Friuli-Venezia Giulia; on the Yugoslav side, the main interlocutor was the network of institutes for the History of the Workers' Movement, and the Ljubljana branch in particular.
4. Among these, the associations of Giulian-Dalmatian exiles in particular.
5. M. Cattaruzza pointed this out in 1992, in 'Considerazioni sulla storiografia giuliana a margine del "Trieste e gli Asburgo" di Angelo Filippuzzi', *Quaderni*

giuliani di storia, 12: 1–2 (1992), 231–3, emphasising how, in the absence of a true nationalist historiography, the myth of Trieste as a 'most Italian city' and the myth of the 'Slav menace' were propagated by 'the numerous publications of reminiscences and memoirs (national-liberal initially, and nationalistic-fascist later) which had an enormous impact on public opinion'.

6 Of the copious bibliography concerning the problem of the relationship between Italian and Yugoslav Communists, see especially M. Galeazzi, 'Togliatti fra Tito e Stalin', in M. Galeazzi (ed.), *Roma-Belgrado. Gli anni della guerra fredda* (Ravenna, 1995), pp. 98–126; R. Gualtieri, *Togliatti e la politica estera italiana* (Roma, 1995); L. Gibianskij, 'L' Unione Sovietica, la Jugoslavia e Trieste', in G. Valdevit (ed.), *La crisi di Trieste. Maggio-giugno 1945. Una revisione critica* (Trieste, 1995), pp. 39–78; G. Valdevit, 'La questione di Trieste fra i comunisti italiani e jugoslavi', in E. Aga Rossi and S. Pons (eds), *L' altra faccia della luna: i rapporti fra PCI, PCF e Unione Sovietica* (Bologna, 1997), pp. 173–208; E. Aga Rossi and V. Zaslavskj, *Togliatti e Stalin: il PCI e la politica estera staliniana negli archivi di Mosca* (Bologna, 1997); G. Valdevit, 'I comunisti italiani e Trieste fra guerra e dopoguerra:. un rapporto disturbato', in G. Valdevit (ed.), *Il dilemma Trieste: guerra e dopoguerra in uno scenario europeo* (Gorizia, 1999). See also Nevenka Troha's remarks in *Komu Trst: slovenci in italiani med dvema drzavama* (Ljubljana, 1999).

7 On the Italian model of occupation during the Second World War, see D. Rodogno, *Il nuovo ordine mediterraneo. Le politiche di occupazione dell'Italia fascista in Europa (1940–1943)* (Torino, 2003); for a summary of the Italian occupation of the Balkans see B. Mantelli (ed.), *L'Italia fascista come potenza occupante: lo scacchiere balcanico*, a monographical issue of the journal *Qualestoria*, 30: 1 (2002); on the occupation of Slovenia see especially M. Cuzzi, *L' occupazione italiana della Slovenia (1941–1943)* (Roma, 1998); T. Ferenc, *La provincia 'italiana' di Lubiana. Documenti 1941–1942* (Udine, 1994); T. Ferenc, *'Si ammazza troppo poco'. Condannati a morte – Ostaggi – Passati per le armi nella provincia di Lubiana 1941–1943. Documenti* (Ljubljana, 1999).

8 See among others J. Vodusek, *Prvzem Oblasti 1944–1946* (Ljubljana, 1992).

9 See the works mentioned in Note 5.

10 The complete text of the joint declaration reads as follows: 'The Governments of the Italian Republic and of the Republic of Slovenia (Croazia) – mindful of the deep and fruitful political, economic and cultural relations which have developed throughout the course of history on both sides of the Adriatic Sea – with a view to further reinforcing and developing their friendly bilateral relations on a basis of better mutual understanding and a spirit of cooperation, hereby decide to establish a historico-cultural Mixed Commission with the task of carrying out a global study and investigation of all the important aspects of bilateral cultural and political relations in the course of this century, agreeing to this end to facilitate the work of the Commission by giving it unrestricted access to all relevant documents, to historical monuments and sites, as well as to cultural institutions and any other site of specific interest. They also decide that the Commission should concentrate on the positive elements which unite the two peoples, thereby helping to throw light on those events which created

difficulties in their relations in the past; the Commission will be composed on each side of a co-president plus six members, chosen by their respective Governments from among recognised experts at the national level in their respective fields; the Commission will be completely independent in its work, deciding independently on its own procedures and on the proper sphere of its activities, on the understanding that that fist two meetings will be held in Rome and in Ljubljana (Zagreb); the Commission will produce a Final Report which will be confidential in nature, and this will be submitted to the two Governments as quickly as possible.'

11 *Qualestoria*, 28: 2 (2000), 145–67; *Storia contemporanea in Friuli*, 30: 31 (2000), 9–35; *Tempi e cultura*, 5: 9 (2001), in the insert entitled 'Dieci anni per un documento'.

12 The preface by Dimitrij Rupel, who was Slovenian Foreign Minister at the time, lends the publication a more official aura.

13 *Associazione-Zdruzenje Concordia et pax, Proceedings* (2003), no. 1.

14 See G. Valussi, *Il confine nordorientale d'Italia* (Trieste, 1972); M. Bufon, *Sviluppo etnico e regionale delle aree di confine: il caso degli Sloveni nel Friuli–Venezia Giulia* (Trieste-Gorizia-Cividale, 1990); M. Bufon, 'Cultural and social dimension of borderlands: the case of the Italo-Slovene trans-border area', *Geojournal*, 30: 3 (1993), 235–40.

15 The founding members of the Work Community were the special statute region of Friuli–Venezia Giulia, the Veneto Region, the Socialist Yugoslav Republics of Slovenia and Croatia, the Austrian Länder of Corinzia, Styria and Upper Austria and, as active observers, the Austrian Land of Salzburg and the German Free State of Bavaria. Subsequently, there were other members from Italy, Austria, Germany, Hungary and Switzerland. See also *Alpe Adria. Una regione europea* (Milano, 1988); M. Antonsich, 'Il Nord-Est tra Mitteleuropa e Balcani: il caso del Friuli–Venezia Giulia', in *Geopolitica della Crisi. Balcani, Caucaso e Asia centrale nel nuovo scenario internazionale* (Milano, 2002), pp. 141–248.

16 The original members of the Italian delegation were Sergio Bartole (co-president), Elio Apih, Angelo Ara, Paola Pagnini, Fulvio Salimbeni, the writer Fulvio Tomizza and Senator Lucio Toth. Prof. Bartole was eventually replaced (also as co-president) by Giorgio Conetti, Fulvio Tomizza by Raoul Pupo and Elio Apih by Marina Cattaruzza. The original members of the Slovenian delegation were Milica Kacin-Wohinz (co-president), France Dolinar, Boris Gombac, Branko Marusic, Boris Mlakar, Nevenka Troha and Andrei Vovco. Boris Mlakar resigned and was replaced by Aleksander Vuga; subsequently, after the resignation of Boris Gombac, Boris Mlakar came back to replace him.

17 The specific difficulties encountered by the Italian and Slovene delegations as regards this point are naturally part of the wider context of the methodological problems posed by the dissolution of Yugoslavia and the tendency for the nationalising historiographies of the successor states to re-read the Yugoslav experience not only in highly critical terms, but also often attributing either to the federal government or to other ethnic groups most of the responsibility for the darkest episodes in Yugoslav history in the postwar years.

18 See for example the debate in the Chamber of Deputies on 11 February 2004,

when a bill was presented proposing 'A day in commemoration of the foibe, the exodus, and the complex events occurring on the Eastern border'. As was to be expected, all the nationalist stereotypes promptly re-emerged and the national secretary of Democrats of the Left (the party descended from the Italian Communist Party) threw his weight behind the figures of 15,000 Italians thrown down foibe and 350,000 Italians forced to leave Istria and Dalmatia, both incompatible with reliable estimates.

19 Among the Italian historians, Marina Cattaruzza in particular (apart from the works already mentioned in Note 2, see also, in the volume edited by the same author, *Nazionalismi di frontiera. Identità contrapposte sull'Adriatico nord-orientale 1850–1950* (Soveria Mannelli, 2003) and R. Pupo 'Le foibe giuliane: 1944–1946. Interpretazioni e problemi', *Quaderni giuliani di storia*, 12: 1–2 (1991), 93–120; 'Violenza politica tra guerra e dopoguerra: il caso delle foibe giuliane 1943–1945', *Clio*, 32: 1 (1996), 115–36; 'L' esodo degli italiani da Zara, da Fiume e dall'Istria 1943–1956', *Passato e presente*, 15: 40 (1997), 55–81. Among the Slovenian historians, see Neveka Troha, and in particular 'Aretacije, deportacije in usmrtitve v Julijski krajini', *Razgledi* (1994), 16; 'Oris polozaja v Koprskem okraju cone B Julijske krjine v letih 1945–1947', *Prispevki za novejso zgodovino* (1996), 36, 67–94; 'Optanti za italijansko drzavljanstvo z obmocja, prikljucenega Sloveniji leta 1947', *Prispevki za novejso zgodovino* (1997), 37, 359–70.

20 In Italy, the Regional Institute for the History of the Liberation Movement in Friuli–Venezia Giulia, the Cultural Consortium for the Monfalcone Area, the Trieste National Library and for Slovene Studies, and the Slovenian Research Institute; in Slovenia, the Museum of Nova Gorica, the Polytechnic of Nova Gorica, the University of Primorska – Centre for Scientific Research of Capodistria – and the Institute of Contemporary History in Ljubljana. The project was presented within the sphere of the European Community Programme INTERREG III Italy – Slovenia 2000-6.

21 B. M. Gombac, *Slovenija, Italija. Od preziranja do priznanja* (Ljubljana, 1996).

22 With this idea in mind, in 2004 the Regional Institute for the History of the Liberation Movement in Friuli–Venezia Giulia organised a series of seminars, dealing with the formation of mass national identities between the nineteenth and early twentieth centuries in what was then the Austrian coastal lands, and with the development of 'crisis' of the region's economy in the twentieth century.

9

The state, the historians and the Algerian War in French memory, 1991–2004

Raphaëlle Branche

French colonialism in Algeria ended in 1962 following eight years of war which revealed deep divisions in French society, repressive police and army methods, and violent opposition among Algerian nationalists.[1] The war was waged both in Algeria and in France, where it led to the collapse of the Fourth Republic in 1958. As specified in the Evian Accord in March 1962, a ceasefire was combined with a general amnesty that prohibited the prosecution of any Algerian nationalist or French soldier, policeman or politician for crimes related to the war. This effectively curtailed debate on Algerian war crimes for many years and meant that before the 1990s, discussion of the war was largely confined to specific lobby groups, such as veterans' organisations.

By contrast, recent years have been marked by the growing importance of the Algerian War in French public debate. This has primarily focused on the repressive methods used by the French, the criminal dimensions of which seem to have been suddenly discovered. Some of the individuals affected are demanding compensation for the trauma caused by their mistreatment. While there is a new concern to understand the processes that led to criminal behaviour in the conduct of the war motivated by anti-racist or human rights perspectives, the Algerian question has not been focused around the 'never again' position that has, for example, characterised Holocaust history. Instead, debates about the war have been concentrated on a series of individual cases or events, through revelations in the press and in the courtroom. The specificity of the French case primarily lies in the way the French state has dealt (or perhaps has failed to deal) with the legacy of a difficult recent past. In contrast to the question of looted Jewish assets and property, issues resulting from the Algerian war were not channelled through a large-scale, authoritative investigating commission. When in the late 1990s, after a long period of silence, French involvement in the Algerian War became a hot topic in the media, this resulted in a series of trials (mostly trials for defamation) which indirectly called the state into question. To some extent unwillingly, historians were then also involved in the matter, not just as individual scholars conducting their own research along the lines that they think are appropriate but as expert witnesses in court and commentators in the media. It is a situation that has raised important ethical questions for French historians, and this chapter will reflect upon the difficulties facing the profession recently.

Vichy and its impact on perceptions of the Algerian War

It is important to understand that these developments took place at a time when the relationship between French historians, government and society had been affected by debates surrounding the Vichy regime and the German occupation of France during the Second World War (1940–44).[2] The debate on Algeria was influenced by this controversy; the two became intertwined and underwent similar stages. The first point of intersection concerned the question of Vichy and the definition of 'crimes against humanity'. In 1987, Jacques Vergès, the lawyer defending the Nazi Klaus Barbie, drew parallels between the actions of the Nazis in France and those of the French in Algeria. The response of the Cour de Cassation (the Supreme Court) was clear: it modified the definition of a crime against humanity by narrowing its application to a crime committed 'in the name of a State practising a policy of political hegemony'. This implied that crimes committed by the French in Algeria could not be defined as crimes against humanity because France was not considered to have been a state practising such a policy. During the trial, Vergès continued to press the comparison, however, arguing that colonialism as a project constituted a policy of political hegemony.[3] Witnesses, including historians, were questioned along that line. At the same time, the historian Pierre Vidal-Naquet, a specialist in ancient Greece who had been active from the very start of the struggle against the use of torture during the Algerian war, argued in an article in *Le Monde* that 'It is obvious that we Frenchmen have committed numerous crimes against humanity in Algeria, of course, and even before that in Indochina and in Madagascar.'[4] He even went so far as to wish that French political and military leaders should have their amnesties annulled so that charges could be brought against them.[5]

The year 1991 marked the thirtieth anniversary of the repression of the Front de Libération Nationale (FLN) boycott of the blackout imposed on Parisian Algerians on 17 October 1961 – a repression that came at the cost of at least dozens of deaths. This occasion prompted several groups – composed mainly of children of Algerian immigrants – to encourage public discussion of the French *devoir de mémoire* over the Algerian War. In 1991–92, the anniversary of the end of the Algerian War resonated with the French, coinciding

The state, the historians and the Algerian War in French memory 161

as it did with the first Gulf War. Public awareness of the anniversary was particularly influenced by a four-part television documentary, 'Les Années Algériennes', broadcast on the public channel. Produced jointly by historian Benjamin Stora and several television directors, it evoked the 'Algerian years' in France between 1954 and 1962. While it did mention the internal struggles of the Algerian nationalists, this documentary was devoted especially to the French experience of the war. In the same way, as the Algerian War resurfaced in French public debate, it was principally the French dimension that was explored.[6]

While the comparison with Vichy had been contained within a fairly contained framework in 1987, it came to national attention ten years later during the trial of Maurice Papon, accused of having organised the deportation of four convoys of Jews from Bordeaux to the death camps while serving as Secretary General of the prefecture of the Gironde between 1942 and 1944. This time, the comparison was posed by the historian Jean-Luc Einaudi, who was called as a witness.[7] Einaudi, author of *The Battle of Paris* (1991), which focused in particular at the events of 17 October 1961, reminded the court that Papon had been serving as the Paris Prefect of Police in 1961, arguing that he bore responsibility for the repression of Algerians in Paris. Although it was far from the trial's main subject, the testimony of this non-professional historian (although Jean-Luc Einaudi is a trained educator, he is the author of several history books on the Algerian War) had important repercussions. His testimony connected Vichy to Algeria through the career of one individual, who had eventually held a ministerial post.[8] This suggested a continuity of men and methods over time, opening the way to a judicial reading of the Algerian War.

A second parallel between Vichy and Algeria raised as a consequence of the Papon trial concerned the official discriminatory practices instituted by the French state: directed at Jews under Vichy (and independent of any German demands), on the one hand, and directed at Algerians on the other. That an authoritarian regime and a Republican regime could undertake similar policies was disconcerting and disturbing. Gérard Noiriel's study, *Les origines républicaines de Vichy* (1999) posed this troubling question for the period preceding the Vichy regime.[9] But the Algerian example was more disturbing because it had occurred after the lessons of Vichy should have been learnt, and during the history of this regime. For the French, it was as though the existence of another France had been revealed. Alongside the traditional republican France, with its values of liberty, brotherhood and equality, there was another, darker, colonial France. Indeed, while the Vichy question faded in the French media and courtrooms following Papon's trial, the Algeria question received increasing attention, particularly from 2000. The primary question raised by Papon's trial, the longest criminal trial in post-war France,[10] was the extent to which an individual could be held responsible for crimes committed as an agent of the state – crimes against humanity, but also, and of central relevance in the case of Algeria, crimes of war. What ultimately was at stake was the state's responsibility for having pursued policies that led to criminal behaviour.

The evolution of official attitudes towards the Algerian War

Under French law, it proved to be difficult to establish the criminal culpability of the state and its individual agents because prosecutions could only be brought for crimes against humanity, which as we have seen was narrowly defined.[11] By 2000, however, there were calls for an official state apology over Algeria. At first, this stemmed less from victims of torture than from other groups with painful memories, in particular Christian veterans, often priests. While at first confined to a small minority, demands grew for a state admission of responsibility. In October 2000 twelve people appealed to the President of the Republic and the Prime Minister to 'condemn the torture that was undertaken [in the name of France] during the Algerian War', attracting press attention for several weeks and attracting many further signatories.[12] In Parliament, Communist MPs relayed this call in vain. The Prime Minister reacted by declaring that it was necessary 'to remember that in dark hours, the institutions of our country failed.'[13] He would not go further than that and refused explicitly to consider any act of collective repentance.[14]

From the beginning, French authorities had refused to characterise the operations they undertook in Algeria as a 'war.' This has had complex legal consequences. Veterans, for example, were awarded honours and decorations that were distinct from those awarded in time of war; likewise, the title of veteran was not even granted them until 1974.[15] Even so, the concept of a war was still not officially acknowledged by the state; this would only come gradually. In 1992 the government had moved forward by not only recognising the status of the individuals involved but also by acknowledging responsibility for them. It was announced that Algerian veterans would be classified as having war-related post-traumatic stress syndrome provided that a line of direct and decisive causality could be established between the imputability of the neurosis and an event that occurred while in service (even if the traumatic event had been underestimated or minimised at the time).[16] Trauma caused by war was being implicitly recognised, opening the doors to compensation. In admitting this, the Government was moving towards an official acknowledgement of responsibility for the war and its consequences. The decree, however, did not quell the uneasiness of many people at the continued official use of term 'operations for the maintenance of order' to designate what they had experienced as warfare. It was as if the government was more comfortable admitting individual histories rather than a collective history. Veterans associations and other groups persistently demanded the official use of the term 'war', which historians as well as the French public had long before adopted. This was finally successful in October 1999, when deputies and senators voted to replace the phrase 'operations for the maintenance of order in North Africa' with 'the Algerian War'. That unanimous decision, however, concealed enormous differences between politicians regarding the events in question. There was not even agreement on the date of the war's end. On the one hand, it was widely assumed to be 19 March 1962, following the signing of the Evian Accords. But many others argued that the thousands of deaths that occurred after the ceasefire made a later date more appropriate. Lobby groups formed along these lines, promoting their alternative interpretations. In January 2002, the secrétaire d'Etat had announced to the veterans that March 19, date of the ceasefire, would become the official anniversary if there was a two-thirds majority vote for it in Parliament. Only 278 deputies, however, voted for that resolution while 204 voted against it. The administration therefore abandoned the idea of proposing a definitive vote to the Senate, which was adjourning, as well as to itself, given the lack of any sufficient consensus.

Considering the emotional re-opening of old wounds and the extraordinary media attention given to the historical trials in the past two decades, it is striking to observe how both governments and deputies have failed over the years to take the initiative on the Algerian War issue, waiting instead to be forced when public opinion has grown too strong to ignore. The official policy – of both the right and the left – on this matter seems to continue in the spirit of the original amnesty laws: to forget the past in order to go on living together, regardless of whether that applies to the Algerians or the French, the former French deserters, the former members of the Organisation armée secrète (OAS), or even the generals behind the failed putsch of April 1961. But by trying to draw a line under the past without any attempt formally to confront the war crimes committed during the Algerian War, the state imposed a silence that became heavier as demands for recognition – and by implication, for reparation – emerged. This silence on the Algerian War enabled equally sensitive questions about other aspects of colonial history to be avoided, questions that were particularly pressing for the descendants of the populations that had come from the former colonies.

Trials, experts and witnesses: history judged

The failure to appoint a commission to investigate these matters meant that the courtroom became the primary site where questions could be posed about the past, providing an outlet for political protest.[17] Two types of trials in particular played this role: the criminal trial for crimes against humanity (for which the Papon trial was emblematic) and trials for defamation. It was only in this context that the state could be held to account, and forced to respond to political questions that were biased by the judicial process. The past few years have seen several trials in particular that involved the Algerian question.

In the first, professional historians were not directly involved. In an action brought in 1998 in the pension court by an Algerian, Mohamed Garne, against the French state following his discovery at the age of 30 that he had been conceived as a result of rape committed by French soldiers. Expert psychiatric testimony attested that Garne had been deeply traumatised by this discovery, and supported his claim for compensation. In a detailed report, the psychiatrist concluded that the French state was 'the only identifiable father of Mohamed Garne'. A highly regarded specialist in war-related post-traumatic stress syndrome, he had served as a military physician in Algeria at the time, and his judgments were clearly shaped by these memories. Judges in this process also made interventions based on their own historical interpretations, taken entirely in the absence of expert historical opinion.[18]

The second trial was a libel action brought by the extreme right wing politician Jean-Marie Le Pen against the historian Pierre Vidal-Naquet in 1999. Le Pen, who had at one time publicly acknowledged having practised torture during his time in Algeria in 1957, later denied it when the allegations were used against him when he became a presidential candidate in 1974. The action was one of a series of suits brought by Le Pen over the years, and followed the publication of Vidal-Naquet's memoirs. In the courtroom, the historian and his lawyer cited the words of the young deputy in 1957 and 1962. The judges, who were not required to pronounce on the substance but instead on the defamatory nature of the offending words, ruled that one could not consider oneself defamed for actions about which one had otherwise prided oneself. The judgement otherwise avoided ruling on Le Pen's past record; it was ruled that the use of the term 'torturer' needed to be discussed, not within the context of a libel trial, but rather in the broader context of 'ethics, the debate of ideas, political discussion that should be permitted in a democratic society'.[19] Thus, while supporting the historian, the court was unwilling to take responsibility for making a historical judgment.

This problem was even more evident during the third trial, the libel action brought by Maurice Papon against Jean-Luc Einaudi in 1998. The former sued the latter for following an article that appeared in *Le Monde* in which the historian claimed – as he had in his original testimony – that there had been 'a massacre perpetrated by the police force acting under the orders of Maurice Papon' in Paris in 1961.[20] Public attention focused on the evidence of these events, and a ruling was anxiously awaited. In court, the deputy prosecutor accepted that the repression of the Algerian demonstration had constituted a 'massacre' but criticised Einaudi's 'unsupported personal judgment' that the police had been acting on Papon's orders. He argued that Papon 'was neither the only, nor the person most responsible' and that one must not forget 'the murderers themselves' or the 'intermediary hierarchy' of the police. This was not accepted by the court, which on 26 March 1999 discharged Einaudi on the grounds that he had acted in good faith. Again, the court had avoided ruling on the issue of responsibility. However, as discussed above, the recognition that there had been a 'massacre' marked the end of the long official silence on the events of 1961. It was not until October 2001 that the new Paris city government placed a plaque on the Pont Saint Michel 'to the memory of the Algerians, victims of the bloodstained repression of a peaceful demonstration,' and this happened only after heated debate and numerous modifications of the text, carefully omitting any indication of the authors of the repression. No additional official acknowledgement was made.[21]

By default, the courtrooms were thus the only place with a national audience where responsibility for the excesses of the repression of Algerian nationalism between 1954 and 1962 has been debated. For the defamation trials especially, the judges had to come to an understanding of the historical reality in order to rule on whether the contested statements were libellous. Historians were thus required in the courtroom, but they were convened as witnesses and faced the same difficulties as those confronting the historians involved in Papon's criminal trial. Their role was ambiguous. They were not official experts, because they were denied access to items in the trial dossier, and they were not witnesses, because they had not been present during the events under question. They were summoned by the court to tell the 'truth' in a context that by its nature excluded the process of historical interpretation or its consideration.[22]

The magistrates have been bewildered by historians who refuse to testify, as it seems reasonable to call upon an historian when expert advice is needed in order to evaluate controversial statements regarding a past historical event. It is however, undeniable that these trials have compromised the scholarly status of the historian by placing him or her on the same plane as other witnesses. Judicial rulings replace historical judgements. The law imposes its own distorting norms on the past according to criteria that are foreign to those of historical research. This was especially evident during the trial of General Aussaresses, for example. He and his editor were sued in 2001 by human rights campaigners, who alleged that the certain statements in his memoirs about the Algerian war constituted 'complicity in apologising for crimes of war'. The action was essentially a political trial by proxy of the illegal methods used in Algeria that had been defended by the general in his book, and it was intended not only as an opportunity morally to condemn him, but also as a means to bring public attention to those methods. The only historian willing to testify was Pierre Vidal-Naquet, whose militant views were long-established. Others felt that the political use of the legal process was not in accordance with the role of the professional historian. By testifying, one would be participating in a distorted process, whose real objectives lay outside the courtroom. This was confirmed when the trial concluded with a condemnation of his apologetic approach to the use of torture. It was not the final ruling itself, but the way that the trial had unfolded which was the real story of this episode.

By contrast the libel trial of Ighilahriz and Pouillot V. Schmitt, brought by two actors from the war against General Maurice Schmitt for statements made on television regarding them and in which he had called into question the veracity of their testimony. In this case, the burden of proof lay with the complainants, while General Schmitt was able to call witnesses as well as to consult documents deposited in the trial dossier. One of his witnesses was General Faivre, a man who has spent many years in the archives in his efforts to defend former Algerian 'harkis' (non-professional soldiers), and who was called in his capacity as a 'historian'. In the absence of a professional historian, there was no competent authority in the courtroom to analyse historical evidence provided. The court ruled in favour of the complainants.

This case raises an ironic result of the media attention surrounding the issue of torture. On the one hand, the focus on specific events or issues that occurred during the war was unsatisfactory because it was divorced from the wider historical context. The paradox for the historian was that defenders of the use of repression and notably torture typically demanded that the wider context should be taken into account as a means of justifying the use of extreme measures. In an atmosphere of moral condemnation, calls for an understanding of the historical context became associated with the defence of brutal behaviour. Media coverage on the other hand, was based on only a few cases and individuals. One can see here how difficult it was for historians to make their work understood. Legal actions have served all who wanted to believe that war crimes were perpetrated by only a minority of individuals, by reducing the war to a series of particular events. The personalisation of the Algerian War through court action, has displaced public attention from the general to the particular, and in the process the broader political issues surrounding the war have been lost sight of. Even when appointed as an officially approved expert witness, the historian will only serve individual histories, and it is questionable whether that should be the historian's most important social role.

The ambiguous position of historians in these trials – dealing with a past that is sufficiently close so that witnesses from that period are still alive, but too distant for the judges to feel they are competent in every respect – is inevitable. Especially in a case like that of the Algerian War, where the past is so fiercely contested, the process is hampered by the absence of scholarly authorities or agreed professional standards for witnesses called as 'historical experts'.

Access to archives, the media and the historians' role

Following the model used for the Vichy question, historians of the Algerian War have been granted selective but expanded access to the withheld archives from the period. For a period as recent as that of the Algerian War, French law governing access to archives is clear. Public documents are not open until thirty years have past since the date of their creation, corresponding in fact to the last date of the period considered, in this case 1962.[23] Therefore it was not until 1992 that files on Algeria began to become available. Since then the Algerian War has been the subject of more serious historical research. Earlier, historians had produced important works, but archival access changed things considerably.[24] Where public archives are concerned then, the historiography of the Algerian War is relatively young. The number of theses and scholarly works produced using public archives is small, although growing, and the number of university researchers established in this area of specialty is also limited, in France as in other countries. On this point, Algeria differs from Vichy, which has a large and established scholarly literature. The burden on historians of Algeria was therefore heavier by comparison.

Access to archives remains, however, a sensitive subject. The 1979 Act introduced a sixty-year rule for files relating to private life or national security. Researchers had to seek special permission to gain access in such circumstances, and until recently the rules governing the granting of such permissions remained vague and arbitrary. This policy encouraged conspiracy theories and an atmosphere of distrust. For example, in 1996 the National Archives were rocked by controversy concerning accusations over the existence of a supposedly withheld 'Jewish file of the Prefecture of Police'.[25] The government finally responded to this by deciding to grant general rather than individual access, following a review of withheld files from the period of the Occupation.

Strengthened by this precedent, the government thus reacted relatively quickly when the pressure began to release withheld files relating to the Algerian War. This was partly due to lingering public suspicion that a refusal to grant access to the archives could only be explained by a deliberate political decision to hide the truth – although, as professional historians are aware, the archives are more likely to raise questions than to give simple answers. In 1998 Einaudi complained publicly that the Prefecture of Police had refused him access to key files relating to his defence. In response to Einaudi's complaints the Prime Minister announced in a May 1999 communiqué, the government's desire to 'facilitate historical research on the demonstration organised by the FLN on 17 October 1961 and more generally on the acts committed in countering French Muslims during 1961'. In a limited gesture, he acknowledged the necessity of widening the scope to the entire year of 1961 in order to illuminate the events of 17 October, revelations surrounding which had proved shocking to French public opinion.[26] The willingness to be open was genuine but cautious, in the sense that the decision applied only to 1961.

The day of Einaudi's testimony, the Minister of Culture,[27] Catherine Trautmann, had affirmed her willingness to open files concerning the 17 October 1961 repression. The Minister of the Interior had added, speaking before the National Assembly, that he would ask for a similar undertaking from the Paris Prefecture of Police, which Einaudi had particularly complained about. There was a clumsy attempt to manipulate this process when, at an early stage, two officials (an honorary advocate general of the Cour de Cassation and a Conseiller d'Etat) were instructed to report on what was contained first, in the Archives de la Justice and second, in the Ministry of the Interior's archives. They were not aided by any historian and rendered their conclusions in terms of factual contents, proposing an analysis that was completely devoid of any deep understanding of the historical context of the documents. Both reports were released to the press and presented as the first official unveiling of secret archives, even though several months before a daily newspaper had tried to force the matter by publishing pages from the archives mentioning French Muslims found dead in the Seine in October 1961.[28] Nevertheless the commitment had been made to permit greater access to the archives. How well did this process work for historians, who were simultaneously being confronted by growing public demands for 'the facts' regarding the Algerian War? Between the government, which was relatively cautious, and the increasingly feverish public speculation, historians found themselves constantly being pulled in conflicting ways.

From 2000, the increasingly emotional temperature of French discussions on Algeria following revelations about the widespread use of torture during the war underlined this problem. The controversy over torture during the Algerian War was launched by the daily newspaper, *Le Monde*, and became the editors' battle horse, as explained below. Declaring an intention to confront an historical taboo and to reveal the 'truth', interviews with witnesses became frequent, accompanied by predictably sensational headlines. The media frenzy began with the testimony of an Algerian female victim splashed on the front page of Le Monde, a few days after the official visit to France of the Algerian president in June 2000. This campaign spread to other media sources, and soon held national attention. Historians were not silent while this was happening, but scholarly views were largely overtaken by the weight and forms of this news coverage. Historians were invited in the press to provide expert opinion. Historical analysis was increasingly treated as just another subjective resource. The papers favoured dramatic witness accounts to balanced analysis, and polemic to the complicated unveiling of reality.

Historians lost control of the process, and failed to convey an appropriate degree of methodological professionalism and scholarly rigour. The role of the historian was made more difficult because recent research on Algeria and war crimes has been controversial within the Academy. Historians of Algeria have been accused of being ideologically motivated and biased in their approach, and it is true that debate has tended to slide from reasoned scholarship into politically motivated trials or to be based on the personal experience of some academics. The Algerian War has proved to be an emotional topic for contemporary historians as well as for the French public. In the media, historians were pressured to take positions on topics outside of their scholarly competence. This was difficult enough, but became even more disturbing as historians became involved in the inevitable courtroom battles that followed, as we have seen. The persistence of such stories in the news put pressure on politicians to respond in some way. In the Assembly, increasing public concern posed an embarrassing political problem that was not taken frankly into account by many deputies. French Communist Party MPs were the only parliamentary group to propose to a commission of inquiry, and the idea was not pursued. Meanwhile, both Prime Minister Lionel Jospin and the President Jacques Chirac proposed their vision of history. Despite the wide differences in their use of words and factual presentation, they were in agreement about the need to minimize the significance of the acts of torture, dismissing them as marginal actions, and thus refusing any consideration of them as part of a systematic policy of repression.

The Prime Minister was first to make his views known, stressing the necessity of allowing historians to do their work: 'The government, as it has done in the past three years with regard to access to archives of the Second World War or documents related to the events of Otober 1961, is ready to support scientific and historical work.'[29] This was an initiative of an entirely different magnitude than previously conceded. In an April 2001 Report responding to the introduction of a right of appeal to a special commission for those denied access to official records, Jospin included a section on 'access to public archives relating to the Algerian War'.[30] This responded point by point to various problems: the length of time it took for a decision to be made once a request was submitted, the reluctance of some agencies to grant access, the absence or closure of catalogues for many significant collections, and the way that control over documents was jealously guarded by services which were slow to hand files over to the archives. Most significantly the Prime Minister set an objective of putting certain collections on an equally open footing as those from the Occupation. This was certainly a step forward for historians, but it was first and foremost a response to media pressure. This is clear, even in the convoluted preamble:

> The return to the events connected to the Algerian War, such as the recent discussions that have developed on this subject, show the level of interest that has undertaken to see that the facts corresponding to this period receive the illumination of historical research. In fact, only such an approach, with the exigencies of the rigour and historical method that are inherent to it, will permit giving these events a clear and impartial understanding.[31]

While respecting historical methodology, Jospin saw it as the historians' role to pacify public feeling by supplying authoritative answers on the conduct of the Algerian War.

The subsequent presidential communiqué of 4 May 2001 was even more explicit, stating that it was necessary for 'historians [to] be in a position to bring the truth to light rapidly on all questions of responsibility by having access to the archives from the period' and that 'the entire truth must be [revealed] on these unjustifiable acts.[32] The President had decided to endorse popular calls to 'establish who was responsible' for acts that were no longer dismissed as the 'acts of a minority' because they had been accepted as morally 'unjustifiable'.[33]

Epilogue

Essentially, Jospin and Chiraq had invoked history as a means of buying time while the furore ran its course in the news. This recourse to historians permitted the government to signal a willingness to account for the past while completely dispensing themselves of any need to make public statements regarding it. It was a dilatory and hypocritical response, for the political authorities seemed to pass along to historians – the 'professionals' of the past – the responsibility of telling 'the truth' about French history. In reality, however, politicians remain happy to pronounce on this past when it suits them to do so. What they did not wish to do at all costs was to accept responsibility on behalf of the state which might entail a reparations obligation that could set a precedent with almost unlimited application to other controversies. This was particularly true of torture allegations; the Prime Minister has continued officially to ignore the historical scholarship on this subject that would permit one to question the argument that the use of torture was but a minority activity.[34] Other groups and individuals have continued to speak out on the question of responsibility, and it is difficult to know how historians should respond to this challenge, and in particular how to convey the subtleties of historiographical debate to a public that wants black and white answers. Because narrative understanding is considered to be partisan, it is difficult to imagine that it would be possible even to agree on appropriate historians to appoint to a commission, should there be the political will to do so. Debate has hinged upon morally loaded terms like 'honour', 'good' and 'evil'. In the case of the Algerian War, as with comparable controversies in other parts of the world, it has proved to be difficult to come to terms with the reality that torture was condoned in a democratic state, because the past is still too contemporary to contemplate with detachment.[35] It sometimes looks as if 'never again' is put on a forgotten agenda, and that the lessons of the Algerian War will continue to be ignored.

Notes

1 I would like to thank Judith Miller (Emory University) who has been so helpful with the translation of this chapter.
2 See H. Rousso, *Le syndrôme de Vichy, 1944–198...* (Paris, 1987); B. Stora, *La gangrène et l'oubli* (Paris, 1991) and R. Branche, 'Désirs de vérités, volontés d'oublis: la torture pendant la guerre d'Algérie', *Cahiers Français*, 303 (July-August 2001), 70–6.
3 *Chronique du procès Barbie pour servir la mémoire* (Paris, 1988).
4 *Le Monde* (16 June 1987).
5 He added that in Algeria, France had not committed the crime of genocide – foreseeing a change in French criminal law that would take place in 1994. In that year, the concept of 'crimes against humanity' was severed from the 1987 understanding of 'a state practising a policy of ideological hegemony', and the crime of genocide was then distinguished from crime against humanity.
6 This chapter does not attempt to discuss Algerian perspectives, which have been largely excluded from recent French public debate.
7 During the same period, historians had also been working in historical commissions including the commission on Paul Touvier and the Catholic church (R. Rémond (ed.), *Paul Touvier et l'Eglise – rapport de la commission historique instituée par le cardinal Decourtray* (Paris, 1992)); the 'Jewish file' commission (R. Rémond (chairman), *Le 'fichier' juif': rapport de la commission au Premier ministre*, Paris, 1996)); and more recently, the mission on the spoliation of Jews in France (commission Matteoli).
8 Maurice Papon was the Minister of the Budget from 1978 to 1981.
9 G. Noiriel, *Les origines républicaines de Vichy* (Paris, 1999).
10 From 8 October 1997 to 2 April 1998.
11 On the specificity of French state and administration, see M.-O. Baruch and

V. Duclert (eds), *Serviteurs de l'Etat* (Paris, 2000). See also, in this book, C. Laborde, 'Penser l'Etat en Grande-Bretagne', pp. 69–82.

12 The appeal appeared in *L'Humanité* on 31 October 2000. The twelve signatories were: Henri Alleg, former editor of *Alger républicain*, author of *La Question* (Paris, 1958); Josette Audin, the wife of Maurice Audin; Simone de Bollardière, the widow of général Pâris de Bollardière; Nicole Dreyfus, lawyer; Noël Favrelière, recalled reservist, deserter; Gisèle Halimi, lawyer; Alban Liechti, recalled reservist, draft dodger; Madeleine Rebérioux, historian, secretary of the Audin Committee; Laurent Schwartz, mathematician, president of the Audin Committee; Germaine Tillion, ethnographer, resistance fighter, author, notably of *L'Algérie en 1957* (Paris, 1957); Jean-Pierre Vernant, historian, resistance fighter; Pierre Vidal-Naquet, historian, author, notably of *La torture dans la République. Essai d'histoire et de politiques contemporaines* (1954–1962) (Paris, 1972). The debate attracted much attention, and was fed by the daily Communist paper *L'Humanité* and by *Le Monde* during the two months that followed.

13 The remarks were made in a speech at the annual dinner of the Conseil Représentatif des Institutions Juives de France on 4 November 2000. His declaration echoed that of President Chirac who, several months after his election, on 16 July 1995, had declared with regard to the round up of the Vel d'Hiv and the participation of the French State in the deportation of Jews: There are moments that are difficult to evoke 'because these black hours stain our history forever and are an offence to our history and our traditions.'

14 Jospin's exact words were: 'La torture en Algérie, les exactions qui ont pu avoir lieu à l'occasion de ce conflit colonial, ne relèvent pas d'un acte de repentance collective mais de la recherche de la vérité'.

15 Law of 9 December 1974. In 1982, a new law improved the conditions under which a combatant's card could be accorded.

16 *Journal officiel* of 12 January 1992. On this decree, see L. Crocq, *Les traumatismes psychiques de guerre* (Paris, 1999), pp. 343–9, and J. Marblé, 'Le décret du 10 janvier 1992 est-il applicable?', *Annales médico-psychologiques*, 156: 1 (1998), 63–6.

17 A. Garapon, 'La demande de responsabilité', in *Le crime contre l'humanité. Mesure de la responsabilité?* (Paris, 1998).

18 It was notably the case when the court corrected the expression 'concentration camps' used by the expert to designate the consolidation camps in Algeria and added: 'to meet the needs of the so-called policy of pacification, large portions of the Algerian civil population had been gathered in these camps called "consolidation camps" (characterised not without some excess as "concentration camps", a term with a specific connotation); camps where the living conditions were precarious and humanity and compassion were largely absent.' The court had thus made its own historical interpretation.

19 *Le Monde* (15 September 1999).

20 'Octobre 1961: pour la vérité, enfin', *Le Monde* (20 May 1998).

21 Several months later, in March 2002, the mayor of Paris unveiled the plaque on the memorial that the capital had decided to dedicate to its soldiers, dead or missing, in North Africa from 1952 to 1962.

22 That ambiguity concerning the status of the discourse involved pushed Henry Rousso, during the Bordeaux trial, to refuse to testify. He explained his refusal in *La hantise du passé* (Paris, 1998), translated as *The Haunting Past: History, Memory, and Justice in Contemporary France* (Philadelphia, 2002).
23 Law no. 79–18 of 3 January 1979.
24 This only applied to the French historiography based on French documents. See R. Branche, *La guerre d'Algérie: une histoire apaisée?* (Paris, 2005).
25 In 1996, an inquiry commission presided by the historian René Rémond determined that there was no official file but instead an assortment of disparate pieces of information.
26 Circular of 4 May 1999 and the communiqué of 5 May.
27 In France, public archives are under the authority of the Ministry of Culture, with the exception of the two ministries that hold their archives independently, the Ministries of Defence and of Foreign Affairs.
28 *Libération* (22 October 1997). Pages from the register of the Parquet de Paris of 30 October 1961. They were leaked to the journalist by an archivist.
29 National Assembly, 28 November 2001.
30 On archives in France, S. Cœuré and V. Duclert, *Les archives* (Paris, 2001).
31 Circular of 13 April 2001 that appeared in the *Journal officiel* of 26 April 2001.
32 Communiqué of the President of the Republic, 4 May 2001, published in *Le Monde* on 6–7 May 2001. President Chirac had also reacted in the autumn but took a more limited position than his Prime Minister, most notably on the question of the archives.
33 I permit myself to indicate that the works of Pierre Vidal-Naquet as well as my own doctoral thesis defended in December 2000 had already illuminated to an extent the question as to who was responsible.
34 R. Branche, *La torture et l'armée pendant la guerre d'Algérie* (Paris, 2001: forthcoming, translated and published by Nebraska University Press, 2007).
35 See the disputes over the occupied territories, terrorism and the Israeli methods, or even the underlying themes of the speeches that followed September 11, notably in the United States, where reputable newscasters on the influential American television show on CBS, 'Sixty Minutes' – astonishingly – even interviewed General Aussaresses as an expert on the 'war against terrorism' and torture. General Aussaresses was presented on the show as the former chief of the French secret service in Algeria, having 'tortured dozens of presumed terrorists' (*Libération*, 23 January 2002).

10

The German historians' debate about the upheavals of 1989

Martin Sabrow

Caesurae are the lifeblood of contemporary history.[1] In Germany there arose, following defeat in 1918, a preoccupation with the causes of the War within the academic establishment, which was used as a political weapon by those demanding revisions in the terms of Versailles, and received substantial public attention. However, it was the cataclysm of 1945 and the need to come to terms with the twelve years under a barbaric regime which, in West and in East Germany, led to the establishment of a recognised professional sub-discipline: Contemporary History, and which has since with increasing intensity become the focal point of the political culture in Germany. The downfall of the SED regime and the end of the Cold War in 1989/90 temporarily bestowed upon the subject an orientation function, making the personalities, work, and institutional set-up of the GDR historians' profession a subject of passionate debate and influencing the internal adjustments required to unite the previously divided halves of the country after 1989.

My contribution here first tries to clarify the reasons for the exceptionally strong attention which historiography enjoyed as a discipline in the process of German unification until the mid-1990s in the public sphere far outside the walls of academia. Secondly, I will address the much less observed phenomenon that the attention in the second half of the 1990s has, in contrast to studies of the first German dictatorship, diminished and today the history of the GDR and its nemesis in 1989 is in danger of becoming a little-visited sideshow in the historiographical circus. In so doing I will pay particular attention to the repercussions arising from the contemporary historian adopting the roles of participant in political events and object of his own analysis. My contention is that this role identification of the contemporary historian not only distinguishes the debate about the events of 1989 from other controversies in contemporary history after 1945 in Germany and Europe, but also obstructs the objective reality of the extraordinary historical and political culture of the 'artificial state' established within the borders of

The German historians' debate about the upheavals of 1989 175

the GDR before its demise, and it prevents a proper understanding of the profundity of the upheaval in 1989.

Peculiarities of the upheaval debate

Whereas other debates on German historiography such as the 'Fischer Controversy' in the 1960s on the German responsibility for the outbreak of the First World War or, thirty years later, the debate about the crimes of the German *Wehrmacht* in the Second World War were concerned with events that happened almost two generations back, the debate about 1989 not only began there and then, but was also affected in its course by historians: a scandalous contribution to the SED organ *Neues Deutschland* on the infallibility of the KPD from the pens of two 'cadre historians' of the SED Party College in May 1989[2] eroded the legitimacy of the SED state and was too much for some prominent GDR historians who, between July and December 1989, made cautious statements distancing themselves from the regime. The call for the foundation of the *Unabhängiger Historikerverband* [UHV: Independent Historians' Association] by protesting young GDR historians on 10 January 1990[3] with its condemnation of the prevailing historiology as an 'inedible mash of lies and factoids' set a signal which reached far beyond the profession and strongly influenced the political handling of the East German profession's heritage. Likewise, historians significantly influenced the opinion of the German *Bundestag*, through two parliamentary inquiries into the presentation of the second German dictatorship to which they contributed reports, expertise and opinion.

Moreover, never before had a generation of historians faced such a massive challenge in passing judgment on themselves. Far more than their predecessors after 1945, the GDR body of historians was after 1989 confronted with the demand to describe a change which had existentially affected every single one of its members in their professional careers and their professional self-conception, and to account for themselves, often in public, on their past actions as historians. At the same time in Western Germany, a fierce dispute broke out amongst those contemporary historians and political scientists who were engaged in GDR analysis, for instance on the questions 'Why did the old GDR research fail?' and whether the profession had submitted to the political zeitgeist in the years prior to 1989 to an unacceptable extent.[4] The topic is also characterised by an unusually marked lack of scholarly distance. For former GDR historians and others, at the time of German unification and the immediate aftermath, the battle for the analytical autonomy and hegemony of judgment went hand in hand with the battle to safeguard one's institutional position and consequently one's social position. The opening of GDR files, but not those of the FRG, the enduring wrangling over the law on

Stasi files, the many attempts to gain non-academic influence on the work of research institutes of contemporary history in unified Germany[5] – these and many other examples show vividly the diversity of interests, overlapping at times, which make the subject of '1989' seem sometimes like a case study in co-operation, but at other times a demonstration of the strained relationship between political, professional integrity and historical truth.

The fact that in the coming to terms with the upheavals of 1989 scholarly historisation and public politisation were intertwined in a unique manner was initially not felt to be a problem by all parties involved. 'As a historian I only felt obliged to comment on political questions at a time of upheaval' explained Joachim Petzold, a GDR historian who became well known for works on fascism and the Weimar Republic, in his autobiography published in 2000.[6] Also the inquiry commission of the German *Bundestag* on the 'Critical review of history and consequences of SED dictatorship in Germany' was happy to describe itself as a body in which 'political processes for the formation of opinion and scientific processes for finding the truth intermingle in a peculiar manner'.[7] Eventually, even East German historians who were close to the civil rights movement professed unselfconsciously to a scholarly ideal which included political partisanship as a matter of course and that looked down, not without derision, on the erudite in their ivory towers who did not see the writing on the wall.[8]

The question of the historians' engagement with the upheavals of 1989 is complex. It simultaneously refers to a historiographical problem of interpretation and a political task of accomplishment; it includes the actions during the upheavals as well as the reflection on the events. Furthermore, it involves a train of events without a clear beginning and end. The beginnings may be extended backwards, so that for example the political unreliability of an FDJ group of young historians at the *Akademie der Wissenschaften der DDR* in 1978 leads in a direct line to the foundation of the *Unabhängiger Historikerverband* in 1990; and it may be seen as continuing to the present day where the enduring debate about the involvement of the historical profession with National Socialism prior to 1945 can appear to be a consequence of the debate about the role of GDR historians in the SED system. Research on this latter issue has not yet been completed and therefore is not included in this volume.

The paradox of storm and calm

These two features need to be borne in mind when explaining the historiographical process, that is to say the sharp contrast between the breadth and intensity with which the debate about 1989 was conducted at times, and its quiet subsistence in the present day. In the early days, members of the UHV characterised their colleagues who had supported the regime as 'a special breed of armchair strategists who delivered the historical legitimisation for Wall, the Stasi, and the order to shoot for border guards';[9] another author seriously asked whether Mnemosyne had been prescribed 'the Pill',[10] and a third one entitled his study on East German historians 'Party Workers at the Historical Battlefront'.[11] Mirroring this was the dispute about the 'failure' of those western historians who were allegedly so enamoured with détente that they ignored the reality. This side also had its share of polemics and accusations, such as Jens Hacker's list of 'palliators and abettors' of the SED dictatorship amongst his colleagues or the 'analyses of a delusional landscape' of GDR research before 1989.[12] Even the *Evangelische Akademie Berlin* thought it appropriate in the first half of the 1990s to pose the question of who ought to and should be allowed to research GDR history in the future;[13] and even the more level-headed representatives of the trade such as Wolfgang J. Mommsen or Jürgen Kocka complained about 'intellectual colonisation' and 'disgraceful reproaches of the old boys' network' or, as Rainer Eckert anxiously asked the question: '[Are we] coming to terms with the past or is the past overcoming us?'[14]

The historians' contribution to the upheavals of 1989, that unusual mixture of action and reflection, reached the wider intellectual and political public with a rare degree of intensity and polarisation. Two opposing camps quickly became apparent under the banners of accusation and exoneration, and remained more or less in place for the five years from 1990 until 1994, on one side pursuing normative-accusatory patterns of valuation and on the other emphatic-qualifying ones with sometimes apologetic tendencies. In the accusatory camp were a number of younger, mostly East German historians who were close to or members of the UHV and, as victims of political repression or new to the profession, were untainted by political or professional concessions to the SED regime. These were augmented by some colleagues who had defied the impositions of the 'contagious state' as marginalised 'niche historians'.[15] On the other side stood the many established colleagues who had represented the GDR historiology system in its multiple facets in various levels of the hierarchy, and who reacted to the collapse of the outer and inner frame of their dealing with the past with a multitude of conceivable attitudes ranging between pitiless self-questioning and unperturbed self-affirmation. There was a third group, made up of German and international historians, whose engagement with the debate oscillated between participatory observation and active participation. They were called on by both East German camps as expert witnesses in presenting their cases, and occasionally played a double role, combining interest and insight via retrospective accusations of collaboration and prospective reproaches for colonisation. Initially their qualified stock-taking of the changed circumstances of the subject met with comparatively little interest.[16] Finally, an inward quarrel *sui generis* was conducted by the West German GDR research as an independent academic discipline, which, after the end of the East German partial state was asked why it had not foreseen the downfall of SED rule, but instead had propagated an interpretation model according to modernisation and convergence theories, which had been disavowed by historical reality in a very dramatic way.[17]

Notwithstanding this crude polarisation or perhaps because of it, contemporary history achieved the unofficial status of a leading discipline in the Federal Republic in the years after 1989. The demise of the GDR coincided with a period in German life that was increasingly conscious of recent history, a phenomenon described by Hermann Lübbe as *Sündenstolz* or 'pride of sin', where the principle of 'reconciliation through truth' replaced the previous policy of 'integration through silence [about the past]'.[18] It is surprising then that in the second half of the 1990s the two opposing camps appeared to merge almost fully into a third camp where antagonism was replaced by professional communication. At the same time they began to disappear from the wider public arena, not entirely but to a great extent. Clearly, both phenomena are closely linked. Whereas outside the academic community two different perceptions of history seem to have evolved, with different value structures on either side of the old East and West divide, a converse development has taken place within the academic community. Regardless of lingering theoretical and methodical differences, the former adversaries shifted themselves quite harmoniously into the large base camp of a reflective historisation, at least in their pretence to insight. Here, openly apologetic voices as well as the shrill attacks of old on the new formation of the old boys' network no longer have a place within the heart of the profession, but appear clearly as fringe views.[19] Meanwhile, the field of historical theory and methodology is also ploughed with academic placidity where such grave questions as the character of the communist dictatorship or the options and limits of its comparative investigation are being dealt with.[20]

The progressive reconciliation within the profession went along with a progressive devaluation of its subject matter outside; that is to say there was a great diminution in the public prominence that the *querelles allemandes* about the place of the GDR in German history had formerly attracted. One decade after the GDR's demise, a former GDR historian need not have feared that his old scripts would give rise to new reprovals, because the daily press did not print exposing articles of this type anymore; and it did not constitute a reputation-damaging self-denunciation anymore if an East German historian had a photograph of himself as 'flag carrier on the occasion of the Second SED Party Conference in 1952' in his autobiography.[21] Even the crucial area of contact with the State Security could be handled autobiographically with sober dispassion, giving little clue as to how explosive revelations or suspicions of former activities as an IM (*Inoffizieller Mitarbeiter*: unofficial associate) would previously have been seen in the 1990s.[22]

After the turn of the century, the ostracism of large parts of the East German historians' body from the professional discourse seemed to some outside observers so sinister that it demanded redress.[23] Personal animosities might have outlasted the change of the German-German zeitgeist, but they should not obscure the fact that the old antagonisms are history. Today one can find, as an encyclopaedia that was published in 2002 on parties and organisations in the GDR testifies,[24] essays by former civil rights activists as a matter of course in publications by the PDS and institutions linked to it. Similarly, the critical review of GDR history is promoted by research groups whose publications range from the rather conservative *Jahrbuch für Extremismusforschung* to the booklets of the PDS-linked trust 'Helle Panke'.[25]

The debate about 1989 in the politico-cultural field

How can the paradox of storm and calm be explained that was the remarkable change in historians' dealing with the upheavals of 1989? One has to keep in mind that the dynamism of the debate about '1989' is fed by the interplay of action-orientated and insight-orientated factors. First of all, there are obvious historic-political and politico-cultural reasons for the excitement and aggressiveness of the disputes that broke out in 1990, which transformed historians in East and West into scholars at odds. The emotionally charged atmosphere is primarily explainable by the fact that professional historisation and scientific-political evaluation clashed, the *argumenta ad rem* was by the nature of the debate also *argumenta ad personam*. The discussion about historical truth became at the same time a discussion about the truthfulness of historians.

The complex western-eastern division meant that the double task of scholarly research and securing political patronage was prey to those seeking to settle old accounts. Most notably this was demonstrated by two headlines in the *Frankfurter Allgemeine*, which had given substantial column inches to a campaign against the *Forschungsschwerpunkt Zeithistorische Studien*, founded in 1992 on the recommendation of the Science Council to centralise the positively evaluated research projects of a number of East German historians. 'Inquisitors on the sloth farm' and 'The Bielefeld Way' introduced attacks by two East German members of the UHV, denigrating both the West German notables associated with the Bielefeld School and East German notables tainted by association with the cultural politics of Walter Ulbricht, known as the 'Bitterfeld Way'.[26]

It was not so much the protagonists themselves who were responsible for the wide publicity of this highly charged debate up to 1993/1994, but more the resonance of the historical-cultural sounding board on which they articulated themselves. The public arena was, however, at this time still largely divided between East and West. For the public in the West, the debate on 1989 occurred at a time when society had a newfound sensibility in relation to the previously unmentioned past and 'second guilt' of Ralph Giordano. The speech of Federal President Richard von Weizsäcker in 1985 on 5 May marking it as a Day of Liberation, the Historians' Dispute of 1986/1987, the peculiar speech on the fiftieth Anniversary of the 1938 Pogrom against the Jews by Philipp Jenniger, president of the Bundestag who was subsequently forced to resign, were all milestones in the epochal transition from, broadly speaking, national pride to guilt pride and a society that had learnt to rate the memory of the victims higher than the integrity of the perpetrators. The debate about '1989' was fuelled by the belief that history could convey warnings and help to avoid repeating the mistakes of the past by exposing Stalin's henchmen where the parents' generation had failed to expose Hitler's henchmen – to the detriment of the democratic integrity of the country.

For the public in the East of the re-uniting Germany, other factors played a more important role, namely the suitability of the historians' debate for proxy outrage. Alongside the public uproar about the bigwig privileges of the SED leaders who had preached water and enjoyed wine and video in their dachas, the scandalous agitation about SED historians who had systematically betrayed themselves, their colleagues, and the public through the creation of selective narratives and concerted falsification of facts had a purgative effect: it permitted the public to distance itself from an unloved, but still experienced GDR past on the road to externalisation, and from this necessity there arose a remarkably unreflective narrow lead of historisation and moralisation: 'The upright powers are largely gathered in the UHV and have the moral competence to write, after decades of historiography to the court, the true picture of the GDR – as it really was.'[27]

Finally, in East and West there emerged the same underdog phenomenon that can also be encountered in other historians' debates: the desire to see those historians perceived to be powerful made feeble, to drag the cardinals of the profession to the confessional with the lever of media attention. At times, the debate about the failure of the GDR historians was led by political scandalisation. Examples are the workings of the Gauck Commission and the daily press reports revealing suspected co-operation with the GDR State Security[28] or the publishing by the media of incriminating excerpts of historic accounts of GDR historians,[29] and also the attempt to discredit prominent West German colleagues as fellow travellers who had fostered closer connections to the GDR side than they would admit.[30]

GDR historiography served in the debate about the character of the GDR as a focus and at the same time as scapegoat, because it was as a factual science more easily condemned for its omissions and falsifications than other disciplines like philosophy or German studies, and because the term 'historical truth', together with the possibility of referring to sources, seemed to provide an unequivocal litmus test with which to determine professional competence. The public remained entirely untouched by the discussion of the *linguistic turn* which was happening at about the same time amongst theoreticians of history and heavily criticised this kind of naïve realism.

The depth of confusion within the discipline

The second viewpoint from which to look at the debate about 1989 moves away from the highly charged public-political arena and examines the implications for the self-perception of the discipline. At a first glance, contemporary history seems to have come out strengthened by the turbulence of arguments and counter-arguments. The profession might seem to have passed the test in the early 1990s, freeing itself from the institutional straightjacket it had worn in East Germany since the 1950s; and had showed that history which has living subjects is capable of producing scientific insights of durable status. Irrespective of temporal closeness to its subject matter and the rich complexity of politics and record, it would thus have regained its rank as a critical science of truth and eventually produced a generally accepted historisation in the face of political interference and public criticism and misrepresentation.

This view is appealing and may be able to count on acceptance. But on closer inspection it becomes clear that it is at least lopsided. There are good grounds for proposing the counter-thesis that the upheaval of 1989 constituted a fundamental threat to history's identity which has so far been insufficiently recognised within the profession, but is strongly reflected in historians' dealings with '1989', and is to be drawn on as a second explanatory dimension for the paradox of storm and calm addressed earlier.

As a starting point we need to recall here how much of a turning point the downfall of the GDR was for the divided German historiology as well as for its stepsister GDR-research, which had been laid out directly as a concomitant political consultancy. This caesura is unparalleled in Germany since the birth of historiology: Whilst '1918' brought contemporary history as a discipline into being, '1933' left the structures of the profession largely untouched; and '1945' simply heralded, after a short interruption, the continuation of the morally tamed historism and his institutions; '1989' meant initially the complete dissolving of everything which carried the name 'GDR historiology'.

From the transplanting of the West German academic system into the new federal states there followed after an assessment of capability, on western terms, the almost complete phasing out of the institutions of GDR's historiography. For every historian this meant invariably the possible or definite loss of position, coercion towards a new professional orientation, and the abandonment of the 'other historical view', which Georg Iggers had detected even in 1989/1990 in GDR historiology.[31] In the year 2000 there were 428 tenured professorships in the humanities in the area of the former GDR, of which 65 per cent were held by West Germans and only 33.5 per cent by East Germans. East German humanities staff has had very little luck anywhere after 1989 in transferring from temporary contracts to permanent posts; in 1995, 42 per cent of historians from the East who had previously had permanent contracts now had temporary ones. To take one institution as an example, the situation at Berlin's Humboldt University developed as follows: On 3 October 1990, its Historical Institute counted a total of 68 professors and assistants. Five years later, on 3 October 1995, this number had shrunk to fourteen, and eleven of those had only short-term contracts.[32] The point here is not how legitimate this development was in moral, political, and professional terms, or how much the East German historians, now free from SED pressure, contributed to it or opposed it; but simply the fact that the great majority of East German historians lost, within a very short space of time, their institutional and professional framework for thought.

It is often overlooked that in the watershed, West German institutions and research branches also ceased to exist. Institutions that suffered the same fate as East German establishments were for example the *Gesamtdeutsches Institut* in Berlin, the *Institut für Gesellschaft und Wissenschaft* in Erlangen, and the *Zentralinstitut 6* at the *Freie Universität* Berlin. Moreover, 'old' interdisciplinary GDR research survived in name only; in reality contemporary history took possession of the subject in 1989/1990, which prior to this date had existed as an idiosyncratic shadow discipline in the cross section of contemporary history, sociology, political science, and futurology.

Similarly, the writings of western contemporary historians on the divided Germany were in the course of events no less devalued than those in the East. The fall of the GDR caught contemporary history in West Germany unawares and forced a national paradigm – Germany as one nation – onto it, whose abandonment had been seen as liberation from outdated patterns of thinking only a short time before. When in 1986 the *Bundeszentrale für politische Bildung* published a 'Federal German History' whose subject matter was the 'History of the Federal Republic since 1945',[33] the people in charge would certainly not have thought it possible that fifteen years later, historians of a new generation would designate not reunification, but the progressive de-nationalisation of the West German conception of history as the grand delusion of the political class; nor would countless colleagues who, in unison with Jürgen Habermas and Günter Grass, with Karl Jaspers and Günter Gaus in their lectures, seminars, and publications had declared the idea of a German unified state historically obsolete or at least indefinitely postponed. Similarly, when in 1984 Alexander Demandt, who watched the navel-gazing of contemporary historians with the serenity of a scholar of ancient history, argued for 'What-if History' [*Ungeschehene Geschichte*], he included in his 'Treatise on the question: What would have happened if ... ?' the possibility that for example Pontius Pilate could have pardoned Jesus, Charles Martell not halted the Arabs, the German Peasants' War been successful; but he excluded from his contra-factual history several possibilities which seemed to him too absurd – such as the farcical speculation that a Soviet General Secretary could denounce Marxism and that the Eastern Bloc could relinquish its power voluntarily.[34]

For German contemporary history, '1989' represented a change in the true sense of the word: it brought what were believed to be discredited theories back to the fore and transformed the profession's latest trends in no time at all into wastepaper. Would Karl-Wilhelm Fricke have dreamt that his taboo-breaking report on opposition and resistance in the GDR, with which he as a non-academic attempted 'with the instrument of political journalism ... to wrest certain things from oblivion' that had been 'pushed away as past in this country,'[35] would make him half a decade later a pioneer of a contemporary history that does justice to reality? Or would Gert-Joachim Glaeßner have believed that his prognosis in 1989 for a crisis-free development of the GDR until the turn of the century[36] would after a few months be enough for professional discreditation?

The professional change that followed the political change rehabilitated an interpretative model which had previously been closely connected with the Cold War and might have been expected to founder with it: totalitarian theory. It took an elaborate approach, which in the 1970s had been a quantum leap in the methodological and theoretical process and the foundation for a whole school of GDR research, based on the premise as set out by Peter-Christian Ludz, that the GDR must be interpreted within its own framework.

Such a sudden change of tack cannot be explained as simply the adaptation of a research discipline to changed conditions. It is a severe indictment on the disciplinary understanding of historiography as a whole. The change of 1989 exposed to contemporary historians in West and East the limitations to these claims of truth and objectivity. It showed clearly that in the end it was not the accumulating research yield and the careful conclusions according to professional standards, nor a system of insight bound to historical materialism that determines our picture of the recent past, but predominantly changes in the political situation, cultural paradigms, and historical caesurae which define the beginning and ending of topics under research.

Strategies of coming to terms with the upheavals

This is a disturbing diagnosis: it identifies a conflict between biographical continuity and professional discontinuity that reflects badly on our integrity as historians.[37] In the same way it brings into question the very identity of the discipline: the belief, staunchly defended in both East and West but attacked by forces outside academia, in the universal validity of its professional norms. In the 1970s and 1980s there had even been attempts to build bridges between the two systems by exploring the basic questions of objectivity and partisanship that would span both systems.[38] If contemporary historians aspire to biographical accuracy and professional integrity, it is naturally that they should, as far as is possible, reconcile past and present in order to formulate generally accepted and timeless professional principles, which they and the discipline as a whole can defend, from the many caesurae evident in a historical account arising from events in the life of the actors and in the development of institutions.[39]

This is true for historians' dealings with '1989'. It shows, in retrospect, that the sub-discipline of contemporary history is seeking to fend off, relativise or completely suppress its third big challenge of the twentieth century after the caesura of 1945 and the challenges to the discipline as a whole in the 1970s. The strategies of suppression that were adopted or sometimes also imposed are particularly evident in historians from the former GDR, but also in their colleagues from the West.

The most prevalent strategy in this respect is of course to fall silent. Either as a shamefaced retreat into anonymity, or helpless resignation in face of the incomprehensible changed reality, or as an enforced loss of voice resulting from cancelled publishing contracts, returned essay manuscripts, and missing invitations to academic conferences – in every case the discipline came to terms with its professional crisis by either disassociating itself to an unprecedented degree from any colleagues, especially the East Germans, who had become a professional embarrassment or quietly shunting them away to the increasingly crowded siding of fringe literature. What counted in either case was the written and attributed word. If in 1988 one likened the 17 June 1953 uprising to an attempted fascist putsch, one's job would certainly be on the line in the first few years after 1989;[40] whereas the majority of East German school teachers were better protected thanks to the transience of the spoken word and could mostly hope to keep their jobs despite far less subtle hijacking of the past in the classrooms to serve the SED-ordained present.

To a lesser extent the same mechanism took hold in the West. Most spectacularly was the closure of the superb library of the *Zentralinstitut für sozialwissenschaftliche Forschung* at the Freie Universität Berlin, which was the heart of GDR research in Berlin, but a few years after unification ended up as the book archive of the *Gedenkstätte Deutscher Widerstand*. Threatened GDR researchers changed universities to avoid probing questions on their 'German errors', or failed to find a place for their specialist research after the closure of their institutes. Following the revelation of his long lasting collaboration with the State Security, Dietrich Staritz was not protected by his distinguished rank as a GDR researcher, but was quietly excluded by the scholarly community and dropped from the editorial board of the *Zeitschrift für Geschichtswissenschaft*, without the editors giving a single word in explanation.

An alternative strategy to silence was to do the opposite: to make an emphatic confession to personal error. Günther Schabowski is a prime example of this public conversion and self-accusation. His careful distancing from the SED's ruling elite seems almost improbable given the merciless severity with which he had 'enforced' day by day the Party line, both as chief editor of the *Neues Deutschland* and also as the Central Committee's secretary.[41] An analogous example within the discipline are the historians who felt their own thinking of old to be so out-dated in the new time that they demanded to have their works that were published around the time of the upheavals pulped,[42] or who would now declare the previously rejected totalitarian theory as a model worthy of further discussion.[43] But a similar dispute happened within the West German scientific community, which was carried out in the *Deutschland Archiv* and culminated in the self-accusatory discussion on the question why the GDR research prior to 1989 had 'failed'.

The morally charged atmosphere and the personalisation of professional error increased the incidences of scholarly remorse. The changes, whether enforced or embraced as a liberation from old dogmas, in the professional analytical framework from a 'partisan' to an 'objective' historiology, transformed the work done under GDR conditions into examples of either success or failure and thus stigmatised contemporary historians of the GDR, who stood accused of legitimising the regime, as an inferior cohort to their colleagues of, for example, mediaeval studies, who were apparently more committed to the international norms of scientific fidelity.

A further strategy finally appeared in a willingness to interpret and to understand the moral adaptation to the new circumstances as an intellectual learning curve and the ideological u-turn as scholarly progress. This was often combined with an attempt to shift back the start date of one's own conversion as far as possible before 1989. Thus, Günter Schabowski dated his own Damascene experience to January 1989, when he was given Paul

Levi's biography of Rosa Luxemburg for his birthday: 'Running over the pages I got stuck on text passages which the former owner had marked with fastidious pencil lines and exclamation marks. I felt as if I looked into a forbidden chamber. Rosa Luxemburg's dispute with Lenin on the relation of dictatorship and democracy seemed to be custom-made for us. The "Heresy" described our problems.'[44]

In the second half of the 1990s, the new realities of a unified Germany and a unified discipline became a 'question-less' normality, a self-evident factual starting position, whose acceptance is no longer seriously threatened by the memory of the former paradigms. As an example, in 1997 this new normality allowed the president of the Berlin-Brandenburgische Akademie der Wissenschaften to pronounce in all equanimity that even bad people can be good historians.[45] The most profound reason for this change of climate does not lie in the generational change or the boredom of the reading public, but in the fact that contemporary history has absorbed its short-term uncertainties so successfully and without any residue. Sure enough, it confirmed the prophecy of an astute observer in July 1990: 'At this point in time we still know that much of the recent course of events has come as a surprise. For those coming after us, all this will become expected, well, "the way things were" it will be impossible to have imagined it otherwise ... And already we can see in the present day the unavoidable process of reinterpretation at work.'[46] The commentator also suspected that the maelstrom of retrospective evaluation would involve the professionalised historiography: 'Yes, the historians, who as a rule only legitimise past perfect and who disavow any alternatives of a past present, will soon explain to us why history could only happen in this way and in no other.'[47] And one may add: They will soon explain again why today's historians could only write history as they did and in no other way.

Notes

1 This chapter has been translated by Christopher Brock.
2 H. Wolf and W. Schneider, 'Zur Geschichte der Komintern', *Neues Deutschland* (6/7 May 1989).
3 A. Mitter and S. Wolle, 'Aufruf zur Bildung einer Arbeitsgruppe unabhängiger Historiker in der DDR', in R. Eckert, I.-S. Kowalczuk and I. Stark (eds), *Hure oder Muse? Klio in der DDR. Dokumente und Materialen des Unabhängigen Historiker-Verbandes* (Berlin, 1994), p. 22.
4 M. Sabrow, 'DDR-Bild im Perspektivenwandel', in J. Kocka and M. Sabrow (eds), *Die DDR in der Geschichte. Fragen – Hypothesen – Perspektiven* (Berlin, 1994), pp. 239–51.
5 The conflict about the *Zentrum für Zeithistorische Forschung* (formerly *Forschungsschwerpunkt Zeithistorische Studien*) in the mid-1990s is documented in the

edited volume by Eckert, Kowalczuk, Stark, *Hure oder Muse?* The row about the *Hannah-Arendt-Institut für Totalitarismusforschung* is highlighted in U.V. Hehl, '"Eine deutsche Affäre?" Beobachtungen zum Verlauf des Konflikts am Hannah-Arendt-Institut für Totalitarismusforschung', in M. Hettling, U. Schirmer and S. Schötz (eds), *Figuren und Strukturen* (Munich, 2002), pp. 121–40, and K.-D. Henke, 'Ein Lehrstück konzertierter Krisenregulierung in den Geisteswissenschaften am Beispiel des Dresdener Hannah-Arendt-Institutes 1999–2002', *Zeitschrift für Geschichtswissenschaft* (ZfG), 51 (2003), 205–37.

6   J. Petzold, *Parteinahme wofür? DDR-Historiker im Spannungsfeld von Politik und Wissenschaft* (Potsdam, 2000), p. 361.

7   J. Kocka, 'Von der Verantwortung der Zeithistoriker', *Frankfurter Rundschau* (3 May 1994).

8   'What now do the historians have to contribute on the subject? ... They were only seldom seen in the fray of the upheavals. But that is not untypical for historians.' S. Wolle and A. Mitter, 'Wenn die Geschichte in die Gegenwart drängt ...', *Der Tagesspiegel* (25 September 1994). See also R. Eckert, 'Replik. Politisches Engagement und institutionelle Absicherung: Die Geschichtsschreibung über die DDR', *Berliner Debatte Initial*, 1 (1995), 99 ff; I.-S. Kowalczuk, 'Geschichtswissenschaft im Dissens. Gespräch zwischen Wolfgang Küttler und Ilko-Sascha Kowalczuk über methodische Differenzen bei der Erforschung von DDR und DDR-Historiography', *Berliner Debatte Initial* (1994), 99–104, p. 99.

9   Wolle and Mitter, 'Wenn die Geschichte ...'.

10 B. Florath, 'Mnemosyne war die Pille verschrieben. Oder: Über die Schwierigkeiten der Historiker sich selbst zu begreifen', in *Initial*, 2 (1991) 150–8.

11 I.-S. Kowalczuk, *Legitimation eines neuen Staates. Parteiarbeiter an der historischen Front. Geschichtswissenschaft in der SBZ/ DDR 1945 bis 1961* (Berlin, 1997).

12 J. Hacker, *Deutsche Irrtümer. Schönfärber und Helfershelfer der SED-Diktatur im Westen* (Berlin and Frankfurt/ Main, 1992); K. Schroeder and J. Staadt, 'Der diskrete Charm des Status-quo: DDR-Forschung in der Ära der Entspannungspolitik', in K. Schroeder (ed.), *Geschichte und Transformation des SED-Staates. Beiträge und Analysen* (Berlin, 1994), pp. 309–46.

13 R. Eckert, I.-S. Kowalczuk and U. Poppe (eds), *Wer schreibt die DDR-Geschichte? Ein Historikerstreit um Stellen, Strukturen, Finanzen und Deutungskompetenz* (Berlin, 1995). Cf. also R. Eckert, 'Nicht ohne Reue. Noch einmal: Wer soll die Geschichte der DDR erforschen?', *Frankfurter Allgemeine Zeitung* (22 September 1993), imprinted in Eckert, Kowalczuk, Stark (eds), *Hure oder Muse?*, pp. 271–3; G. Herzberg, 'Wer soll die DDR-Geschichte erforschen?', in ibid, pp. 438–46.

14 W. Mommsen, 'Von der Bevormundung zur intellektuellen Kolonialisierung', *Frankfurter Allgemeine Zeitung* (25 August 1993), imprinted in Eckert, Kowalczuk, Stark (eds), *Hure oder Muse?*, pp. 270 ff.; J. Kocka, 'Infamer Seilschaftsvorwurf', *Frankfurter Allgemeine Zeitung* (2 October 1993), imprinted in Eckert, Kowalczuk, Stark (eds), *Hure oder Muse?* p. 291; R. Eckert, 'Vergangenheitsbewältigung oder überwältigt uns die Vergangenheit? Oder: Auf einem Sumpf ist schlecht bauen', in ibid., pp. 201–6.

15 C. Maier, 'Geschichtswissenschaft und "Ansteckungsstaat"', *Geschichte und Gesellschaft*, 20 (1994), 616–24.

16 See for example L. Niethammer, 'Nun muß zusammenwachsen, was sich auseinanderentwickelt hat. Zur Lage von Historischer Orientierung und Geschichtskultur in Deutschland am Ende seiner 40jährigen Teilung', in J. Calließ (ed.), *Historische Orientierung und Geschichtskultur im Einigungsprozeß (Loccumer Protokolle 8/91)* (Loccum, 1991), pp. 21–38; J. Kocka, 'Überraschung und Erklärung. Was die Umbrüche von 1989/90 für die Gesellschaftsgeschichte bedeuten könnten', in M. Hettling *et al.* (eds), *Was ist Gesellschaftsgeschichte? Positionen, Themen, Analysen* (Munich, 1991), pp. 11–21; idem, 'Folgen der deutschen Einigung für die Geschichts- und Sozialwissenschaften', *Deutschland Archiv*, 25 (1992), 793–802; G. Hockerts, 'Zeitgeschichte nach der Epochenwende', in J. Calließ (ed.), *Historische Orientierung nach der Epochenwende oder: Die Herausforderungen der Geschichtswissenschaft durch die Geschichte (Loccumer Protokolle 71/93)* (Loccum, 1993), pp. 95–104; W. J. Mommsen, 'Die Geschichtswissenschaft nach der "demokratischen Revolution" in Ostmitteleuropa', *Neue Rundschau*, 105 (1994), 75–88; G. A. Ritter, *Der Umbruch von 1989/91 und die Geschichtswissenschaft* (Munich, 1995).

17 P. Eisenmann and G. Hirscher (eds), *Dem Zeitgeist geopfert. Die DDR in Wissenschaft, Publizistik und politischer Bildung* (Munich, 1992); H. Jäckel, 'Unser schiefes DDR-Bild. Anmerkungen zu einem noch nicht verjährten publizistischen Sündenfall', *Deutschland Archiv*, 10 (1990), 1557–65; H. Kreutzer, 'Warum hat die Forschung das Offensichtliche übersehen?', *Deutschland Archiv*, 6 (1992), 629–32. Critically defending the achievements of 'old' GDR research: R. Thomas, 'Leistungen und Defizite der DDR- und vergleichenden Deutschland-Forschung', in H. Timmermann (ed.), *DDR-Forschung. Bilanz und Perspektiven* (Berlin, 1995), pp. 13–27; idem, 'Von der DDR-Forschung zur kooperativen Deutschland-Forschung. Bilanz und Perspektiven eines umstrittenen Wissenschaftsfeldes', *Zeitschrift für Parlamentsfragen*, 1 (90), 126–36, imprinted in H. Timmermann (ed.), *DDR-Forschung. Bilanz und Perspektiven* (Berlin, 1995) pp. 299–313.

18 M. Sabrow (ed.), *Heilung durch Wahrheit? Zum Umgang mit der Last der Vergangenheit* (Leipzig, 2002).

19 As a particularly scurrile example one might instance a combat organ published in 2002 by former secret service officers with the designative title 'The Security': R. Grimmer *et al.* (eds), *Die Sicherheit. Zur Abwehrarbeit des MfS* (Berlin, 2002).

20 See for example a debate held in 2003 in the feature pages of the *Frankfurter Rundschau* and imprinted in *Deutschland Archiv* on the trade balance of GDR research: J. Kocka, 'Bilanz und Perspektiven der DDR-Forschung. Hermann Weber zum 75. Geburtstag', in *Deutschland Archiv*, 36 (2003), 764 ff.; H. Bispinck *et al.* (eds), 'DDR-Forschung in der Krise? Defizite und Zukunftschancen – Eine Entgegnung auf Jürgen Kocka', in ibid., pp. 1021 ff.; T. Lindenberger and M. Sabrow, 'Zwischen Verinselung und Europäisierung: Die Zukunft der DDR-Geschichte', *Deutschland Archiv*, 37 (2004), 123–7.

21 See for example F. Klein, *Drinnen und draußen. Ein Historiker in der DDR* (Frankfurt/Main, 2000), p. 195.
22 W. Bramke, 'Freiräume und Grenzen', in K. H. Pohl, *Historiker in der DDR* (Göttingen, 1997), p. 29; Petzold, *Parteinahme wofür?*, pp. 258 ff.; Klein, *Drinnen und draußen*, pp. 193 ff., 287 ff. and 356 ff.
23 So S. Berger in late 2002 under reference to critical comments by P. Bender, J. Kocka, and L. Niethammer, 'Wie Aussätzige behandelt. Die ostdeutsche Geschichtswissenschaft 12 Jahre nach dem Ende der DDR', *Neues Deutschland* (11/12 December 2002). By the same token: idem, 'Former GDR Historians in the Reunified Germany: An Alternative Historical Culture and its Attempt to Come to Terms with the GDR Past', *Journal of Contemporary History*, 38/1 (2003), 63–83. A revised version of this contribution was published in German with the title 'Was bleibt von der Geschichtswissenschaft der DDR? Blick auf eine alternative historische Kultur im Osten Deutschlands', *ZfG*, 50 (2002), 1016–34. The federal government of Berlin considered on this foil in 2003/04 intermittently even a formal rehabilitation of the phased out academics of the former *Akademie der Wissenschaften der DDR* who lost their jobs as a result of German unification.
24 G.-R. Stephan et al. (eds), *Die Parteien und Organisationen der DDR. Ein Handbuch* (Berlin, 2002).
25 An impressive synopsis of the current state of GDR research above former scientific and scientific-politico boundaries offers the volume edited by R. Eppelmann, B. Faulenbach and U. Mählert (eds), *Bilanz und Perspektiven der DDR-Forschung* (Paderborn, 2003).
26 A. Mitter and S. Wolle, 'Inquisitoren auf der Faultierfarm. Gestern Bielefeld und Ost-Berlin, heute Potsdam: Wie flexibel dürfen Historiker sein?', *Frankfurter Allgemeine Zeitung* (9 September 1993), imprinted in Eckert, Kowalczuk, Stark (eds), *Hure oder Muse?*, pp. 276–81; idem, 'Der Bielefelder Weg. Die Vergangenheitsbewältigung der Historiker und die Vereinigung der Funktionäre', *Frankfurter Allgemeine Zeitung* (10 August 1993), imprinted in Eckert, Kowalczuk, Stark (eds), *Hure oder Muse?*, pp. 260–5. 'The new understandings of western and eastern functionaries, especially as far as historians are concerned, prolongs the East German weakness. The Potsdam *Institut für Zeithistorische Studien*, headed by Jürgen Kocka, one of the leading exponents of the Bielefeld School, is a prominent example.' added the editorial staff of the *Frankfurter Allgemeine Zeitung* in an accompanying article as a help for those readers who might be too dim to understand the subtle insinuation of the title. On the scientific aims of the campaign, see H. Zimmermann, 'Alte Seilschaften, neue Elite. Ein Historikerstreit nicht nur ums DDR-Erbe', *Frankfurter Rundschau* (13 January 1994).
27 G. Herzberg, 'Wer soll die DDR-Geschichte erforschen?', in Eckert, Kowalczuk, Stark (eds), *Hure oder Muse?*, pp. 438–46, p. 438. From this arose the demand for an interprofessional integrity commission, from which in the future any colleague who 'knowingly conceals the truth, lies, directs his knowledge along a party line, and creates despite knowing the sources "white blotches", should be

'disqualified as a matter of principle'. R. Eckert, 'Ein gescheiterter Neuanfang?', *Geschichte und Gesellschaft*, 20 (1994), 609–15, p. 614.

28 In 1994, particular prominence was achieved by the public exposure of the former deputy head of the *Zentralinstitut für Geschichte der DDR-Wissenschaftsakademie*, Olaf Groehler, as an IM during a conference on the German Resistance against Hitler in the Brandenburg Parliament. Cf. Paul Stoop, 'Der Ministerpräsident zieht sich staatsmännisch aus der Affäre. Bei der Tagung über den 20. Juli schweigen Stolpes Kritiker. Die Vorwürfe gegen Historiker Groehler', *Der Tagesspiegel* (25 June 1994); H.-G. Golz, 'Wem gehört der Widerstand? Eine Tagung zum Geschichtsbild der vergrößerten Bundesrepublik', *Deutschland Archiv*, 27 (1994), 1087–90.

29 Such a strategy was embarked on in August 1993 by the authors of the article 'The Bielefeld Way' in the *Frankfurter Allgemeine Zeitung*, by reproaching their former colleague at the *Akademie der Wissenschaften*, Peter Hübner, to have portrayed the Soviet response of the June Uprising of 1953 as the protection of workers' liberty even in 1988. Hübner responded with a contribution that shed light on the foils of his omission, which in the meantime he had come to regret, and which described GDR historiography as an arena for negotiation. P. Hübner, 'Ein Labyrinth, in dem es nur falsche Wege gibt. Wie Historiker sich durch Konzessionen die Wissenschaftsfreiheit zu sichern versuchten. Erklärung eines Betroffenen', *Frankfurter Allgemeine Zeitung* (8 September 1993), imprinted in Eckert, Kowalczuk, Stark (eds), *Hure oder Muse?*, pp. 273–6.

30 Such a strategy, in this case directed against Jürgen Kocka and Lutz Niethammer, was embarked on at times for example by the *Forschungsverbund SED-Staat* at the Freie Universität Berlin. K. Schroeder and J. Staadt, 'Die Kunst des Aussitzens', in K. Schroeder (ed.), *Geschichte und Transformation des SED-Staates* (Berlin, 1994), pp. 346–54.

31 G. G. Iggers, *Ein anderer historischer Blick. Beispiele ostdeutscher Sozialgeschichte* (Frankfurt/Main, 1991).

32 Those figures in M. Sabrow, 'Der Untergang der DDR und die Historiker', in M. Sabrow (ed.), *Grenzen der Vereinigung. Die geteilte Vergangenheit im geeinten Deutschland* (Leipzig, 1999), pp. 55–72.

33 H. Kistler, *Bundesdeutsche Geschichte. Die Entwicklung der Bundesrepublik Deutschland seit 1945* (Bonn, 1986).

34 A. Demandt, *Ungeschehene Geschichte. Ein Traktat über die Frage: Was wäre geschehen, wenn... ?* (Göttingen, 1984), pp. 40 and 73 ff. In a later edition, Demandt amended it in the light of his own experience 'Aussichtslose Unternehmungen der Vergangenheit sind leichter zu erkennen als solche der Zukunft' in idem (3rd edn 2001), pp. 60 ff.

35 'The author did not want to write a scientific work. Yet he was keen to make his book worth reading for historians and political scientists.' K. W. Fricke, *Opposition und Widerstand. Ein politischer Report* (Opladen, 1984), p. 9.

36 G.-K. Glaeßner, *Die DDR in der Ära Honecker. Politik – Kultur – Gesellschaft* (Opladen, 1988), p. 11. The following year, the same author argued that the GDR had been concerned with 'consolidating its achievements and setting the course for a crisis-free development of GDR society until the turn of the

century. It is rightly able to strike a self-confident balance of the Honecker era.' G.-J. Glaeßner, *Die andere deutsche Republik. Gesellschaft und Politik in der DDR* (Opladen, 1989), p. 73. Even Zbigniew Brzezinski, together with Carl Joachim Friedrich the founder of the variety of the best-known version of the totalitarian theory, claimed in 1989 in his settlement of accounts with the 'failed communist experiment' the GDR as the only Eastern bloc country with still relative stability and potential for economic development. Z. Brzezinski, 'Das gescheiterte Experiment. Der Untergang der kommunistischen Systeme' (Vienna, 1989), p. 239.

37 For an impression of such uncertainty, see for example J. Petzold, 'Die Lampes und die Hampes. Zum Konflikt zwischen Parteidoktrinären und Geschichtswissenschaftlern in der NS-Zeit, in der SBZ und in der früheren DDR' and the angry reaction by G. Neugebauer, both in *ZfG*, 42 (1994), 101–17 and 448 ff.

38 Not by accident did the first volume of the study group 'Theory of History', founded by Reinhard Wittram and Theodor Schieder, address the subject 'Objectivity and Partisanship'. The volume collected contributions by Wolfgang Mommsen, Koselleck, Rüsen and others on the dependency on location and perspective of statements on history, and built a bridge from there to the meaning of partisanship for GDR historiology.

39 On historians' autobiographies, cf. M. Sabrow, 'Der Historiker als Zeitzeuge. Autobiographische Umbruchsreflexionen deutscher Fachgelehrter nach 1945 und 1989', in K. H. Jarausch and M. Sabrow (eds), *Verletztes Gedächtnis. Erinnerungskultur und Zeitgeschichte im Konflikt* (Frankfurt/Main and New York, 2002), pp. 125–52.

40 'Either this historian really believed this in 1988, then he is academically discredited; or he wrote it because of opportunism, in which case he is morally intolerable.' Mitter, Wolle, 'Der Bielefelder Weg'. In his answer, the superior of the accused colleague also thought it 'an open question, how frequent or how massively scholarly contortions must have happened in order to discredit a historian despite his otherwise considerable complete works of recognised quality', J. Kocka, 'Auch Wissenschaftler können lernen', *Frankfurter Allgemeine Zeitung* (25 August 1993), imprinted in Eckert, Kowalczuk, Stark (eds), *Hure oder Muse?*, pp. 266–9.

41 On Schabowski's attitude as secretary of the Central Committee, see for example D. Klein, 'Ostinterne Folgen einer Begegnung mit Egon Bahr', in D. Küchenmeister and D. Nakath (eds), *Architekt und Brückenbauer. Gedanken Ostdeutscher zum 80. Geburtstag von Egon Bahr* (Bonn, 2002), pp. 71–7, p. 74.

42 This concerns the work by Lozek and his colleague Hans Schleier, *Geschichtsschreibung im 20. Jahrhundert. Neuzeit-Historiographie und Geschichtsdenken in Deutschland/BRD, Frankreich, Großbritannien, Italien, USA*, which had been published in 1990 by the East Berlin publishing house Akademie-Verlag, but was withdrawn before dispatch on Schleier's objection, as the publisher's chief reader evinced by letter: Schleier has 'forbidden the publication of the ... book with all resoluteness, since in connection with the societal changes in Germany its contents must be regarded as antiquated despite certainly existing merits'.

Quoted from W. Berthold, 'Rezension eines (noch) nicht erschienenen Buches', *Universitätszeitung Leipzig* (13 July 1991).

43 G. Lozek, 'Totalitarismus – (k)ein Thema für Linke? Die Totalitarismus-Auffassung in der europäischen und deutschen Geschichte vor und nach 1945', *Pankower Vorträge*, 1 (Berlin, 1995).

44 G. Schabowski, *Der Absturz* (Reinbek, 1992), p. 159.

45 D. Simon, 'Wem gehört die DDR-Geschichte', *Potsdamer Bulletin für Zeithistorische Studien*, 6 (1996), 19–29, p. 25.

46 A. Esch, 'Geschichte im Entstehen. Der Historiker und die Erfahrung der Gegenwart', *Frankfurter Allgemeine Zeitung* (14 July 1990), imprinted in U. Wengst (ed.), *Historiker betrachten Deutschland: Beiträge zum Vereinigungsprozeß und zur Hauptstadtdiskussion* (February 1990–June 1991) (Bonn and Berlin, 1992), pp. 17–29, p. 27.

47 Ibid., p. 22.

Conclusion

Harriet Jones, Kjell Östberg and Nico Randeraad

The popular understanding of history and how it works is often at odds with how professional historians understand their methodology and the appropriate purposes to which it can be applied.[1] There is, so it seems, a gap between the experts and the popular expectations of what they can deliver. When important questions arise in public debate that involve recent historical controversy, it is only natural to turn to the contemporary historian – in the same way that people would consult a doctor when ill, or a mechanic when the car breaks down. Historical experts sitting on commissions of inquiry, for example, are appointed because there is a sufficient degree of public trust in his or her knowledge and impartiality to hand over the job of providing answers to troubling and contested questions. But this implies that it is the task of the historian to provide definitive answers about the past when memories conflict (for example in an investigation or a commission), or to instruct and educate the public in the 'appropriate' ways to learn from the past (as in programmes of education or through textbooks). This is a view of history which is highly simplistic and misleading.

In the same way it is risky to compare the historian's work to that of a judge. On the surface it would appear that the processes are similar: the sifting of facts, the weighing of evidence, the presentation of the arguments, and the arrival at a conclusion. Popular perceptions of what historians do largely reflect this deceptively simple construction. But historians know that they are not so much in the business of arriving at a verdict as in trying to understand and to explain what understandings and points of view led to the actions of decision makers or the behaviour of individual actors or societies. These explanations are almost always tentative and subject to revision as new factors are taken into account, given the enormous complexity that lies behind any snapshot of the past.

Misunderstandings about the role of history and the historian have serious implications for the practice of history, especially at a time when the 'historical expert' has come to play an increasingly active role in public and political debate. When the state utilises the judgement of historians to establish a common understanding of the past, it overlooks the fact that historical interpretation is not fixed but constantly changing, and that a healthy historiography can only develop in circumstances in which challenging new interpretations are embraced and open to scrutiny within the profession. It was with such considerations in mind that on 12 December 2005 a group of nineteen distinguished historians wrote a petition published a day later in Libération protesting what they perceived to be the French politicisation of history in a series of laws which, while motivated by good intentions, were felt to have serious implications for the practice of history in France. Worth reproducing at length, the signatories declared that

> History is not a religion. The historian does not accept any dogma, does not respect any restriction, does not know taboos. He can be disturbing.
>
> History is not a set of morals. The historian does not exalt or condemn, but explains.
>
> History is not enslaved by topicality. The historian does not impose present ideological understanding on the past, and does not apply today's sensibilities to events of other times.
>
> History is not memory. The historian collects memories, compares them, checks them against documents and evidence, and establishes the facts. History holds memory to account, it is not reduced to it.
>
> History is not something that can be decided legally. In a free state, it is not the task of parliament or the courts to define historical truth. The role of the state, even when motivated by the best of intentions, must not interfere with the role of the historian.[2]

As French historians have discovered, the engagement of the profession in political debate is not a one-way process whereby the historian instructs the non-expert and then returns to the archive. If the result of the process inspires a new law (for example, that slavery was a 'crime against humanity'), or a government sponsored programme of research (for example, on holocaust education), then the outcome can be ultimately to limit or constrain the nature and direction of historical research. It is in this sense that historians across Europe have begun to question the extent to which the role of the 'historical expert' has had the unintended consequence of putting history on trial.

The chapters of this book concentrate on the emergence of contested episodes from a recent past in public debates. The authors assess the different ways in which contemporary history weighs on the public consciousness, and focus on the repercussions that this appearance of the past has for the work of professional historians. As Peter Mandler has reminded us, the revival of history calls again into question the responsibility of the historian. Apart from the general contributions by Mandler and Karlsson, the chapters offer particular examples of situations in which the responsibility of the contemporary historian is challenged. Three contributions deal with official commissions investigating controversial episodes in the recent histories of Belgium, Sweden and the Netherlands (Verbeeck, Molin and Blom); two are about juridical processes which involve historians as expert witnesses (Bew and Branche); two concentrate on bilateral historical commissions trying to overcome national prejudices appearing in textbooks (Cattaruzza and Zala, and Pupo); and one highlights the inner conflicts of the historical profession when confronted with a 'regime change'(Sabrow). We realise, of course, that this selection is not exhaustive, but the issues raised are indicative of the different problems facing contemporary historians when dealing with popular and politicised demands.[3]

This volume has drawn particular attention to the experiences of contemporary historians in countries where official commissions have been asked to investigate painful episodes. On the one hand, generally speaking, such fact-finding commissions have been common to many countries since the nineteenth century, but on the other, it can hardly come as a surprise that the commissions discussed here have been set up in countries with a strong tradition of compromise, such as Sweden, the Netherlands and Belgium. Despite the common roots of these commissions in a tradition of accommodation, there are clear differences between them. The commissions have researched markedly different issues (the activities of the secret service in Sweden, the mass killing of Muslims in Srebrenica, and the murder of Lumumba), although it is possible to argue that all three directly or indirectly stemmed from the waning of the Cold War. Following our typology laid out in the introduction we could point to the fact-finding purpose they share. Molin refers to the public description of the Swedish investigation as a 'truth commission'. The NIOD commission's task was simply to investigate 'the events preceding, during and after the fall of Srebrenica'. The Belgian commission had a wider though implicit aim from the start, as it was expected to prepare the ground for a change in foreign policy. The commissions themselves, however, were not meant to pass verdicts. It was up to the national governments and parliaments to act upon the results of the inquiries. The Netherlands witnessed the most dramatic consequences, as the publication of the report prompted the government to step down. In Sweden measures were taken to reform the secret service. Belgium offered an official apology to the family of Patrice Lumumba and to the entire Congolese people, and set up development funds for the economic recovery of the country. Apart from these direct consequences the commissions certainly contributed to a more general acknowledgment of the role of the states in question, which had not been very positive to say the least. A major difference between the three commissions was their composition. In Sweden and Belgium historians were part of a larger team, which also included state officials. The only truly historical commission was the one created by the NIOD, which is somewhat surprising since the events in question were so recent in comparison. The likely explanation is that NIOD as an institution was perceived in official circles to be competent to undertake an inquiry of this kind; handing the Srebrenica question over to a group of historians was also a convenient way to de-politicise the subject while the inquiry team was undertaking its research.

The French and British cases presented in this volume shift the focus to the courtroom and the media culture surrounding it. Clearly, the outcome of a juridical process has more binding consequences than a report by a commission. Commissions can work undisturbed by the media, whereas a controversial trial is bound to attract a lot of attention. Commissions try to understand and to explain; judges eventually have to pass a verdict. Historians acting as expert witnesses, therefore, may feel a greater direct responsibility than historians sitting on commissions. Sometimes the historian in the courtroom is simply asked to ascertain the truth (did someone belong to a military unit), but in general his or her role is to provide context, and context adds complexity. This is not necessarily what the public wants, and can conflict with the need to pass judgment. Moreover, witnesses are selected by the plaintiff or the defence according to the ways in which the testimony will strengthen the case – as Branche has pointed out in regard to several of the trials concerning war crimes in Algeria. It is of course the responsibility of the opposing counsel to question the impartiality of the witness, and that should ensure that the most flagrant abuses of historical testimony are avoided. But surely no historian is entirely unbiased. That is not to say that historians cannot serve as witnesses without integrity; but the role is not unproblematic. If the purpose of the legal proceeding is primarily to pass judgment, then historical context can confuse and even, in the case of unsound testimony, mislead. But if the more general purpose of the proceeding is to come to terms with the past, then historical context is essential. In that sense, the professional historians play a critical role in the process of truth and reconciliation, and this is where the focus of their responsibility lies.

Reconciliation is most clearly the purpose of the bilateral commissions discussed by Pupo and Cattaruzza and Zala. In these instances national bias threatens to prolong conflicts that are possible to resolve because of changing political circumstances. Both chapters reveal that this is a tricky process. As Pupo points out, the Italo-Slovene bilateral commission was relatively successful because there was a willingness on both sides to view the region from a post-nationalist perspective accept the coexistence of different points of view. By contrast, the Italo-Croatian issue proved more difficult to resolve in this way. Cattaruzza and Zala discuss the long history in Europe of using the model of the bilateral commission as a tool for conflict resolution, in the aftermath of political upheaval.

Sabrow's chapter differs from the rest in the sense that it discusses the internal professional challenges faced by historians following the reunification of Germany in 1992. It is difficult to conceive of a comparable situation in which historians of the same nationality are so sharply divided ideologically. But this is an interesting case, because unlike the other cases considered here, German historians were not only challenged to assist the public understanding of a past event, but also had to confront within their own community the consequences of past events.

To some extent then, in each of our examples expert historians have risked being put 'on trial' themselves, if not literally then in the sense that the highly controversial nature of the questions they have been asked to consider makes their methods and interpretations vulnerable to public scrutiny and debate. This is not necessarily bad news, and there have been clear benefits, especially for the discipline of contemporary history, which is still, after all, relatively young. It requires a level of continuous reflection on sources and research methods, for example, which has undoubtedly benefited the development of the methodology of contemporary history in general. This has been particularly evident for oral history; public history has assisted in the development of new methods of interviewing politicians responsible for the abuses investigated, perpetrators of terrorist acts, colonial cruelties and war crimes, and the traumatised victims of past atrocities. Inevitably, rigorous public inquiry has had an important impact on contemporary historiography as well, drawing scholarly attention and new sources of funding to areas of contention and placing special emphasis on evidence and fact-finding. Popular pressure leading to some form of public scrutiny – be it a trial or a commission – has often proved to be a more successful method of getting at withheld documents in the archives, than has professional lobbying from the profession, even when, as has been the case in the UK for example, this has been a relatively well organised and co-ordinated process. On the other hand, in contrast to the experiences in many other countries, Swedish historians still cope with closed archives, despite an apparent tradition of freedom of information and the efforts of more than one official commission. In the end, needless to say, contemporary historians as a whole have also benefited from the advantages of the heightened public interest in the recent past which has both led to and resulted from these processes.

However, in some respects public inquiries differ from 'traditional' historical research, and these differences are not always comfortable. One obvious reason why commissions or other forms of inquiry are initiated is that there have been embarrassing lacunas in contemporary historical research. There may well be good reasons why that is the case: restricted access to archives, an unclear division of work between academic disciplines, or lack of funding. As argued in this volume, public processes can help to redress all of these problems. Nevertheless contemporary historians should be prepared to discuss the extent to which their research topics have been influenced by the dominating discourses of their culture and society. Plenty of contemporary historians enthusiastically participate in top-down initiatives that define the topics of their research. But is the profession really happy to live with the consequences of the fact that it is the state that is setting the agenda, directing the funding and determining the conditions for the release of the documents? The French historians cited above certainly are not, and their experiences do not bode well for contemporary historians in other parts of Europe as attention begins to shift away from the Second World War to issues such as the legacy of colonialism or the crimes of communism.

Most of the experiences described here involve historians in working as part of a team of experts, a process which is generally unfamiliar to them. There are no doubt great benefits in such multi-disciplinary projects, which may fertilise the work of historians. If, however, the result of the work is expected to be a common statement or report, this will necessarily include either a process of negotiation and compromise, or the risk that historical testimony is simplified or exaggerated. Paul Bew and Karl Molin, for example, discuss the complexity of this process, when working with experts from other professions, be they lawyers, civil servants or politicians. The subtle complexities of historiographical debate are inevitably lost, to the detriment of historical understanding. Even in cases where a team of historians is assembled to conduct an inquiry, as was the case with Srebrenica, for example, the necessity for consensus can be a troublesome thing. When the ambition is to 'educate' and 'integrate' colleagues from other traditions there is a need for careful reflection, a problem stressed by Cattaruzza and Zala, Pupo and Sabrow. This is especially true for European historians today, given the new phase of European integration and expansion that puts pressure on us to integrate historical narrative – and historians – in the context of a turbulent and conflict-ridden common past.

The implications of the rise of the historical 'expert' are only beginning to be understood and it seems clear that, as new controversies and explosive questions appear on the agenda of public debate, this new role for historians is not going to go away. The public need to make sense of the recent past is not nearly exhausted yet – certainly not in Europe, as it deals with the legacies of the troubled twentieth century. On 25 January 2006 the Parliamentary Assembly of the Council of Europe adopted a resolution on the need for international condemnation of crimes of totalitarian communist regimes. Article 5 points out that the collapse of communism 'has not been followed in all cases by an international investigation of the crimes committed by them. Moreover, the authors of these crimes have not been brought to trial by the international community, as was the case with the horrible crimes committed by National Socialism.' And in article 7, it is resolved that 'the Assembly is convinced that the awareness of history is one of the preconditions for avoiding similar crimes in the future.' The Assembly stressed that moral condemnation of the crimes of communism should play an important role in the education of young people, and called on communist or post-Communist parties 'to reassess the history of communism and their own past'. Delegates agreed that the construction of a common understanding and an unambiguous rejection of the crimes of communism will pave the way to further reconciliation in Europe.[4] Contemporary historians will inevitably play an important role in this process, as new waves of public indignation, new media hypes, new programmes of education, new commissions, and new trials begin to grapple with these issues. It is essential that we continue to reflect upon our role in this context because there is going to be a lot more work for the expert historian.

Notes

1   We are indebted to Raffaele Romanelli who kindly shared his notes for his oral presentation concluding the preparatory meeting for this book in 2002.
2   The signatories were: Jean-Pierre Azéma, Elisabeth Badinter, Jean-Jacques Becker, Françoise Chandernagor, Alain Decaux, Marc Ferro, Jacques Julliard, Jean Leclant, Pierre Milza, Pierre Nora, Mona Ozouf, Jean-Claude Perrot, Antoine Prost, René Rémond, Maurice Vaïsse, Jean-Pierre Vernant, Paul Veyne, Pierre Vidal-Naquet and Michel Winock.
3   See also the recently published collection of articles edited by G. Zelis, *L'historien dans l'espace public. L'histoire face à la mémoire, à la justice et au politique* (Tournai, 2005).
4   Resolution 1481(2006). See http//assembly.coe.int/documents/adopted text/ta06/eres1481.htm (retrieved 27 January 2006).

Index

Adams, Gerry 63
Afanasev, Yurii 36
African-Americans 4, 20
Algeria 159–73
anti-Semitism 5, 28–9
Apih, Elio 157n.16
Ara, Angelo 157n.16
archives, access to 53, 67–8, 94, 107, 167–70, 198
von Aretin, Karl Otmar Freiherr 130–1
Arthur, Paul 63
Association internationale d'histoire contemporaine de l'Europe 131
Austria 5, 139
Azéma, Jean-Pierre 199n.2

Badinter, Elisabeth 199n.2
Bartel, Horst 132–3
Bartole, Sergio 157n.16
Becker, Jean-Jacques 199n.2
Bédarida, François 9
Belgium 46–61 *passim*
Berndt, Günter 128
bilateral historical commissions
   Austro-Slovenian 139
   Austro-Yugoslav 128
   East German-Czechoslovakian 133
   East German-Soviet 131–3
   Franco-Germanic 124–7
   German-Czech 137–8
   German-Polish 125–6
   German-Slovak 137
   Italo-Croatian 138, 144, 148, 156n.10, 196–7
   Italo-Slovenian 138, 144, 148–54, 156n.10, 196–7
   Italo-Yugoslav 138, 148
   Polish-East German 133–4
   Polish-Russian 135
   Polish-Soviet 134–5
   Soviet-Hungary 135
   West German-Polish 128–9, 136–7, 140
Blair, Tony 62, 66
Boëthius, Maria-Pia 38
Bolshevism 18, 130
   see also communism
Bosnia-Herzegovina 104–22 *passim*
Braeckman, Colette 57
Branche, Raphaëlle 16
Britain *see* United Kingdom
British Historical Association 126
Bulgaria 134

Callaghan, James 62
Canada 3
Carr, E.H. 98
Cattaruzza, Marina 155n.5, 157n.16, 158n.19
Chandernagor, Françoise 199n.2
Chirac, Jacques 169–70
Churchill, Winston 19
Clarke, Liam 68, 75–8

Cold War 2, 4, 8, 20, 33, 36, 53, 82, 101n.1, 125, 136, 146, 195
colonialism 46–61 *passim*, 159–73 *passim*
communism 2, 4, 8, 29, 35, 39, 49, 52–3, 88, 92–3, 130–6 *passim*, 146–7, 174–87 *passim*, 199
Conetti, Giorgio 157n.16
Congo 46–61 *passim*
Conze, Werner 130
Council of Europe 125, 199
Croatia 138, 144–58 *passim*
Czech republic 137
Czechoslovakia 133, 136–7

Davies, Norman 33
Decaux, Alain 199n.2
de Jong, Louis 104–5
Demandt, Alexander 183
Deutsche Historiker Gesellschaft 132
De Vos, Luc 60n.19
De Witte, Ludo 49, 59
Dolinar, France 157n.16
Dostoevsky, Fyodor 83
Droz, Jacques 125
Dumoulin, Olivier 2–4

Eckert, Georg 126
Eckert, Rainer 177
Einaudi, Jean-Luc 16, 161, 164–5, 168
Eliasson, Ulf 91
Engelberg, Ernst 126
Erdmann, Karl Dietrich 130
Evans, Richard 3, 16

feminist historians 16
Ferro, Marc 199n.2
Flink, Carole 1
France 3, 5, 9, 109, 125–7, 159–73, 194
Fricke, Karl-Wilhelm 183
Front de Libération Nationale (FLN) 160, 168
Fukuyama, Francis 9

Gallerano, Nicola 1
Gaus, Günter 183

genealogical approach 31
Gerard, Emmanuel 60n.19
Gérard-Libois, Jules 60n.19
Germany, Germans 9, 15, 31, 33, 83, 86, 124–38 *passim*, 174–87 *passim*
  East Germany 9, 124–38 *passim*, 174–87 *passim*
  West Germany 31, 124–38 *passim*, 174–87 *passim*
Giordano, Ralph 180
Glaeßner, Gert-Joachim 183
Gombac, Boris 157n.16
Gorbachev, Mikhail 37
Governmental commissions (general) 5–8, 195–9
  Bergier Commission (Independent Commission of Experts) 5
  The Bloody Sunday Tribunal (Saville Tribunal) 24, 62–79 *passim*
  Bundestag commission on the SED dictatorship 176
  Commission on Compulsory Sterilisation, Sweden 86–7, 99
  Commission on Norwegian security services 88
  NIOD commission on Srebrenica, Netherlands 105–21
  Parliamentary Inquiry Commission (on the murder of Lumumba), Belgium 50–9
  The Raoul Wallenberg Commission, Sweden 83, 86
  SÄKO (Commission on the Swedish Security Services) 81–103 *passim*
  Swedish commission on trade with Germany during WW2 83
  The Widgery Tribunal (on Bloody Sunday) 64–5, 77
Grass, Günter 183
group identity 16–20, 31–3, 42

Habermas, Jürgen 183
Hacker, Jens 177
Haider, Jörg 23
Halbwachs, Maurice 36

Harris, Jose 17
Havel, Václav 137
Heath, Edward 64
Herzfeld, Hans 125
Hillgruber, Andreas 131
historicism 14, 23, 25n.4, 27
Hitler, Adolf 19, 23, 129, 131
Hjort, Magnus 91
Holocaust 5, 9, 15, 18–19, 27–45 passim
Howarth, Gerald 62
Hübner, Peter 190n.29
Hume, John 65, 71
Hungary 134–5

IB 87–8
identity-groups see group identity
Iggers, Georg 182
International Committee of Historical Sciences (ICHS) 123–4, 130
Internationales Schulbuchinstitut 126, 128, 133
International Institute of Intellectual Co-operation 124, 139
Ireland 62–80 passim
Irish Republican Army (IRA) 62–80 passim
Iron Curtain 2, 140
Irving, David 3, 16
Israel 41
Italy 127, 138, 144–58 passim

Jaspers, Karl 183
Jerussalimski, Arkadi 129–30
Jewishness 18–19
Johansson, Alf W. 91
Johnstone, Kathy 68, 75–8
Jordanova, Ludmilla 1
Jospin, Lionel 169–71
Julliard, Jacques 199n.2

Kacin-Wohinz, Milica 157n.16
Katanga 47–8, 51, 55–6
Kocka, Jürgen 177, 189n.26, 190n.30, 191n.40
Kok, Wim 105, 115–16

Lagrou, Pieter 20, 119
Lampers, Lars-Olof 89, 91
Leclant, Jean 199n.2
Leff, Gordon 22–3
Le Pen, Jean-Marie 16, 164
Lipstadt, Deborah 3
Living History 27–8, 32, 41
Lübbe, Hermann 178
Ludz, Peter-Christian 183
Lumumba, Patrice 46–61 passim

Maier, Charles 29
Major, John 65–6
Markiewicz, Wladislaw 128
Marusic, Branko 157n.16
Mazower, Mark 25
Milza, Pierre 199n.2
Mitter, Armin 186n.3, 189n.26, 191n.40
Mlakar, Boris 157n.16
Mommsen, Wolfgang J. 177
Mussolini, Benito 146

Napoleon 23
NATO 41, 82, 145
Nazism 15, 18, 21, 28–9, 33, 38, 40, 86, 133, 146, 160
Netherlands, The 9, 104–22 passim
Neuenschwander, John 3–4
Noiriel, Gérard 161
Nora, Pierre 36, 199n.2
Northern Ireland 23, 62–80 passim
Norway 88
Novick, Peter 42

O'Dochartaigh, Niall 70–1
Ozouf, Mona 199n.2
Pagnini, Paola 157n.16
Pan-Africanism 19
Papon, Maurice 3, 16, 161, 164–5
Perrot, Jean-Claude 199n.2
Persson, Göran 27–8, 30, 41, 91, 102n.10
Petzold, Joachim 176
Poland 124–38 passim
Popper, Karl 14
Prost, Antoine 199n.2

racism 15, 23, 28
Rathbone, Richard 25
Raxhon, Philippe 60n.19
Rémond, René 173n.25, 199n.2
Renouvin, Pierre 125
Ritter, Gerhard 125–6
Romanelli, Raffaele 199n.1
Rosenzweig, Roy 36
Rothman, David 3
Rousso, Henri 3, 173n.22
Royal Historical Society 12, 24
Ruin, Olof 85
Runia, Eelco 122n.13
Russian Federation 28–9, 37–8
Rwanda 33, 50, 58

Salimbeni, Fulvio 157n.16
Santayana, George 14, 25n.4
Saville, Mark (Lord) 63, 65–8, 75–7
Sayle, Murray 79
Schabowski, Günther 185–6
Schilfert, Gerhard 134
Schmidt, Walter 133
Schorske, Carl 27, 30
Simmons, Ruth 4
Slavery 4, 137
Slovakia 137
Slovenia 138–9, 144–58 *passim*
Soviet Union 2, 30, 35–9, 47, 86, 99, 125–38 *passim*
Stalin, Josef 19, 40, 129–31, 144
Staritz, Dietrich 185
sterilisation 32, 38, 86–7, 99
Stora, Benjamin 161
Sweden 5, 9, 21, 27–45 *passim*, 81–103 *passim*
Switzerland 5

Thelen, David 36
Thierry, Augustin 23–4
Thomson, David 19

Tito, Josip Broz 144, 146–7
Töllborg, Dennis 97
Trimble, David 62–3
Troha, Nevenka 157n.16
Truth Commissions 5–6, 52, 195

Ukraine 29–30
Unabhängiger Historikerverband 175–80 *passim*
UNESCO 7, 125, 127–9, 139
United Kingdom 9, 12–13, 18–24 *passim*, 62–80 *passim*, 126
United States 3–5, 19

Vaïsse, Maurice 199n.2
Venezia Giulia 145–6, 150–2, 154, 155n.1
Verband der Historiker Deutschlands 130, 132
Vergès, Jacques 160
Verhofstadt, Guy 58
Vernant, Jean-Pierre 199n.2
Veyne, Paul 199n.2
Vidal-Naquet, Pierre 16, 160, 164, 166, 172n.12, 199n.2
Vichy regime 3, 160–1
von Ranke, Leopold 9, 123
von Weizäcker, Richard 180
Vovco, Andrei 157n.16
Vuga, Aleksander 157n.16

Wallenberg, Raoul 83, 86
welfare state 32, 38, 81, 101n.1
Widgery, John 64–5, 77
Winock, Michel 199n.2
Wolle, Stefan 186n.3, 189n.26, 191n.40

Young, James 29
Yugoslavia 119–20, 128, 144–58 *passim*
Zaremba, Maciej 38

EU authorised representative for GPSR:
Easy Access System Europe, Mustamäe tee 50,
10621 Tallinn, Estonia
gpsr.requests@easproject.com

www.ingramcontent.com/pod-product-compliance
Ingram Content Group UK Ltd.
Pitfield, Milton Keynes, MK11 3LW, UK
UKHW021835140426
5217IPUK00021B/1456